Islam and Bosnia
Conflict Resolution and Foreign Polic
in Multi-Ethnic States

Islam and Bosnia re-examines the conflict of the 1990s from the perspectives of international relations, conflict resolution, and history as well as psychology, anthropology, and cultural studies. Rejecting the primordialist, or "ancient hatreds," interpretation as the root of the conflict, the authors detail how a complex cultural transformation led to the erosion of what had been the common inclusionist base of a multi-ethnic state and brought about a new exclusionist nationalism. By pulling together the individual elements of culture, society, and foreign policy and analysing their interaction, *Islam and Bosnia* demonstrates how the secular romantic nationalism of the nineteenth and early twentieth centuries, centred on history, language, and landscape, was overthrown in favour of one that highlighted religion, race, and territory.

Islam and Bosnia shows how the Bosnian conflict bears on the wider contexts of cultural paradigms, deadly conflicts, and the formulation of foreign policy. It argues for a new perspective in foreign policy-making, one that would embrace and incorporate better and deeper knowledge and understanding of culture, history, and ideology.

MAYA SHATZMILLER is a professor in the Department of History and former director of the Centre for Nationalism and Ethnicity, University of Western Ontario.

Islam and Bosnia

*Conflict Resolution
and Foreign Policy
in Multi-Ethnic States*

EDITED BY

MAYA SHATZMILLER

McGill-Queen's University Press
Montreal & Kingston · London · Ithaca

© McGill-Queen's University Press 2002
ISBN 0-7735-2346-4 (cloth)
ISBN 0-7735-2413-4 (paper)

Legal deposit fourth quarter 2002
Bibliothèque nationale du Québec

Printed in Canada on acid-free paper that is
100% ancient forest free (100% post-consumer
recycled), processed chlorine free, and printed
with vegetable-based, low VOC inks.

This book has been published with the help of
a grant from the J.B. Smallman Publication Fund,
Faculty of Social Science, The University of
Western Ontario.

McGill-Queen's University Press acknowledges the
financial support of the Government of Canada
through the Book Publishing Industry Development
Program (BPIDP) for its publishing activities.
We also acknowledge the support of the Canada
Council for the Arts for our publishing program.

**National Library of Canada Cataloguing
in Publication Data**

Main entry under title:
Islam and Bosnia: conflict resolution and foreign
policy in multi-ethnic states
Includes bibliographical references and index.
ISBN 0-7735-2346-4 (bound). –
ISBN 0-7735-2413-4 (pbk.)
1. Bosnia and Hercegoniva – History. 2. Islam –
Bosnia and Hercegovina. 3. Bosnia and
Hercegovina – Ethnic relations. 4. Conflict
management – Bosnia and Hercegovina. 5. Yugoslav
War, 1991–1995 – Diplomatic history. 6. Yugoslav
War, 1991–1995 – Bosnia and Hercegovina.
I. Shatzmiller, Maya
DR1750.I74 2002   949.742   C2001-904014-8

Typeset in New Baskerville 10.5/13
by Caractéra inc., Quebec City

Contents

Abbreviations

CSCE	Conference on Security and Cooperation in Europe
EC	European Community
EU	European Union
HDZ	Croatian Democratic Union
HVO	Croatian Defense Council
ICFY	International Conference on the Former Yugoslavia
ICTY	International Criminal Tribunal for the Former Yugoslavia
JNA	Yugoslav National Army
LCD	Local Election Commission
NATO	North Atlantic Treaty Organization
NGO	non-governmental organization
OHR	Office of the High Representative
OSCE	Organization of Security and Cooperation in Europe
PEC	Provisional Election Commission
RFER	Radio-Free Europe Research
SANU	Serbian Academy of Arts and Sciences
SDA	Party for Democratic Action (Muslim)
SDS	Serbian Democratic Party
SFR	Socialist Federal Republic
SUC	Serbian Unity Congress
TANJUG	Telegraphic Agency of the New Yugoslavia
UN	United Nations

UNESCO   United Nations Educational, Scientific, and Cultural
          Organization
UNHCR   Office of the United Nations High Commissioner
          for Refugees
UNPROFOR United Nations Protection Force

Contributors

TONE BRINGA, University of Bergen

AMILA BUTUROVIĆ, York University, Toronto

JOHN V.A. FINE, University of Michigan, Ann Arbor

PETER W. GALBRAITH, Former US ambassador to Croatia

GRAHAM N. GREEN, Former Canadian ambassador to Croatia

NADER HASHEMI, University of Toronto

JOHN M. REID, Information commissioner for Canada

ANDRÁS RIEDLMAYER, Harvard University

MICHAEL A. SELLS, Haverford College

DONALD W. SMITH, Canadian ambassador to Croatia

VAMIK D. VOLKAN, Centre for Study of Mind and Human
Interaction, University of Virginia

Introduction

This volume contains essays written for a conference held at the University of Western Ontario in London, Ontario, Canada, in May 1999 under the title *Islam and Bosnia: The Historical and Cultural Paradigms of Conflict Resolution and Foreign Policy Making in the Case of the Multi-Ethnic State*. Organized under the auspices of the university's newly created Centre for Nationalism and Ethnicity, the conference's objective was to use the war of 1992–95 in Bosnia as a research engine by which to study the case of Bosnia and its bearing on the wider context of cultural paradigms, deadly conflict, and the formulation of foreign policy. In terms of conflict resolution, this approach was intended to complement the analysis of short-term contingency management, which diplomats administer, by investigating the roots of the conflict, to which academics attend. By combining the two perspectives, it was hoped that a new approach to foreign policy making would emerge, one that the record of the West and of the international community and its institutions on the Bosnia crisis seems to require.[1] The new approach would suggest that more meaningful and useful paradigms for the formulation of foreign policy would result from expanding the terms of reference to include disciplines such as history, sociology, anthropology, psychiatry, literary criticism, and art history. While the conference was a long time in the making, the actual meeting took place during the NATO bombardments of Kosovo, which provided a constant reminder of the urgency and relevance of such an approach. I invited both academics and veterans of Foreign Affairs, who were directly involved in the formulation and implementation of us, Canadian, and international policy and diplomacy in the region, to reflect and interact. The result is the collection of essays offered here, which includes a wide array of thematic and chronological conceptualizations of the events, surveying both the long "historical past" and the short history of the "diplomatic past." Treatment of the former begins as early as the Middle Ages and at times collapses the period between medieval and modern while making use of all its *longue durée* evidence. The latter, which began with the war and ended with the Dayton Peace Accords and their aftermath, is recounted as private history based on the personal experience of the participants. The mixture of participants and disciplines also resulted in a diversity of methodological approaches and various themes. The authors from academic disciplines adopted a more detached and comprehensive approach, with the customary scholarly apparatus, while practitioners wrote from a unique perspective of personal involvement and experience.

I initially suggested to the participants three general paradigms to be used as a thematic and methodological framework for their essays: Islam and Europe, the disintegration of the multi-ethnic state, and the role of foreign policy making in the resolution of a deadly conflict. Bosnia seemed to incorporate all three. It was unique, both within the former Yugoslavia and in Europe, for its Islamic component and for the social and economic integration of its three ethnic communities: Muslims, Serbs, and Croats. However, judging the presence of Islam in Europe in historical or global terms was not without its problems. Islam's multi-faceted, but initially negative, image had enabled Europeans to reject and resist the idea of a pluralistic society.[2] The initial denial of the existence of willing converts to Islam had provided Europeans with an intellectual, political, and cultural challenge, giving them the opportunity to define themselves vis-à-vis another culture.[3] Europe's perception of Muslims had taken on a new physical dimension with the recent arrival of Muslim immigrants in Western Europe and had forced the reopening of the debate.[4] As the war in Bosnia has demonstrated, no matter how the secular Bosnian Muslims viewed themselves, their neighbours and other Europeans regarded them, in the first place, as Muslims.

Islam, however, only became the divisive and decisive factor in the conflict when it was combined with ethnic nationalism. The former Yugoslavia was not the only multi-ethnic state where the Islamic component was involved in a civil war, nor was Bosnia the only place where political power among co-citizens was shared along confessional lines. The idea of the multi-ethnic state that gained ground at the end of wwII as a democratic vehicle for economic prosperity and progress had failed to provide the structural framework needed to outweigh and replace the narrower base of race and religion, and was thus insufficient for the creation of a civil and just society. The breakdown of the multi-ethnic state of the twentieth century in Europe, Asia, and Africa suggests that rather than becoming a tool for conflict prevention, it became a scene of ethnic strife. The disintegration of the political system in Lebanon, or the Soviet Union, and the ethnic massacres in Rwanda and Indonesia provide examples of the demise of the multi-ethnic state. Western foreign policy makers were caught by surprise by the disintegration of the multi-ethnic states in the early 90s, failing to see how the new conditions changed the nature of the deadly conflict. Modern deadly conflicts are no longer international but intrastate and rarely involve two homogenous nation states. This poses a whole set of new problems, not only as concerns a just society, but also for outside intervention. Since the recent conflicts involved co-citizens, intervention initially appeared to be a violation of sacred principles to the legally minded Western policy makers and legally inspired international bodies born from the centuries-long evolution of the concepts of international law and state sovereignty. In many instances human rights violations perpetrated by the state against its own citizens are still depicted as an "internal matter," and civil war is defended as "national interest." The point at which human rights should take precedence over those of the state is only now being recognized by international bodies, albeit hesitantly, as cause for military intervention.[5]

Working within this thematic framework, the authors in the first section of the book focus on the construction of cultural identities of ethnic groups, both the identities these groups give themselves and those given them by others, as a component in the conflict. The first two papers, by Professors Fine and Bringa, deal with the important question of the content and context of the Islamic identity of the Bosnian Muslims. Both authors agree that a pronounced Islamic identity for Bosnia's Muslims developed as recently as 1990. Both also agree that the elements informing this identity are so unique that it should not be lumped together with the contemporary Islamic radical movement but understood on its own terms. Professor Fine's paper makes two important points. The first is that the particular historical process by which Christianity made inroads in the Balkans conditioned the formation of a religiously tolerant society in Bosnia, where religious zeal had never manifested itself. The relaxed attitude to religion after the Ottoman conquest of the fourteenth century contributed to a conversion rate to Islam in Bosnia larger than in other regions of the Balkans and to the formation of a strong Muslim component.[6] The state secularism of the communist regime maintained this characteristic, making Bosnia a society free of religious/ethnic cleavages, a fact born out by the 40 per cent mixed marriage rate found just before the war. The second point made in the paper is the crucial role played by Western policy makers and diplomats in forcing the Bosnian Muslims to accept a division along religious/ethnic lines, a concept foreign to them and that they opposed. However, once the framework for such a division was established, the Bosnian-Muslim identity was quickly filled out with real content imported from Islamic countries, where fundamentalist movements already possessed the material culture, whether literature, dress, or arms. The invigoration of the Islamic identity among urban and rural Muslims grew faster as a direct outcome of the war, during which their identity as enemies was conceptualized in religious terms. The new conditions strengthened the hands of individuals, who had formerly been marginalised and minoritarian within the Bosnian-Muslim community, and who now claim vindication of their previous position and demand invigoration of Islamic character and practices for their society and state.

Looking into the formation of an Islamic identity in Bosnia, Professor Tone Bringa, an anthropologist at Bergen University, Norway, adds another dimension to Professor Fine's argument by evoking the unique character of the Islam practiced in Bosnia's rural areas. The Bosnian landscape was a component shared by all the communities, but religion was the main cultural factor distinguishing one community from another. Bosnian Muslims were no different, and the creation of a collective identity took place via religion, though it was a religion that incorporated common local notions of history and territory shared with non-Muslim Bosnians. In other words, Bosnia did have a collective cultural identity in which all Bosnians, including Muslims, shared, but Dr Bringa adds another factor that contributed to the Islamic revival observed recently among Bosnian Muslims, namely the opening of the former Yugoslavia to influences from the other Islamic countries with whom Yugoslavia interacted during the 80s. Yet she shares the view of the particularly nasty role played by the West, which adopted the terms and images used by Serb propagandists against the Muslims, terms that were fabricated especially to strike a nerve with a Western audience. Well acquainted with the situation on the ground as a result of her anthropological field work, Dr Bringa is optimistic about the role Bosnian Islam is capable of playing as a bridge-builder between the Islamic world and Christian-defined Europe.

Illuminating a shared Bosnian national identity without a religious component, Amila Buturović, a professor of literature at York University, provides a splendid illustration of the forms, symbols, and content that such an identity embraced by examining the work of Mak Dizdar (1917–71), the well known Bosnian-Muslim poet. Studying Dizdar's most acclaimed poem, *Stone Sleeper*, Professor Buturović shows how Dizdar creates a universe filled with images from Bosnian history and Bosnian landscape. By engaging with the mysterious medieval tombstones, whose inscriptions commemorate deeds attributed to members of the Bogomil sect , the poet creates a bond between present occupiers of the land and its ancestors buried on its soil. By collapsing the hundreds of years separating the two periods, Dizdar opts for a set of cultural representations that disregard religion and race.

The unique insight that literature can offer into the nation's collective psyche and identity is at the centre of the next two essays by Professors Michael Sells and Vamik Volkan. Both are intrigued by the process of cultural transformation through which historical myths have become powerful tools of hatred and ethnic cleansing. It is hard to see how innocent cultural themes can become vehicles of atrocities and war crimes, but Sells, a professor of Arabic literature at Haverford College, analyzes the transformation process, showing how the discourse of the Slavic Church managed to focus anti-Muslim feelings in the person of all Bosnian Muslims today. The assimilation of the death of Prince Lazar at the hands of the

Ottoman Turks into the imagery of the crucifixion became the central theme in what he terms "Christoslavism." The participation of intellectuals, scientists, and academics in the process of fabricating this crude ideology and mythology – as exemplified in statements made by the Serb geneticist Biljana Plavsić, former head of the Academy of Science, about the "genetic deformed elements which embraced Islam" – serves Professor Sells in demonstrating the monstrous dimensions of this process. In that respect, both the Eastern and Western church were equally part of Europe. Professor Sells's paper forcefully draws together the cultural components of the deadly conflict, both those that fueled the inflammatory discourse of the religious leaders and those that political leaders diffused.

Cultural psychiatry offers a very original analysis of the process by which historical events are translated into a collective sense of victimization and trauma, as occurred during the Bosnia war. Combining history and psychiatry, Dr Vamik Volkan of the University of Virginia demonstrates how one's interpretation of and identification with a group's historical experience would become a potent political tool. The event in question is the battle of Kosovo of 1389, which has come to symbolize the total occupation of Serbia by the Ottomans, thus becoming in the collective psyche "the national trauma." Showing how one historical instant travels through time to transform itself into a set of symbols, Dr Volkan bears witness to the selective creation of a *chosen Serb trauma*. The promotion of mass participation in the rituals surrounding Prince Lazar's death celebrations, first by the church's discourse and then by that of state officials, effectively collapsed the period of 600 years between Lazar's death and the emergence of modern anti-Muslim propaganda. Here, fact and fantasy were used to portray Islam not only as the historical enemy, but also as a contemporary one reincarnated in current affairs. The Serbs were made to feel not only that the defeat in Kosovo occurred yesterday, but also that modern Turkey is the present enemy of Serbia. In this surrealistic landscape the organized rape of Muslim women is historicized as a retaliation for the *Devshirme* system, the Ottoman practice of collecting Christian boys and converting them to Islam. The involvement of religious leaders and religious institutions accentuated the role of religion in the elaboration of a deadly conflict.

How crucial history and material culture were in the formulation of national identity was exemplified in the destruction of Bosnian

archives, libraries, books, records, mosques, bridges, and all standing
monuments recalling an Ottoman and Islamic existence. The physical
elimination would not be complete without eradicating the historical
record of this existence. In a presentation accompanied by many
slides of the monuments destroyed by Serb artillery, all of which,
unfortunately, could not be reproduced here, András Riedlmayer,
of Harvard's Aga Khan Center for Islamic Architecture, described
the deliberate targeting and destruction of cultural, religious, and
historical landmarks by nationalist extremists. This occurred not
only in Sarajevo, which as the regional capital was home to the
Oriental Institute, the National University Library, and national
archives that had held civil records for hundreds of years, all of
which were bombarded and burned to the ground, but also in small
villages, where churches, mosques, and madrasas were dynamited
and their ruins dispersed. Mr Riedlmayer makes the point that the
elimination of the physical symbols was not just a denial that they
ever existed, but also an attack on the record of centuries of pluralism and tolerance in Bosnia, and on its distinct quality as a meeting
place for influences and interactions from East and West.

In the second section of the book a group of diplomats and
foreign policy makers involved in Bosnia's conflict resolution
during its final stages analyze the role played by their governments
and international bodies. The responsibility of the international
community for failing to foresee and prevent the atrocities visited
upon the civilian population has been both acknowledged and
rejected by some of the players in personal memoirs and in committee reports.[7] Unique to the essays here is how the authors'
attempts to define their personal contributions help us to understand the intersection of and differences between institutional and
individual behaviour. The Bosnia war was no different from other
international conflicts in its submission to considerations of global
and regional interests, legal and humanistic principles, and personal and ideological motivations on the part of implicated states,
institutions, and individuals.

The reluctance of the US administration to get involved in the
early stages of the crisis has come under criticism from many quar-
ters. Peter Galbraith, the US ambassador to Croatia from June 1993
until after the signing of the Dayton Peace Accords, presents a
different picture of American foreign policy and diplomacy, one
characterized by a set of defined objectives and strategies. Because

of the key role Ambassador Galbraith played in formulating and executing this policy, his analysis sheds new light on the American involvement. He frankly concedes that no cohesive policy concerning the events that followed the breakup of Yugoslavia existed when he assumed his position, a situation that left him with a measure of independence and influence. When a strategy was finally formulated, the role of the diplomats on the ground remained crucial given the complexity of the issues involved, the multiple partners, interests, and personalities, and the rapidly changing conditions. In chronological sequence he analyzes the series of negotiations that preceded the Dayton Peace negotiations, to which he was party, and shows how they led to the formulation of the final agreement that ended the war. The craft of diplomatic negotiations, he reminds us, might well be formulated in humanitarian principles, but on the ground it is about territorial gains, sticks, and carrots.

One of the objectives of the Dayton Peace Accords was to recreate a state with functioning institutions in Bosnia-Herzegovina through democratic elections. The Hon. John Reid, information commissioner for Canada, was recruited by the Government of Canada as an expert to serve on the commission responsible for organizing the elections in the new federation, and his essay recounts his work and observations. As the only experienced parliamentarian among the members of the committee created by the Organization of Security and Cooperation in Europe, the OSCE, he reflects on the mandate they were given in view of the legacy of the war, the large number of displaced persons, the continuous ethnic cleansing, an uneven distribution of powers between municipal and federal bodies, and the reluctance of local politicians to transfer power by democratic means. Organizing and carrying out the elections was a challenging task, but Mr Reid is aware of the opportunities created by the Dayton Peace Accords for the reconstruction of Bosnian society. The democratic process of self-determination was achieved in spite of the war legacy thanks to the elections, which were viewed as a tool of pacification despite their limited contribution to "the restoration of normality" and law and order. Even if the Dayton constitution did not identify the correct power sharing structures and did not devise an optimal power division, the Accords demonstrate the power and merit of the international community's intervention.

A closer look at the international community's attempts to resolve the conflict in the former Yugoslavia, and in particular the war in Bosnia, is undertaken by Mr Graham Green, former Canadian ambassador to the Republic of Croatia. Drawing on his considerable experience in the work of the United Nations security council, his analysis shows first that the reaction of members of international organizations was too slow to afford them sufficient awareness of what was happening as the crisis unfolded and second that their eventual response was inadequate and confusing, with a multiplicity of plans being formulated by the United Nations, NATO, and the European Community (EC). Timing was also crucial, with factors such as the Middle East crisis of 1991 diverting the gaze of the West eastward, while the process of growing ethnic nationalism in the former Yugoslavia was quickening its pace. The failure to recognize the intensive and pervasive power of this emerging nationalism resulted in the failure to foresee the breakup of Yugoslavia looming on the horizon, which led in turn to the formulation of a European reductionist approach. Not only was a plan of action missing, but the flexibility to address daily and monthly changes on the ground was also lacking. Each new crisis was treated in a piecemeal fashion with no coordinated international policy. Each new development provoked even more discord. The divergence between European and American approaches delayed military intervention and confined action to diplomatic efforts, while discord among NATO members themselves required that radical solutions be sacrificed for the sake of unity. Even though blame could and should be equally distributed, Mr Green offers some thoughts as to when diplomacy should be abandoned in favour of military intervention.[8]

The decision to adopt military intervention as a legitimate means of conflict resolution remains a central issue for foreign policy makers. Ambassador Donald Smith, Canadian ambassador to Croatia at the time of the conference, draws on the lessons from the events of the Bosnia war to debate and generate a broader, far-reaching framework for policy making and diplomacy. He defines four areas in which fundamental policy-making dilemmas exist for the Western nations today. First and foremost is the issue of military intervention. The hesitant and belated military engagement in the Balkans can be traced to the fact that both Europe and the US and Canada shared a postwar reluctance to engage in military intervention. The Western democracies are aware that any military intervention will be exposed to media coverage, and they accept this; all share the need to maintain the same transparency in their military actions as they do in civilian matters. However, given the West's unfailing commitment to act against human-rights abuses, western countries are inclined to intervene militarily to enforce human rights, except in situations in which internal conditions make it difficult to act. Such intervention, nonetheless, must interact with and complement diplomacy. As the case of Kosovo has shown, given that "Milosević believed for a long time he could call NATO's bluff," the threat of military intervention should be credible if military force and diplomacy are to coexist. Credibility must be maintained if diplomacy is to work. More fundamental dilemmas for diplomacy and policy making occur as a result of changing conditions, such as when the International Criminal Tribunal issued indictments against Milosević at a time when some in the West thought it would harm the possibility of reaching a negotiated solution with him. The extent to which policy makers are bound by constraints and commitments made in other areas cannot be overlooked, Smith suggests. All lessons learned from previous mistakes, particularly those pointing to factors that might inhibit cohesive and clear-sighted policy, should be considered within the larger framework of foreign policy making. A dilemma of another sort cited by Ambassador Smith results from ignoring the psychology and values of opponents, yet, when Western values require taking action in response to human-rights abuses, those values should not limit the option of using military force. As for Canada, if it is to adopt humanitarian law as a foreign-policy objective and guideline, this dilemma needs to be resolved.

Mr Nader Hashemi, an intern with Canadian Foreign Affairs, mounts a strong attack on Canada's foreign policy role in the Bosnia war. Armed with declarations made by Canadian prime ministers, ministers of Foreign Affairs, generals, and other officials, he comes to the conclusion that "Ottawa's actions prolonged the war in Bosnia." Among the actions he considers failures of Canadian policy, he counts the enforcement of the embargo on arms to Bosnia, the pressure on Bosnians to capitulate to Serb demands, and the reluctance to support calls for air strikes against the Serbs. He faults Canadian policy makers for being too obsessed with peacekeeping to develop their own independent stand and for adhering to decisions made in other capitals: The "main concern was not to be left out."

The contribution of the collection's papers as a whole resides in drawing together the individual elements of culture, society, and foreign policy making and in analyzing their interaction. The analysis points to some new developments in this framework, the most visible and powerful among them being the transformation that has taken place in the context and content of nationalism in the region. The analysis of the transformation process has unearthed a nationalism that went through a redefinition of its identification ideology. The new nationalism that transpired was no longer the classical nationalism of the nineteenth and early twentieth centuries, a secular and romantic movement centred around history, language, and landscape; instead it was one that highlighted religion, race, and territory. This new nationalism rejected the notion of inclusion that language, landscape, and history offered, a notion that was dominant in the prewar construction of Bosnia's national identity, and opted instead to adopt concepts that were exclusionist. What the changes in the new nationalism actually mean is that the old conceptualization failed to produce an identity-forming focus for people in the region The role played by history in this process deserves a special place in the analysis. The identity-forming power of history was not diminished by the new nationalism, on the contrary, it was highlighted. Both the formation of the Serb national trauma and the use of medieval tombstones to forge a sense of shared ancestry employed history in the process of identity formation, except that the former employed it for exclusion, the latter for inclusion. The juxtaposition of these two cases shows the important role history played in shaping national identity in the region, but the analysis of how history was used demonstrates that the process can be manipulative, selective, and perverse. The ability to collapse a period of hundreds of years and successfully generate identification with medieval heroes and territory was used by the new nationalistic discourse, except that it selectively translated religious struggle into hateful stereotypes.

The papers show how a process of cultural transformation changed the content and context of what was once the common base of the multi-ethnic state and eroded the identity-forming power of previous ideologies. They also show that the transformation process and the new cultural notions of nationalism affected Western politicians and the Western media as well. The anti-Islamic images retrieved and generated by the new nationalism were not rejected in the West, and the suggestion that the concepts were neither new nor foreign continued to influence international response to the war. The unscrupulous and irresponsible manipulation of anti-Islamic sentiment in the region, by political and religious national leaders, had an equivalent in the Western reaction to the Kosovo crisis, when some argued that the NATO bombing of Kosovo should cease – and the Kosovo Muslims be left undefended – because it was harming the opposition to Milosević! The centrality of religion in the process of cultural transformation, as highlighted in the papers, also suggests the likelihood of a more cautious approach to the process of state building in Bosnia, which has now begun under the auspices of the Dayton Accords. The Bosnian Muslims were the last to abandon their age-old secular identity, having been forced to do so by what was going on around them, in what could be seen as the last stand against the erosion of the secular foundation of the Bosnian state. The ideological constraints that guided Western policy making, in particular the tacit recognition of the anti-Islamic notions by US right-wing politicians, also became a symbol of the final victory over communist secularism. Will the Dayton Peace Accords be what sows the seeds of future wars and a prelude to the division of Bosnia along ethnic lines? The ultimate reply is that the changing cultural paradigms require new thinking in foreign policy making, a new approach that will embrace a deeper understanding of culture, history, and ideology in the hope of achieving more than just a victory of pragmatism.

The conference was supported by grants from the Holmes Fund for the formulation of Foreign Policy, which is administered by Canada's Foreign Affairs and International Trade ministry, from the Canadian Social Science and Humanities Research Council, and from the Faculty of Social Science at the University of Western Ontario. In addition, many people gave the conference both moral and practical support. At Western, Professor Michael Keating suggested venues for raising the necessary funding and made himself available whenever his competent advice and clear vision were needed. Professors Thomas Sea, chair of the History Department, and Brian Timney, associate dean of the Faculty of Social Science, provided material support and encouragement when it was crucially needed. Professors Michael Carroll and John McDougall, and John McGarry of the University of Waterloo, who served as session chairs, discharged their duties with grace and firmness, reining in the participants in the sometimes heated debates. Emmanuel Brunet-Jailly and Jelica Zdero, Ph.D. candidates in the Political Science and History Departments respectively, carried out their organizational tasks efficiently and competently. In the early stages of the conference's development, conversations with Serge Marcoux, then Canadian ambassador to Bosnia, and Gordon Smith, then deputy minister of Foreign Affairs, neither of whom could take part in the conference, helped me to appreciate the Canadian involvement in Bosnia and also suggested people to call upon. Katarina Pejakovic of Ottawa, a cultural consultant, activist, and writer, offered precious insights on the Balkan situation and advice on dealing with Canadian agencies involved in the Balkans. May they, as well as the granting agencies, find here the expression of our warmest gratitude.

Robert Lewis, our copy editor, did a superb job, eliminating repetitions, clumsy rhetoric, and confusing syntax and, by forcing us to carefully rethink some statements, made the essays more worthy of the project.

Maya Shatzmiller
Montreal, February 2001

NOTES

1 As James Gow notes in reviewing the large number of books that appeared in the aftermath of the Yugoslav war, "the events of the 1990s revealed major gaps in the literature, and that these gaps could also be taken as contributing to the initial failures to grasp what was happening" (1997, 469).

2 The role of Islam was intended to provide the negative pole in the Augustinian dualism that dominated the intellectual formation of Christian thought. The idea that Europe needed that contrast in order to define itself cultivated a view of the world that saw Islam as the antithesis to Christianity (Ballard 1996, 15–51).

3 See Daniel 1960. For a chronological and thematic survey of Europe's scholarly approach to Islam, see Hourani 1991.

4 The new Islamic realities in Europe gave rise to numerous publications, among them the following collections of articles: Shadid 1996, Nonneman 1996, and Vertovec 1997.
5 See *Preventing Deadly Conflict*, Final Report, Carnegie Commission on Preventing Deadly Conflict (New York, 1997).
6 New data on the conversion to Islam in the Balkans can be found in a recent Ph.D. dissertation by Anton Minkov, *Conversion to Islam in the Balkans*, The Islamic Studies Institute, McGill University, 2000.
7 See Boutros-Ghali 1999, Holbrooke 1998, and the Carnegie Commission report.
8 Mr Green's essay sounds a sympathetic note with the complaints raised by Boutros-Ghali, the UN's secretary-general at the time, in his memoirs of the events. See Boutros-Ghali 1999, 231–8. Boutros-Ghali offers a simple answer to the question "Why was Bosnia a failure? Because the United States was so deeply involved politically and so deeply determined not to be involved militarily" (246–7).

Islam and Bosnia

The Various Faiths
in the History of Bosnia:
Middle Ages to the Present

JOHN V.A. FINE

The conflict that began wracking Bosnia in early April 1992, when the international community recognized Bosnia's declaration of independence from a self-destructing Yugoslavia, though often called an ethnic or religious one, is hardly that. At the start it was only partially ethnic, and in its first years religion – other than being brought in as a subject of propaganda by Serb and Croat separatists – had no role at all. The government of Bosnia, though often called in the press the Muslim government, stood for the multi-ethnic entity Bosnia had been as a republic within Tito's Yugoslavia, representing toleration of all religions and nationalities. And this toleration has marked Bosnia's entire history, except when foreigners or locals stirred up by foreign governments or foreign movements have incited the Bosnians to other paths.[1]

In the Middle Ages the independent banovina and later kingdom of Bosnia was home to three religions. Bosnia lay between Catholic Dalmatia and Orthodox Serbia; often called a meeting ground between the two great churches, it was more a no-man's land between them. Bosnia proper was claimed by Rome and put under the archbishop of Dubrovnik. Bosnia's Catholics had few priests; Latin was unknown, and its services were in Slavic. Various errors crept into the local Catholicism, which Hungary, seeking to assert control over the independent-minded Bosnians, was able to depict as heresy. In 1235, having persuaded Rome of this claim, the

Hungarians launched a crusade against the so-called Bosnian heretics. A vicious war followed that brought Hungary temporary gains until the Tatars swept into Hungary in 1241, putting an end to the crusade. The Hungarians were not able to resume the venture but did persuade Rome to take Bosnia away from the lax supervision of Dubrovnik and assign it to a Hungarian archbishop in Kalocza. The Bosnians, determined to have nothing to do with the Hungarians, rejected the change, broke with international Catholicism, and in the 1250s formed their own Bosnian Church. For the next century, except for peripheral areas added to the state in the west and north, where Catholics were to be found, and in Hum (modern Hercegovina), most of which was conquered by Bosnia in 1326, where Orthodox were to be found, practising Bosnian Christians attended the Bosnian Church. This church has often been depicted as a dualist, neo-Manichee, or Bogomil church; however, all the local (including Dalmatian) evidence shows it to be a mainstream church, with standard Christian/Catholic views. Unlike dualists, the Bosnian Church accepted an omnipotent God, the Trinity, church buildings, the cross, the cult of saints, religious art, and at least part of the Old Testament. Furthermore, had the Bosnians been dualists, the cordial relations the sources depict between Bosnian Churchmen and Catholic officials (and even clerics) in Dalmatia, particularly in Dubrovnik, could not have occurred.

To avoid another threatened crusade the Bosnian ban, Stjepan Kotromanić, in about 1340, allowed a Franciscan mission into the central part of Bosnia; by the end of that decade Kotromanić had accepted Catholicism, and all of his successors (with one exception) up to the Ottoman conquest in the 1460s were Catholic. But despite the acceptance of Catholicism, the rulers remained entirely tolerant; members of all three faiths could be found at court, and other than efforts by the Franciscans to proselytize, which was freely allowed by the state, the Bosnians left religion to the wishes of individual Bosnians. The basic geographical division also remained: Orthodox were to be found in Hum/Hercegovina to the south and along the Drina; Catholics were to be found in the north and west, with the Franciscan mission in the centre; and the Bosnian Church also existed in the centre, spreading into the north, south, and east. Expansion of the state into Orthodox and Catholic areas did not lead to any significant spread of the Bosnian Church into other parts of Bosnia. And there were no religious persecutions in Bosnia until the last five years of the state. Then, with the Turks at the gate and Bosnia in need of western aid, the papacy made that support conditional upon the elimination of the Bosnian Church. The desperate king gave in, and for the state's final five years conversion to Catholicism or exile was the choice given to the Bosnian Church clergy in areas controlled by the king.

The tolerance that had existed throughout Bosnia's history until this final episode was probably owing chiefly to the indifference of most Bosnians to formal religion, but in any case, unlike what occurred in other areas of medieval and early modern Europe wherever two faiths were in competition, the faith of the Bosnian ruler did not govern the faith of his subjects. Since religion was worn loosely, Bosnians freely and frequently changed faiths to make alliances with more religiously zealous neighbouring nobles or to contract marriages. Keeping matters low-key was the shortage of priests of all three faiths and the fact that most priests were semi-literate (or less) locals. Only the Franciscans tended to be foreigners – mostly Italians – and there were fewer than 100 for all of Bosnia.

The Turks conquered most of Bosnia in the 1460s and the rest in the years that followed. The Bosnian Church, already in decline, was to disappear. The current Bosnian Muslim myth is that with the appearance of Islam, Bosnian Church-members, angry at Catholicism for its policy of persecution in the last five to six years of the state's existence, converted en masse to Islam, making nineteenth- and twentieth-century Muslims the descendants of medieval Bosnia's elite. Moreover, they argued that the Bosnian Church was a state church to which a majority of medieval Bosnians had belonged. They also believe that church to have been dualist, or as they call it Bogomil. However, this picture is false and over simplified. The Bosnian Church had never been a state church, and it is not clear that a majority of Bosnians had actually belonged to it.

Considerable religious change was to occur in Bosnia after the conquest, but it was a complex process. First many Orthodox fleeing Serbia, which was conquered before Bosnia was, settled in Bosnia. By 1500 the Orthodox, originally found only in the south and east, were to be found all over Bosnia. Many Catholics, with Catholic Dalmatia and Croatia not yet conquered, fled Bosnia entirely. So in Bosnia we find the Catholic population declining and Muslims appearing in increasing numbers. Some of these Muslims were migrants, but most were converts. However, they were converts

from all three Christian faiths of medieval Bosnia; there was nothing special about Bosnian Church members seeking Islam. Moreover, other Bosnian Church members became Catholics, while still
others became Orthodox. And many Catholics converted to Orthodoxy and a few Orthodox to Catholicism. This multi-directional
process was gradual and occurred over several centuries. It was not
until the seventeenth century that a majority of Bosnians had
become Muslim.

Why did so much religious change occur in Bosnia (and Albania)
and not elsewhere in the Balkans? Strong Orthodox or Catholic
organizations existed elsewhere in the Balkans that bound their
flocks to those churches through faith/doctrine and a sense of
community. Bosnia, by comparison, had competing churches, none
particularly strong, and all with a scarcity of priests. Thus Bosnians
were much less devoted Christians than most other Balkanites. Islam
appeared as a dynamic new faith, often propagated by dervishes,
and God's favour was shown by Ottoman success. It is not strange
that many shaky Christians would adopt it. (And we can add that
weak Christian Church organizations were also a feature of the interior of Albania, where many – eventually a majority – also converted
to Islam.) Those Bosnians who wanted to remain Christian tended
to become Orthodox, for that church was favoured by the Ottomans. The whole Orthodox hierarchy was within the Ottoman state,
and its leadership had reached an accommodation with the Ottomans, who gave their community recognized status and had a hand
in determining which men were appointed bishops. The Catholic
Church on the other hand was led by a figure in Italy, who also was
the major instigator of attempted crusades against the Ottomans.
Catholic clergy were seen, not surprisingly, as a fifth column. The
Orthodox were regularly allowed to take over Catholic churches in
Bosnian towns, and Orthodox bishops had the right to collect
church taxes from "Christians," whom Ottoman judges usually saw
as including Catholics too. So, if a Catholic did not want to pay both
tithe and Orthodox Church tax and wanted to continue to attend
his church, and suffer less suspicion from Ottoman authorities, it
made sense to become Orthodox; after all, these were uneducated
people who could not have understood the minuscule differences
in theology between one church and the other.

The Ottomans extended toleration to people of the Book (Jews
and Christians) and divided the population into communities

under their respective religious heads, which eventually came to be called millets. The Catholics as an empire-wide body did not get a millet, but the Bosnian Franciscans received a charter to operate and thus on a local scale enjoyed the privileges of a millet, which increased over time as more and more Bosnians (as opposed to Italians and other foreigners) came to staff the local Franciscan operation. The Franciscans were to be the only Catholic clergy operating in Bosnia for the whole post-1340 medieval and subsequent Ottoman periods.

Clearly favoured was the Islamic millet, and Christians were second-class citizens, with various restrictions in dress and occupation and in how much display their services could have. However, they were tolerated, and the Muslim, Orthodox, and Catholic communities lived fairly separate lives under their community notables, tolerating one another and suffering a minimum of friction. Unlike most of the rest of Ottoman Europe, a majority of the local Muslims were native Bosnians who had converted. The Muslims also controlled the land, so in most regions Muslim landlords ran estates manned by serfs. The serfs were not limited to Christians, for peasants who converted to Islam were serfs as well. Social tensions existed. The Ottomans, in dividing the people into millets and favoring the Muslims, did not try to create a state in which all had a stake. The subjects produced taxes, while the Muslim elite ran the state. People were classified by religion; no national or ethnic distinctions were recognized. And the Ottoman leadership was made up of Muslims from the whole empire, with many urban Bosnian Muslims receiving a higher education before going off to become members of the Ottoman establishment. Some of the Bosnians became major figures among the ulema, and several Bosnians served in the role of Shejhul-Islam, the highest position in the religious structure. Nevertheless, although there was an elite Islamic establishment in Bosnian cities that included educated Bosnian aristocrats and also other Ottoman Muslims from elsewhere serving in Bosnia, who were very visible to travellers in the area and important in Ottoman politics, most Bosnian Muslims remained on the periphery in a localized world that overlapped only occasionally with the religious establishment, which took little interest in what the lower orders did.

Excluding the Muslim elite, Bosnia continued to be a society of peasants (or shepherds in mountain areas) with very little education.

Popular Islam and Christianity remained syncretic and full of superstition. And villagers kept up ties across faiths, frequently attending each other's festivals. For most Bosnians, however, particularly the peasants, who made up the vast majority of society, religion (of all three faiths) stood at considerable distance from formal religious institutions; religion remained centred in the villages, where ritual acts (most aimed at obtaining benefits in this world) constituted one's religion. Thus Bosnian peasants' so-called religious concerns chiefly centred on practices rather than doctrine. The interaction between religious communities on the village level during the Ottoman period, supported by the local priests, most of whom were locals, including the village hodjas and the Franciscans, allowed the development of what truly is a Bosnian culture, shared by Bosnians of all faiths and distinct from that of the neighbouring regions (now states). Much of this general Bosnian feeling was still alive and well in the late 1980s. The events of the last decade, with their ideological accompaniments, have since then done much to destroy this feeling. But there is a major tradition and a memory of it that may once again overcome the chauvinist movements that seek to destroy it. Tito's ethnically just Yugoslavia succeeded in just that after the horrors of World War II.

Bosnia remained under the Ottomans from 1463 to 1878. Then, after a major uprising there and in Bulgaria, the Russians intervened, defeating the Turks, and the Treaty of Berlin assigned Bosnia-Hercegovina to Austria-Hungary to administer.

When one looks at the Balkan wars of the 1990s, again and again we hear that these different peoples have been fighting for centuries and that current hatreds are ancient. This is sheer myth for all the Balkan peoples. But let us look specifically at the Bosnian case:

In the Middle Ages the local population saw itself as Bosnian (or had even more localized regional identities); people called Serbs and Croats did not live in Bosnia proper. The state of Bosnia warred against Serbia and Croatia, but these were international wars, led by dynastic-based rulers, with no ethnic aspects. The three religious faiths lived in mutual toleration. There was not a single ethnic or religious war among peoples in medieval Bosnia. The Hungarians in the 1230s crusaded in Bosnia on behalf of Catholicism, and the Ottomans fought in the name of Islam, but these were foreign invasions. The Bosnians themselves did not fight either ethnic or religious wars. This is not to idealize the Bosnians. They were fighting all the time, nobles against king, nobles against nobles, but their wars were over land and hegemony.

Under the Ottomans, ethnicity played no role until the concept gradually began penetrating Bosnia in the nineteenth century. And, until the second half of the nineteenth century, the Ottomans kept the society under control and the millets in mutual toleration. There were foreign wars between Catholic Habsburgs (in whose armies Serbs and Croatians from that empire served) and Muslim Ottomans (in whose armies Bosnian Muslims served). However, these locals did not fight as ethnics, but as parts of imperial armies. And quarrels between Muslim landlords and peasants (often Christian), which became frequent only in the 1850s, were basically social. So in the Ottoman period we have no internal ethnic or religious warfare either. The current tensions are clearly not ancient; in fact, they began after the creation of Yugoslavia in 1918.

The concept of ethnicity itself had raised its dubious if not evil head in Bosnia only in the nineteenth century, when Christian Bosnians began to take up ethnic and national ideas that penetrated Bosnia from Serbia and Croatia. With this development, new dimensions were added to one's religious identity. If you were a Catholic, you were also a Croat; if an Orthodox, then also a Serb. Now, for the first time, the names "Serb" and "Croat" were applied to people in Bosnia. The Franciscans were active in persuading Catholics to take on the new Croat identity since many of them were swept up by the Croatian nationalism rapidly spreading in Croatia in the mid- to late-nineteenth century, and since most Franciscans received their religious education in Croatia. The Muslims at first showed little or no interest in ethnic identities at all; both "Serb" and "Croat" implied Christianity. But it is important to stress that throughout the Ottoman period and to the present, members of the three religious communities and of the present ethnic ones, regardless of label, spoke and speak the same language.

In 1878, when (against the wishes of its Muslim and Serb Orthodox populations) Bosnia came under the control of Austria, a Catholic state, a crisis arose in the Muslim community and also, though people not familiar with Bosnia might be surprised, in the Catholic community. The Muslims found themselves subject to a Catholic state that also imported a strong degree of secularism, including general state schools, in which children of all religions were mixed and followed a modern European curriculum. Educated

Muslims became worried, fearing that such schooling, combined with administration by a Catholic state, would lead to conversions of Muslims to Catholicism. For the first time, they became worried about the loose and ignorant version of Islam that had tolerated so much syncretism with Christian traditions, such as the practice of honouring saints. Might not their lack of sophisticated Islam, combined with both the number of retained Christian traditions and the influence of a Catholic state that was not averse to conversions, lead Muslims to convert to Catholicism? For the first time, the educated Muslim elite, who had totally ignored the practices of their Muslim serfs, began taking an interest in what the village Muslims were doing. Their interference caused major tensions within the Muslim community.

The Catholics underwent a similar clash. Rome worried about the Franciscans' lax administration of the local Catholics and about all the practices the Franciscans tolerated – practices it might be added, whose tolerance was perhaps necessary to ensuring that Catholicism did not lose the majority of its flock to the two other religions. So the pope, supported by the Austrian emperor, appointed Bosnia an archbishop who was a foreigner and also not a Franciscan. Until then, neither the medieval Bosnian state nor the Ottomans had allowed the Vatican to appoint a bishop who could exercise authority in Bosnia. The new archbishop for Sarajevo, Archbishop Josip Stadler, agreed upon by Rome and Vienna, arrived in Bosnia in 1881. The Franciscans, who had laboured there for 500 years and without whom there would no longer have been any Bosnians who were still Catholic, were outraged. Their objections were followed by a compromise: the Franciscans would still be able to administer half of Bosnia's parishes. Though the Franciscan leadership in Rome agreed to this, the local Franciscans, strongly supported by their congregations, balked. Even today (i.e., at the start of the war in Bosnia) the Franciscans still control well over half of the parishes in Bosnia. And the on-going tensions can be seen in responses to the visions of the Virgin at Medjugorje. The Franciscans support the claims and are administering a religious shrine there, while the bishop of Mostar – who has jurisdiction over Medjugorje – calls the whole claim teenage hysteria. This century-long quarrel has no wholly good or bad guys; the Franciscan support of village Catholicism did much to contribute to an all-Bosnian perspective, but the Croatian nationalism with which they were infected caused them to blindly embrace Croatian causes, which would lead them to support the Ustaše in World War II, the most divisive – not to speak of criminal – action they could have taken.

However, the tensions that came to the fore with the Austrian occupation, though highly emotional and fascinating (particularly because they are so little studied), are within religious (becoming ethnic) communities, not between them.

Yugoslavia between the First and Second World Wars was a greater Serbia; most other peoples were clearly second-class citizens, whose regions were run from Belgrade. Dissatisfaction grew, the most vocal being the Croatians, though the Macedonians and Albanians suffered far more. Animosities grew that the Germans were able to play upon after their conquest of Yugoslavia in April 1941. Yugoslavia was partitioned, and Bosnia was joined to the fascist puppet state of Croatia, which was led by a terrorist group called the Ustaše, even though Bosnia had only a small number of Croats; at the time Bosnia's ethnic make-up was roughly 20 per cent Croats, 35 per cent Muslims, and 42 per cent Serbs. The Croatian regime, strongly nationalistic, immediately set about ethnic cleansing, particularly of Serbs. Mile Budak proclaimed Ustaše policy in dealing with Serbs: kill a third, expel a third, and convert a third. Since Bosnia was assigned to Croatia, this policy was applied to Bosnia as well. As the Croats were a minority in Bosnia, the Ustaše decided to woo the Muslims. Nationalists had for the previous decades been claiming that all Bosnians were Croats (or Serbs) and that the Muslims were simply those of that ethnic group who had converted. This idea was pushed hard by the Ustaše, and a few Muslims were won over. Some of the initially persuaded, however, quickly abandoned the cause when they saw what the Ustaše were about. Thus the ethnic warfare of World War II had a definite religious dimension. And one must emphasize and condemn the support that the Catholic Church, including members of the hierarchy and in particular the Franciscans, gave to the Ustaše and their endeavours. Franciscans were active in carrying out the policy of forced conversions, and a couple even had major roles in the administration of concentration/death camps. In this case disagreements within the Franciscan-episcopal hierarchy took a back seat; only the elderly bishop of Mostar, Alojzije Mišić (who died early in the war), condemned the genocide and the forced conversions. His letters to the metropolitan and overseeing archbishop in Zagreb, Alojzije Stepinac – now outrageously being championed by Croat nationalists (and even many in the Vatican) for sainthood – were ignored. The rest of the episcopal hierarchy in Croatia and Bosnia supported the Ustaše and the new so-called independent state of greater Croatia, though a few did express occasional doubts about the means the Ustaše were using. Ustaše terror and destruction of Serb villages provoked a Serb nationalist response (under Serb royalist nationalists who called themselves Četniks), resulting in a violent campaign against Croatian villagers. Nearly two million Yugoslavs died in the course of the war.

This time, in place of the Tatars who had burst upon the scene to save Bosnia from Hungary in 1241, divine providence provided a new saviour in Josip Broz Tito. His popular front movement alone rose above the ethnic strife and called for the peoples of Yugoslavia to cooperate, under the slogan of "brotherhood and unity," in ousting the invaders and their local surrogates. In the long-run Tito and the allies were successful, and Yugoslavia was liberated, put together again, and divided up into six republics (each based on a dominant ethnicity, except for Bosnia, which had Serbs, Croats, and Muslims, with each group to be found throughout its territory). Tito was able to start with a clean slate, for the extreme nationalists had fled or been killed; no Karadžić-es and Mladić-es remained in Bosnia to perpetuate chauvinism. Yugoslavs were sick of ethnic warfare, and Bosnia in particular had seen its horrors, for it had such a great mixture of peoples.

As Yugoslavia progressed (and progress it did) and, as it turned out and to its detriment, followed a policy of increasing decentralization, ethnicity became more and more central to politics. Those of Muslim background, who on the whole still did not see themselves as Muslim Serbs or Muslim Croats, realized that they needed to form an ethnic group and proceeded to do so, becoming an officially recognized nation in 1968 under the label of "Muslim." Since that time, the term "Muslim" has had a double meaning, denoting a religious community and also an ethnic one – the same twin aspects that characterize the term "Jew" in America. And since 1968, the vast majority of references to Muslims in Bosnia have been to the so-called ethnic group.

By 1990, after forty-five years of communism, all of Bosnian society was very secularized, and though all three ethnic groups had their origins in a religion (with the Muslims being only the most recent to follow that path), religion played little role in the lives of any of the elite. Thus one should not see Muslims, Serbs, and Croats as being Muslim, Orthodox, and Catholic, but as being of those three respective backgrounds. And since persons of all three ethnicities were twentieth-century, modern, secular Europeans, led by members of the Communist Party of Bosnia-Hercegovina, there was much intermarriage among different groups in Bosnia's cities. Between the Second World War and 1991 roughly 40 per cent of urban marriages were mixed, and over 20 per cent of urban Bosnians declared themselves in censuses "Yugoslav" or "other," refusing to define themselves in ethnic terms. Thus the first definition for the term "Muslim" after 1968 was ethnic, and few educated Muslims gave Islam much thought. They thought of themselves as Europeans and feared an Islamic focus, for Islamic values clashed with their secular views on life. An urban Bosnian Muslim had more in common with an urban Serb or Croat than with a religious Muslim living in the Middle East. Villages, however, tended to be more conservative, and some villages were made up of people who all belonged to a single ethnicity. The villagers tended to keep up religious practices to a greater extent than most urbanites.

After the irresponsible and unnecessary secession of Croatia and Slovenia from Yugoslavia, which broke up a magnificent country, set off a vicious war in Croatia, and revived many of the Ustaše-Četnik horrors of World War II, Serbia's leaders began seeking a reconfiguration of borders to bring all Serb areas (or what they perceived as such) into a new greater Serbia. Bosnia had many Serbs. As ethnic tensions grew and then warfare exploded in Croatia, it became clear that Bosnia was to be next. It had a small number of Serb and Croat chauvinists among its populace, whose numbers grew as a result of the barrage of slanderous propaganda that Serbia and Croatia directed at Bosnia, hoping for its elimination and subsequent division between their two republics. Indeed, just as war was breaking out between Serbia and Croatia over parts of Croatia, Slobodan Milošević and the equally villainous Franjo Tudjman came together and agreed upon how they would partition Bosnia. In Serbia and Croatia propaganda against one another was stepped up, but both states also directed hate-stirring propaganda at their co-nationals in Bosnia.

By this time three nationality-based parties had emerged as victors in the 1990 Bosnian parliamentary elections, all of whose campaigns had emphasized new economic policies and cooperation among ethnicities, something that was not even briefly to happen once the nationalists had won. Only one party, the SDA, the overwhelmingly Muslim party of Izetbegović, took a multi-ethnic position. After all, the Muslims could not survive in a landlocked state caught between chauvinist and irredentist Serb and Croat states; the only hope for the Muslims was to follow Bosnia's traditions of inter-ethnic cooperation, something Bosnia had long upheld and upon which the survival of the Muslims of Bosnia depended.

Wanting to divide Bosnia between them, the leaders of Serbia and Croatia, who deemed any basis for society other than ethnicity contrary to their goals (and nothing could be worse than multi-ethnic cooperation), turned on the Muslims, slandering them in television transmissions beamed from Zagreb and Belgrade. With the aim of stirring up fears among their co-nationals in Bosnia, they accused the SDA and Izetbegović of seeking to set up an Islamic state and of being Islamic fundamentalists. In reality the SDA's leadership in 1991–92 (excluding Izetbegović) was secular and made up of ex-communists. Izetbegović, unlike the other leaders, was a religious Muslim, but being religious does not mean being a fundamentalist, as Americans who deal with Christians and Christian fundamentalists well know. Though Bosnia did have a small number of very religious Muslims in 1992, these people had little or no role in politics. Moreover, almost none of them could be called fundamentalists, for almost none of them believed the state's law should be based on the Sharia.

However, as a young man Izetbegović had pondered whether Islam could co-exist with the modern world, and in 1969, having concluded that it could, he had written an essay called "The Islamic Declaration" on how an Islamic state could exist, keeping the values of Islam alongside technological progress. The work was a theoretical one and more or less a "Utopia." Bosnia was never mentioned in the text, and Izetbegović also explicitly stated that such an Islamic society could be established only in a state that was overwhelmingly Muslim. Bosnia, then about 45 per cent Muslim, was clearly not such a state. But this work was a great find for propagandists in Zagreb and Belgrade, who used it to stir up fears among their Bosnian co-nationals, claiming that this utopian

Islamic state was Izetbegović's goal for Bosnia. It was not his goal, and though Izetbegović may well have liked the idea of such a state, it was anathema to his SDA associates, who, as ethnic and not religious Muslims, were secular Europeans who did not think that religion had a place in governing a modern state. In any case this anti-Muslim propaganda found many Serb and Croat villagers receptive, and a majority of the early Serb and Croat separatist ethnic warriors, though not their officers, were from villages.

When Bosnia declared its independence from rump-Yugoslavia in April 1992, the local Serbs immediately launched their rebellion to detach "Serb" lands from Bosnia. They were supported by the Yugoslav People's Army (now almost entirely Serb in leadership), which had huge numbers in Bosnia. Thus Serbia did not even have to invade, and in a matter of weeks the Serbs had secured close to two-thirds of Bosnia. The local Croats, fearing the Serbs, briefly supported the Bosnians, but after the Bosnian Croats had armed themselves from Croatia, they stabbed the Bosnians in the back, hacking out their own territory and ethnically cleansing their region as the Serbs had theirs.

Clearly, foreign intervention was called for from the outset; here was an internationally recognized state (whose independence the international community had encouraged) being torn apart by its two neighbours, Serbia and Croatia (though these aggressors were fronted by local surrogates). The Bosnian government was supported not only by the Muslims, but also by many urban Serbs and Croats: the cabinet of 1992 had nine Muslims, six Serbs, and five Croats; a third of those defending Sarajevo against Karadžić's separatist Serbs were other Serbs; and the commander of the defense of Sarajevo, Jovan Divjak, was also a Serb. So it is important to stress that Karadžić spoke only for some of the Serbs. The Bosnian government, desperate in the face of this appalling outbreak of the nationalist disease, took a position that the West and the UN should have supported: ethnic and religious toleration in a multi-ethnic state. But not only did the West and the UN not help Bosnia, but Western negotiators even adopted the ethnic categories of the aggressors, the Serb and Croat chauvinist separatists. The Bosnian government called for a multi-ethnic state, but every peace plan advanced by the international community had a very weak central Bosnia, with a variety of ways being provided for any given ethnic group to completely subvert that central government's effective functioning, and with this weak all-Bosnian state being combined with some form of ethnic partition, be it through ethnic zones or a variety of ethnic cantons. Then Western negotiators, particularly Lord Owen, became enraged at the Bosnians for turning down these solutions that the West was drawing up to allegedly help them. The current solution provided by the Dayton Accords in November 1995 is just such a solution, which, I believe, deliberately or not – though delaying it – simply provides for the eventual ethnic partition of Bosnia, a partition for which all those involved in the Dayton Accords share responsibility.

Meanwhile the anti-Islamic propaganda became a self-fulfilling prophecy. One of the pre-conference notices for the academic gathering at the University of Western Ontario states that "In all of these cases, including Bosnia, a militant Islamic component was involved in the process." For Bosnia, at the start and until the autumn of 1993, that statement is simply not true. An Islamic component has now emerged but was not there for the first couple of years. Then international pressure on Bosnia to accept proposed plans for the country's ethnic partition began to affect some Muslim politicians, who feared that if they did not agree to the international solutions, the international community would leave them to their fate. Indeed, it was becoming increasingly clear in the year preceding the Dayton Accords that in the end there would be an ethnic solution (as in fact the Accords were to provide) with a Muslim zone. If that were to be the case, then the sooner the Muslims backed down and accepted such a solution, the more territory they might be able to acquire for the Muslim people. As the war proceeded, some Muslims for the first time began to embrace the idea of a Muslim nation state. Moreover, for the first time since 1945, owing to the exodus of Christians from the area under the control of the Muslim-led government, religious Muslims found themselves able to enter the sphere of Bosnian politics. As a result, if one was a religious Muslim, new opportunities arose; but if one was a secular Muslim, or a non-Muslim, new dangers emerged.

These dangers and the effects they have had were seen by Tom Gjelten in autumn 1993:

By the fall of 1993, Muslim nationalism in Bosnia had moved closer in character to its Serb and Croat counterparts, with Muslim party leaders arguing that the Bosnian government should give precedence to Muslim national interests over the concerns of Serb and Croat citizens.

Such arguments were given a big boost when international mediators David Owen and Thorvald Stoltenberg promoted the Milošević-Tudjman proposal to partition Bosnia, creating a "union" of three ethnic republics. Owen and Stoltenberg had spoken continually of Muslims, Serbs, and Croats – rather than [of] citizens of Bosnia – in the peace negotiations, and on July 31, 1993, Alija Izetbegović accepted their formulation and agreed to the proposal, at least in theory. Speaking from Geneva via Radio Sarajevo to listeners back home, Izetbegović sounded as if he saw himself no longer as the president of Bosnia but only as the leader of the Bosnian Muslim people. "We are trying to preserve a large piece of Bosnia for our nation," he told them ...

With Izetbegović's tentative acceptance of the idea of a "Muslim" republic existing in a loose union with "Serb" and "Croat" republics, the goal of preserving a multiethnic Bosnian state appeared to have been abandoned, and Sarajevo's standing as a bastion of interfaith harmony and tolerance was put in jeopardy. Conservative Muslim leaders seemed unbothered. "We Muslims don't have much choice," said Selim Hadžibajrić .... "The other sides [Serb and Croat] pushed us into a civil war. We are left alone, and now we must have our own state as well. Serbs and Croats who want to stay and live with us will be free to do so," he said, "but the question of civil authority must be left to the Muslims. We must not be manipulated by Serbs and Croats again.[2]

This change in emphasis from Bosnia to Muslim Bosnia was first prominently seen when Izetbegović presented the Owen-Stoltenberg plan in September 1993 to an assembly of Muslim intellectuals before submitting it to the multi-ethnic Bosnian parliament. The plan, which called for a Muslim entity, found support among some Muslim leaders, including Alija Isaković, the head of that congress. Isaković said, "Now that multiethnic Bosnia has been destroyed, the Muslim state must create its own political and constitutional framework in the same way as the Bosnian Serbs and Croats have done."[3] Non-Muslims were allowed to be present at the assembly only as observers, and many of them feared that this assembly would accept the plan, which would have greatly undercut future hopes for a continuing multi-ethnic society. However, concluding that the territory the Muslims were being offered was badly designed for a viable state, the assembly rejected the plan.

The growing Muslim national feeling in Sarajevo over recent years has been strongly encouraged by the presence of refugees. Since mid-1993, Sarajevo has been full of refugees fleeing the ethnic cleansing by Serbs and Croats. Dislocated and poor, usually from Muslim villages and poorly educated, these people have never truly adopted the values of "brotherhood and unity." Croats or Serbs drove them from their homes, and in Sarajevo they now find Serbs and Croats possessing a portion of the city's limited housing. To them, this situation is unjust, and the city's leaders should rectify the situation. There are refugees in ever-increasing numbers; they are a pressure group and a voting block, and various Muslim politicians have been responding to them. In some cases this is pure opportunism, but the war has also been a strain on the politicians, and its effects have surely made some of them truly less supportive of multi-ethnic values and less tolerant of the local loyalist Serbs and Croats, owing to the behavior of these peoples' co-ethnics.

This declining tolerance has been seen particularly among some of the religious leaders. Mustafa Cerić, the Reis-ul-Islam (head of Bosnia's Muslims), has on occasion publicly suggested that all Serbs share in the blame for what the separatist Serbs have done. When Muhamed Filipović, a leading Muslim who had broken with the SDA, accused Cerić on one occasion of acting more like a politician than a cleric, Cerić replied, "We want a state, a country, in which we as Muslims have no need to apologize for our Islam."[4]

Moreover, even though Bosnia's Muslims were secular individuals, Muslims throughout the world saw them as victims because they were Muslims. Foreign Muslims began volunteering, often very religious ones, and Islamic states (in particular Iran) began smuggling in arms and advisors. So an Islamic presence began to grow.

Furthermore, Izetbegović did want Islam to play a role in the state – particularly as the area under his control became more and more Muslim. New figures (who had no communist past) began rising in the SDA, some of them former associates in Islamic organizations to which Izetbegović had belonged in his youth. Some of these people began clashing with the secularly inclined leaders over multi-ethnicity; hatred for the treatment they had suffered at the hands of Serbs and Croats was too strong. Muslim areas were now overwhelmingly Muslim – due to an influx of new immigrants and the exodus of many Serbs and Croats. Given that the refugees had been expelled from their homes by Serbs and Croats, why were people from these two nationalities occupying apartment space in Muslim-run Sarajevo when the Muslim refugees were more or less homeless? Since government-run territory was overwhelmingly

Muslim, why not keep it so by agreeing to a partition? The issue for many was now to get as much territory as possible for the Muslim statelet. Mustafa Cerić, as the Reis-ul-Islam, now found receptive listeners after the years of being ignored that those in his post had faced under communism. He had funding to bring out and circulate religious magazines and newspapers with his views. And he soon began a campaign against mixed marriages. Enes Karić, appointed minister of culture in mid-1994 (a position that also oversees education), began insisting on the teaching of Islam in the public schools – and secular Muslims, horrified at this, found themselves in the position that Americans face over the issue of prayers in schools, a practice advocated in the us by the religious right. The secular Muslims found themselves and their values threatened; if Sarajevo's schools were going to be interfered with like this, how many Serbs and Croats would return? And, if they did not return and the schools were to be run by religious Muslims, was there going to be a place in Sarajevo for its secular Muslims? The sda also began taking an interest in higher education. The autonomy enjoyed by the universities and respected under communism was quickly challenged, and various regulations cutting into that autonomy have now been adopted as the party quietly gets its people into the top positions of the University of Sarajevo and its various faculties in order to be in a position to take control when the time is ripe for Bosnia to revive its struggling and basically unfunded faculties.

This newly visible and audible Islam, which is pushing newly emerging Bosnian-Muslim leaders into increasing numbers of conflicts with their more secular co-ethnics, is all pervasive. And the term audible is particularly apt, as blaring calls to prayer have now become commonplace in Bosnia's cities.

Religion also began penetrating the armed forces in 1994–95; Islamic symbols and quotations from the Koran started to show up among army units, and in February 1995 a unit of Muslim soldiers was reported praying publicly at a manoeuvre. Whether the soldiers were put up to it by their unit commander or by some higher authority is not clear, but it brought serious protest from the two Serbs, the two Croats, and the one Muslim Social Democrat in the seven-person collective presidency of Bosnia. The five declared, "Nobody has a monopoly on patriotism and the struggle for liberation. Our position remains that the army which defends and guards the state of Bosnia has to be secular and multinational." The two SDA members of the presidency (one of whom is Izetbegović) denied there was an official attempt to make Islam the dominant ideology of the army, saying, "There is no use of religion as ideology. There is only the manifestation of religion and that will continue to be allowed everywhere, including the army." And the two went on to argue that prayer and turning to God would give the soldiers more courage to go into battle. The commander of the Bosnian army, General Rasim Delić, echoed the two SDA presidents: "Any manifestation of religion in the army is free and does not represent any sort of ideological indoctrination."[5] But are these manifestations merely a spontaneous sign of the times, aberrant acts pushed by unit commanders, or first steps in a deliberate policy being advocated at a higher level?

The Serb and Croat ethnics in Bosnia, and their dominant parties, have been as secular as the Muslims first were; in their case religious influence has remained insignificant. These parties, like the original SDA, are dominated by ex-communists. And though at times priests have been paraded out to bless ethnic troops or to make statements on behalf of a national cause, they have had little or no influence on Serb or Croat politics and ideology. In this warfare, the Catholic clergy on the whole has been much more responsible and tolerant than it was during World War II. Much of this may be owing to the admirable archbishop of Sarajevo, Vinko Cardinal Puljić, who has consistently and publicly pleaded for peace and multi-ethnic toleration. And, on the whole, the Franciscans, though many are still nationalist Croats, have also been voices of reason, calling upon the different ethnic and religious groups to live together in peace. The tolerant positions taken by these leading Catholic clerics may explain why the clergy has had so little role in Bosnian-Croat politics. In any case the chauvinist leaders of the Croatian and Serbian entities remain in control of their societies, and though the Bosnians (Muslims) and Croats are supposedly joined together in a federation, the federation barely exists. So Bosnia is in fact three separate mutually hostile entities combined in a non-functioning all-Bosnian state that has jurisdiction over only a small number of functional departments.

This result is certainly not what the Muslims or the SDA initially sought. The experience of the war and its traumatic effects on many Muslims in Bosnia, as well as the contents of the various proposed peace plans and then of the Dayton Accords, followed by the order those Accords created, have combined to gradually (but increasingly over time) push many Muslims in those parts of Bosnia under the Bosnian government in a Muslim direction. But, should the results of war and diplomacy create a permanent entity, defined as a Muslim one, this tragedy will have been an outgrowth of events and not the result of the initial aims of any of the Bosnian government's (or original SDA Party's) leaders. And in no way should such a result be seen as justifying the separatist Serbs' so-called fears, expressed in their propaganda, of Izetbegović's desire to create a Muslim (or as they usually said, an Islamic) state.

Moreover, even if some Muslims now seek or would acquiese in supporting an official Muslim and/or Islamic entity, this trend is not in the interests of the Muslims (including the nationalists) themselves. As Obradović argues:

There can be no doubt, however, that such a division [an ethnic partition of Bosnia] would be fatal to the Muslims above all. A Muslim nation would be a posteriori justification for the war and aggression on both the Serbian and Croatian sides. What the Serbian and Croatian propaganda machines groundlessly called "preventive reasons" for the war and the establishment of ethnic states would become more convincing. Separatist Muslim nation-alism would not only lead to the division of Bosnia and Herzegovina but also to isolation for the Muslim nation. Undoubtedly, an anti-Muslim alli-ance between Serbia and Croatia would be established for the final divi-sion of Bosnia and Herzegovina, the consummation of an idea first introduced in secret talks between Franjo Tudjman and Slobodan Milošević in 1991.[6]

Thus the battle among the Bosnian Muslims to define the mean-ing of "Muslim" and what effect this identity should have on their lives and the state they live in continues. The Muslims are strongly divided over this issue, and the debate over its various aspects is often heated. How Muslim should the state be? And, if Muslim, to what degree is this to be an ethnic state? To what degree does Islam have a role? To what degree should the state cater to multi-ethnicity? And, of course, the context in which the debate takes place is one of great uncertainty. Will all of Bosnia come back together again? Will even the non-existent Bosnian-Croat federation become a reality? Or will the federation fade away to be replaced by a Bosnian-Muslim – and two other ethnic – statelet(s)? Obviously, the eventual result of the war's aftermath – and this result may be decades away – will affect the answers to these questions.

But, if a tiny Muslim statelet does emerge (in those areas presently controlled by Muslims), what role will and/or should Islam play in that territory? That this question can be posed in 1999 would have seemed amazing to a scholar in 1989 or even 1992, when the Islamic side of the Muslim nation was so minuscule that analysts could simply ignore it. The fears expressed by supporters of multi-ethnic Bosnia that Bosnian Muslims might well be driven in a religious direction by the horrific war and the response of the international community – whether that of the condescending and unhelpful West or that of the religiously motivated Islamic East – have been at least partially realized. Of course, if the Bosnian Muslims end up with their own statelet, its lack of a port and the presence of hostile neighbours on all sides might well render it unviable in the long run. But to the degree that it can survive, will it have a place for those of other ethnicities who supported it in the years of wartime crisis, for those of mixed backgrounds, and even for secular non-religious Muslims?

At present it is too early to predict the answers to these questions, particularly since no one can foresee what the future of Dayton-defined Bosnia will be and what will happen if the occupying NATO troops ever leave. Moreover, much will depend upon the direction the SDA takes when Izetbegović no longer leads the party. There obviously will be a power struggle between various factions within the party, and that a religiously driven faction might well come out on top is an amazing result of the war. The influence of the secularists in the party is weaker now, with some of the ablest secularists, like former Prime Minister Haris Silajdžić, having already left the party. But if the secularists are to be defeated, one can only hope that the Islamicists will remain true to Bosnia's historical traditions and at least tolerate those of other ethnicities and also those with other views within their own ethnicity.

In any case, the Western European disease of ethnic nationalism has hit Bosnia with the virulence such epidemics often have on populations with little past experience of them, which means that they have little or no immunity. And this new ideology really does threaten to destroy the toleration that has usually marked Bosnians of all faiths from the Middle Ages up until our own time. Western policy makers must think long and hard now, for as long as the West caters to ethnic-based solutions, whether in the once and future Yugoslavia or elsewhere, it will merely cultivate the disease rather than cure those infected.

NOTES

1 The name of the Republic under Tito and of the current state of Bosnia is the Republic of Bosnia and Herzegovina. For simplicity's sake I shall refer to it as "Bosnia" throughout. On the history of Bosnia see: Donia and Fine 1994, Malcolm 1994, Fine 1975, Fine 1987, Imamović 1997, Hickok 1997, Babić and Zovkić 1986, and West 1994.

2 Gjelten 1995, 227–8.

3 Ibid., 230–1.

4 Ibid., 228.

5 R. Cohen, "Bosnia Debate: Army as Defender of Islam or Multiculturalism?" *The New York Times*, 4 February 1995.

6 Obradović 1994, 13–14.

Islam and the Quest for Identity in Post-Communist Bosnia-Herzegovina

TONE BRINGA

When I started my anthropology studies in the early 80s, I was motivated by an interest in Muslim societies and more particularly in Muslim-Christian encounters. The Muslims of Bosnia-Herzegovina in what was then Yugoslavia who lived in close interaction with their Catholic and Orthodox neighbours appeared as an attractive and fascinating case for my Ph.D. fieldwork. While researching the literature in London's university libraries, however, I found very little on the Bosnian Muslims published in English. What I found was either outdated or did not deal properly with the role of Islam in everyday life in Bosnia. One scholar suggested that the only relevance of Islam to the Bosnian Muslims was that they had once believed that "Allah was the one god and Muhammed his prophet"; all that remained of their faith was their ethnonym "Muslim." His point was that Muslim had become a secularized ethnic identity devoid of religious content (see Gellner 1983). In a Radio-Free Europe Research (RFER) report from the early 1980s, I read that "female imams" had been marching to the local mosque in Pristina (Kosovo) to demand participation in the Friday prayers. Intriguingly, this looked like a kind of Islamic feminism before it became fashionable elsewhere in the Islamic world. In another report I read about the trials against Muslim nationalist political activists or so-called "Islamic fundamentalists" in Sarajevo in 1984 (where among others Alija Izetbegovic, the leader of the Bosnian government

during the recent war, was sentenced). In retrospect, the information I had about the role of Islam in everyday life in Bosnia, and
thus about its meaning to the Bosnian-Muslim identity, before I
gained first-hand knowledge through my anthropological fieldwork, was at best contradictory and at worst misleading. However,
the information I came across in the library of a major European
capital was illustrative in what it revealed about Western European
attitudes towards Muslims and Islam. The lack of informed knowledge and the persistence of biases became even clearer in the course
of the Western media coverage of and humanitarian involvement in
the recent war in Bosnia-Herzegovina. There were in particular two
prevalent themes. First, to some Western observers (including some
scholars), the presence of Islam in Europe (in an indigenous population as opposed to a recent immigrant population) was perceived as something that belonged to the past, a historical remnant
of the Ottoman Empire – a view held by several speakers at international conferences on Bosnia that I attended during 1992–95.
Islam, in other words, was perceived as a foreign body on European
soil that had been (or should have been) eradicated with the defeat
of the Ottomans in the last century. The European Muslims in the
Balkans were associated with the Ottoman conquest of Europe and
considered an anachronism. In the extension of this view is lurking
a more bigoted perception, the idea that Muslims, specifically their
religion and customs, are "backward." This is very much also the
local prejudice that many Christians hold against Muslims in the
former Yugoslavia. Second, reflected in the previously mentioned
RFER reports was an obsession with Islamic fundamentalism. It is
important to note that in Tito's Yugoslavia, Islamic fundamentalism
(or just "fundamentalist") was considered synonymous with Muslim
nationalism and a parallel to Serb and Croat nationalism. The
expression of any nationalist sentiments was regarded as an anti-
state act in Tito's Yugoslavia and therefore punishable as a form of
treason. Since there was an almost complete overlap between the
religious community and the ethnic or national community in
Bosnia-Herzegovina, public expressions of religiosity were as feared
by Yugoslav authorities as any overt expression of nationalism. This
applied equally for all three ethno-religious communities. The difference was, however, in the apparent emphasis on the religious
aspect of Muslim identity by others. I believe there were two reasons
for this, first that "Muslim" as the ethnonym for the Bosnian

Muslims (as opposed to say Bosnian or the recently reinvented Bosniak) stresses the religious identification of the community and its individual members to the exclusion of other identifications. Within the Bosnian context this was not a significant problem, as all three communities in Bosnia had been identified according to religious adherence. This was a legacy of the Ottoman millet system. Indeed, in many rural areas of Bosnia up until the recent war the people identified themselves and were identified by others primarily as members of religious, rather than national, communities. For instance, in the village where I did my fieldwork there were two communities, one Catholic and one Muslim. (According to the official Yugoslav nationalities categorization, the Catholics in Bosnia were also Croats.) Second, while the ethnonym "Muslim" in many Bosnians' minds had become detached from its original meaning of someone who submits to the will of God and believes that Muhammad is his prophet (as Gellner correctly points out), this was certainly not the case in the Europe outside of Yugoslavia. This became apparent when worldwide and particularly European media attention was focused on Bosnia and the plight of the Bosnian Muslims. The information void about the Bosnian Muslims was easily filled by various sources, many of which played right into Western preconceptions and prejudices about Islam.

Indeed, the very word Muslim invoked a set of associations consisting of "fundamentalism," "violence," "backwardness," and hostility towards Christians. When the Serbian propaganda machinery epitomized by the Bosnian-Serb leader Radovan Karadzic repeatedly espoused propaganda that associated the Muslims with concepts such as Islam fundamentalism, terrorism, and a threat to Christian civilization, he knew such images would strike a nerve with a Western audience. He referred to Bosnian Muslims as Turks (an old Christian-Slav slur) and thus categorized them as foreign invaders with no right to the land. He also accused them of committing "demographic genocide" against the Serbs. ("Genocide" was a favorite word in Karadzic's and the Serbian nationalists' vocabulary, on pair with fundamentalism.)[1] Indeed, particularly in the beginning of the war, it was depressing to see how much of the Serbian propaganda was echoed by respectable newspapers and commentators. I observed this particularly in Norway, but it was also apparent among officials within the UN system and among other international representatives.[2]

The Serbian propaganda found resonance in a European tradition of "orientalism" – a term coined by Edward Said to mean the image of the orient as Europe's "other," which Europe ruled culturally and economically and negated (see Said 1978). But it was not only Christian-defined Europe that often misrepresented the Bosnian Muslims; non-European (Middle-Eastern) Muslims did this too. Their perceptions were based on a view of the Bosnian Muslims as ignorant of the true faith and therefore in need of instruction and proselytizing. It was a deeply patronizing attitude. Organizations of Muslim immigrants in Europe understandably identified with the plight of the Bosnian Muslims and often used it to make political points to serve their own interests. In one British-Muslim newsletter that I picked up at a conference, a women representing a small Islamic women's aid organization writes about how she met with Bosnian-Muslim women (some of whom were rape victims) in a refugee camp in Croatia. One woman explained that not all Serbs were bad and that her Serb neighbour had helped her. The interlocutor from Britain was struck by the refugee woman's apparent naiveté and lack of true understanding of what had happened to her and her fellow Muslims. She condescendingly implied that these Bosnian-Muslim women had not yet understood the cause of their suffering and that it was the duty of herself and other Muslims (i.e., non-Bosnian Muslims) to make them see that they had been attacked by Christians because of their religion. In imposing her Christians-versus-Muslims interpretive framework on these Bosnian-Muslim women's suffering, the Muslim foreigner was ignoring, first, the Catholic Croat women who had been subject to the same terror at the hands of Serbs and, second, local knowledge that the violence had been directed against non-Serbs in general, who by their mere presence obstructed the Serb nationalists' aim of creating an ethnically pure Greater Serbia. Indeed, Serbs too who opposed this political project were targets of violence and terror by fellow Serbs.

In the early years of the war in Bosnia, the conflict was sometimes portrayed by outside observers and commentators as being between Muslims and Christians along the fault lines of "Western" and "Eastern" civilizations as outlined by Samuel Huntington in *The Clash of Civilizations* (This is the view of the world that the late president of Croatia, Franjo Tudjman, ascribed to, seeing himself and his country as Europe's bulwark against Islam and Eastern Orthodox civilization. His logic was that the West needed him to prevent Bosnia and its Muslims from becoming too influential.) The "centuries-old ethnic hatreds" much cited by international commentators and policy makers as the ultimate explanation for the war in the former Yugoslavia was in essence derived from that same interpretive model. To some it was a convenient interpretation that would eliminate the complexities of the social and political facts of the war on the ground and gloss over their own ignorance. For others it was a politically expedient view. And for yet others it was a little of both. However, the conflict in Bosnia was not between Christianity and Islam; nor was it even a clear-cut conflict between Christian- and Muslim-identified communities. Both in the beginning of the war and towards the end, Catholic Croats and Muslim Bosnians joined forces against Serbian (Christian Orthodox) forces, which first attacked Croatia and then Bosnia. Nevertheless, there were also instances of cooperation between Catholic Croats and Orthodox Serbs against Muslim Bosnians. Their shared interests, however, were not religious but territorial. Indeed, to be able to understand the dynamics of the war in Bosnia-Herzegovina it is paramount to analyze the relationship between three ethnic/national communities, each defined by a distinct religious system of beliefs, rituals, and symbols. In Bosnia religion is the main cultural distinguishing factor among the Bosniaks (Muslims), Croats, and Serbs, and religion provides each group with a source of cohesive rituals and emotionally powerful symbols. In other words, the role that Islam played in the construction of a Muslim (or Bosniak) identity was similar to that played by Catholic and Orthodox Christianity in the construction of Croat and Serb collective identities respectively. In the Socialist Federal Republic of Yugoslavia there was freedom of expression of religion; however, there were important limitations to such expression. No public display of religious beliefs or rituals was permitted, and devoutness was not compatible with holding membership in the Yugoslav Communist Party (which was a prerequisite for advancing within the state career system). For Muslims there were no designated areas at work, school, or university for performing collective prayers, and canteens would not respect the Muslim dietary requirement of avoiding pork. Furthermore, in the 1950s and 60s Muslim Communist Party members were discouraged from giving their children traditional Muslim names. The "Yugoslav" authorities' curb on the expression of religious beliefs in public was a combination of the basically atheist outlook of their communist ideology and their fear of any expression of separatist nationalism. The authorities were well aware that for many "Yugoslavs" adherence to one particular religion was intimately linked to their identification with one national community (or "nation"). With communist systems collapsing all over east-central Europe, communist ideology was superseded by nationalist movements. Prior to 1990 religious beliefs had been expressed privately, and rituals had been low key; some of the more prominent rituals took place in people's homes and were to a large extent dominated by women (see Bringa 1995). Among Bosnian Muslims there were devout believers who held deep religious convictions, there were people who practiced certain key rituals and honoured major religious holy days out of respect for tradition, there were those who believed in God but had never learned how to practice Islam, and there were those Muslims by "ethnicity" who declared themselves atheists. In other words, among Bosnia's Muslims there was a continuum of degrees of conviction and practice similar to what is found in Christian-defined societies in Western Europe. Towards the end of the 1980s, as communist structures and ideology were losing their hold on Bosnian society, Muslims as well as Catholic and Orthodox Christians were publicly attending religious sermons and rituals in ever greater numbers. In the spring of 1990, during the Bjaram celebrations to celebrate the end of Ramadan, the "Begova" mosque (Gazi-Husrevbeg) in downtown Sarajevo gathered more people than could fit into the mosque and its courtyard. The sermon and the crowds attending were shown on Bosnia-Herzegovina's main television station. Many of those who were present came out of curiosity and did not know the procedures of the sermon or what was being recited, as they had never before attended prayers at the mosque. But the public and open display of religious celebrations was a sign of new democratic times, when both political and religious beliefs could be expressed openly. In particular, ideas that had been dangerous to pronounce, such as those pertaining to nationalism, were now being openly expressed. Unfortunately, religion was also the one feature that stressed the distinctiveness of three ethno-religious communities in Bosnia-Herzegovina. Religion was the antithesis to Tito's all inclusive credo of "brotherhood and unity" among all the peoples and nationalities in the Yugoslavia he had helped to create in that it was exclusive to one group. Furthermore, religion provided nationalists with a rich source of symbols and rituals with which to inspire national identification, separateness, and internal cohesion of the ethnic group. Public space, which prior to 1990 had been inclusive of every "Yugoslav" citizen irrespective of ethnic affiliation through the use of symbols that were shared by all three ethno-religious communities, was being redefined as the territory of one particular ethno-religious group (or nation). For instance, greetings that had earlier been used in private among members of the same ethno-religious community (because they were associated with the particular religious tradition of that group) would be used in publicly defined spaces (post offices, shops, banks, schools, etc.) by members of the group that was in political and military control of a certain area. In other words, those people who did not share the same limited code were made to feel like foreigners who did not belong. The expression of religious beliefs, then, did not only change from a private matter to a public one; it was also politicized.

The public expression of religious beliefs and traditions, and its appropriation by nationalist politicians, changed the dynamics between the three ethno-religious communities in Bosnia, but it also changed the dynamics – i.e., the power and status relations – within the community of Bosnian Muslims. In communist Yugoslavia, Muslims who made it to top positions in society were those to whom Muslim was an ethnic category devoid of any religious content. Those who were devout Muslims were seen as nationalists and were either marginalized or even sentenced to prison. Political changes and democratic elections in 1990 brought those previously marginalized Muslim activists into positions of power until their defeat in elections ten years later.

In Bosnia, Islam attaches people to two symbolic communities, each different in content, function, and scale. On the one hand, Islam (here understood as cultural heritage, historical legacy, a set of practices and moral values) connects people together in a community of Bosnian Muslims (as opposed to Croat Catholics or Serb Orthodox). On the other hand, it unites them with a community of Muslims worldwide (the Islamic umma) as opposed to non-Muslims. For a large majority of Muslims in Bosnia, the identification as Muslims/Bosniaks vis-à-vis Croats or Serbs is, I contend, primary to their identification with a worldwide umma (see Bringa 1995). However, there is in Bosnia what we could call a religious elite or the Bosnian-Islamic establishment (mainly based in Sarajevo and a few other major cities) for whom identification with the Islamic umma is a more important identification. In war and post-war Bosnia those Bosniaks have become not only more visible but also politically influential.

During the last twenty years of Tito's rule, Yugoslavia had wide-ranging cooperation with its non-aligned alliance partners and particularly with oil producing countries in the Middle East. Yugoslav companies were involved in contract projects in the Middle East, and Yugoslavs, including Bosniaks, went to work in the Middle East. However, a far more important cooperation was in education. During the 1970s and 80s a number of Bosnian Muslims studied Islamic theology at renowned Islamic teaching institutions such as al-Azhar in Cairo. These students, usually men, were often from Bosnian families with a long tradition of religious instructors and religiously learned men and women. While before 1990 such individuals belonged to a rather exclusive as well as reclusive section of Bosnian society with low public visibility, the new non-communist, nationalist, independent Bosnia has given these Bosnian Islamicists a public, and in many instances a political, platform. Yet the Islam-icist current in Bosnia did not suddenly appear after 1990.[3] An Islamicist movement had been a feature of the so-called *islamska zajednica* (the official organization of the Islamic community in Bosnia) in the 1980s. Indeed, local Muslim practices that were not considered Islamic by the more scripturalist Islamic instructors were modified or eradicated through preaching and education. In other words, local knowledge and beliefs that had developed in close interaction with belief systems other than the Islamic (i.e., Catholic and Orthodox Christian as well as pre-Christian) were challenged (see Bringa 1995).

Elsewhere, I have argued that Islam is central to the understanding not only of a religious Muslim identity in Bosnia, but also of a secular or ethnic Muslim identity. In addition to informing morality, a range of everyday values, and the annual ritual calendar, Islam is the main ethnic marker between Muslims and their non-Muslim compatriots and the main constitutive factor in both self-ascription and ascription of a collective or "national" identity. However, the marker is not primarily between Muslim and non-Muslim Bosnians but between Muslims vis-à-vis (Orthodox) Serbs and between Muslims vis-à-vis (Catholic) Croats. In Bosnia, then, religious symbols, rituals, and practices are equally important in constituting the three ethnic groups or "nationalities" whether Muslim Bosniak, Orthodox Serb, or Catholic Croat. Yet neither Bosniak, nor Croat, nor Serb identities can be fully understood with reference only to Islam or Christianity respectively but have to be considered in a specific Bosnian context that has resulted in a shared history and locality among Bosnians of Islamic as well as Christian backgrounds. This implies among other things that being Bosniak means possessing expressed or tacit knowledge about a whole range of rituals, beliefs, everyday practices, and values, as well as participating in a set of social structures. Islam informs some of this knowledge, but it is also informed by cultural practices and values that are shared by all Bosnians.

Yet a process of Islamication was already taking place before the war. This process had been facilitated by several interacting factors. First was the extensive cooperation between Tito's Yugoslavia and Islamic countries (which were oil producing members of the non-aligned organization), a cooperation that included education and other religious matters, such as sponsorship of the building of mosques.[4] Second was the more relaxed attitude by Yugoslav officials towards religion as Tito's Yugoslavia was coming to an end and communist states were being challenged from within in central and eastern Europe.

However, the war in Bosnia and the desperate plight of particularly its Muslim citizens did intensify this process, in some instances opening up Bosnia to a new kind of involvement from Islamic countries. I have said elsewhere that war changes people and their perceptions of who they are. For some Bosnian Muslims, who were the main victims (in terms of organized targeting and numbers) in the 1992–95 wars, this has led to a reassessment of identity and a reorientation of group affiliation towards the wider world community of Muslims. This reorientation is expressed through a more assertive Islamic identity, primarily by expanding the use of Islamic discourse and symbols into new domains (e.g., specific Muslim greetings, Islamic holidays becoming state holidays, public broadcasting, education). This does not mean a refusal of a specific Muslim identity anchored in Bosnian society, but it does mean a stronger stress on the Islamic heritage of that collective identity.

These changes should be understood in their proper local context. An Islamication process in Bosnia will be the outcome of circumstances specific to Bosnia. Both its dynamics and expression will be different from those found in Muslim societies outside

Europe. True, some expression will be identical to that of the Islamic movement everywhere (e.g., the increase in women who wear the hijab). In Bosnia, however, the more public use of Islamic symbols has to be seen in relation to the increase in public use of religious symbolism among the Catholic Croats and the Orthodox Serbs. Religion, as already pointed out, is intimately connected to the expression of ethnic/national identity that distinguishes the Serbs, Croats, and Bosniaks from each other.[5]

There has been a revival of both the Catholic and the Orthodox faiths in the former Yugoslavia; not least, the leadership of both Croatia and Serbia have aligned themselves with their respective churches so that being a good Catholic, for instance, has become synonymous with being a good Croat and vice versa. It is telling, however, that Western media seem to pay more attention to the revival of Islamic beliefs and practices among the Bosniak population than to the religious revival among the Serbs and Croats. Yet the revival of religious beliefs and practices as well as their integration into a political (national) public discourse has developed along parallel lines for all three communities in Bosnia (for Bosniaks, Serbs, and Croats alike). Historically, however, the religious organizations and elites of the three communities have played different political roles. The particularistic and nationalist character of the Serbian Orthodox Church (which is inward looking and concerned with the interests of the Serbs) stands in contrast to the universalistic (i.e., not nationally defined) character of both the Catholic (Croat) Church and the Islamic (Bosniak) association. Furthermore, the Islam that took root in Bosnia was an Ottoman version of the faith that grew out of the multi-religious (multi-national) character of the Ottoman Empire. Other religious communities were tolerated (and even politically and economically supported). This is in contrast to the Serbian Orthodox Church, whose very being as a separate church community defined it as a challenger to and enemy of the Islamic community (see Sells 1996).

CONCLUSION

It has been argued that Islam as a social identity cannot be understood properly in the Bosnian context without taking into account the importance of the Catholic and Orthodox Christian belief systems to the identities of the Croats and Serbs respectively. In Bosnia nationality is defined by religion, and a religious revival will be at the core of any development of an aggressive nationalism among either of the three Bosnian nationalities (Serb, Croat, or Bosniak). It is likely that since the war polarized and radicalized members of the different ethno-religious or "national" communities in Bosnia, religious leaders in all three populations may not only play an important role but also hold a particular responsibility in facilitating the process of reconciliation among the three Bosnian faiths. Furthermore, the Bosnian Muslims challenge our Western-European and Christian perceptions of who and what Muslims are. As indigenous European Muslims, they in fact challenge our very ideas of Europe as a Christian entity. Because the Bosnian-Islamic leadership knows and understands Islam and its expression in both the Arab world and the mainly Christian Europe, a revived Bosnian Islam could play a constructive role as a bridge-builder between the Islamic world and the mainly Christian-defined Europe to which the Bosniaks belong, geographically, historically, and indeed culturally.

NOTES

1 Serbian nationalism and Christian orthodoxy have their own very specific tradition of bigoted and denigrating imagery about the Muslim Slavs. For a further discussion of this topic, see Sells 1996 and Bringa 2002.

2 In 1995, I worked as a political and policy analyst at the headquarters of the UN peace keeping mission for the former Yugoslavia based in Zagreb, Croatia.

3 By "Islamicists" I mean those Muslims who want a revival of Islamic beliefs and practices and who favour a scripturalist interpretation, one that would rid the local expression of Islam of practices that are not strictly Koranic. Muslim societies everywhere go through this kind of revival process at different points in their histories (see Eickelman and Piscatori 1990).

4 The new mosques that were and are being built and designed by sponsors in the Middle East are distinctivley different architectually from traditional Bosnian mosques.

5 In Kosovo, where the vast majority of the Albanian population are Muslims, language and history, rather than religion, are the main cultural criteria distinguishing Albanians from their Orthodox Serb neighbours.

Medieval Cemeteries as Sites of Memory: The Poetry of Mak Dizdar

AMILA BUTUROVIĆ

At the centre of this essay lies the poetry of the Bosnian author Mak Dizdar (1917–71). Commonly hailed as the most eminent poet of Bosnia-Herzegovina, Dizdar's place in Bosnian literary culture is inestimable in that he has become a cultural icon to Bosnians of different ethno-national persuasions.[1] His most notable collection of poetry, *Stone Sleeper* (1966), chosen as the focus of this essay, functions as a powerful mytho-poietic meditation on Bosnian culture in its historical and spatial manifestations. Both structurally and aesthetically, *Stone Sleeper* is especially germane for Bosnian Muslims, insofar as it "authenticates" their identity in a space-time that predates, and thus challenges, the one at the root of their official ethno-national identity.[2] In many respects, then, Dizdar's poetry is the poetry of an alternative national sentiment. As a widely celebrated production – *poiesis* – of a cultural and psychological bond between contemporary Bosnia and its medieval past, it is an important testimony to the provisional quality of the official national taxonomy in the former Yugoslavia.[3]

A few words about the poet are due here: born to a Muslim family in Stolac in 1917, Mehmedalija Mak Dizdar began his literary career before World War II. A member of the communist movement from very early on, Dizdar actively participated in history making, as a fighter for the socialist revolution on the one hand, and against the Nazi occupation on the other. Correspondingly, his subsequent engagement in culture-making and culture-writing carried important political overtones. Although he emphatically abandoned the overt socialist-realist style common in post-wwii Yugoslavia, it is quite clear from his writings in general that his poetic creativity never shunned important social issues.[4]

Despite a fecund and successful early career, Dizdar's primary claim to fame rests with *Stone Sleeper.*[5] As the author himself concedes, however, the ideas and poetic elements of *Stone Sleeper* are deeply rooted in the early stages of his poetic career.[6] This observation identifies in Dizdar's collection its Janus-faced quality as a set of poetic segments committed at once to the past and to the future. Moreover, its success is explained in cumulative, not epiphanic, terms, the collection having been manufactured over time through hard work, poetic experimentation, and gradual stylistic maturation. "Poetry is like life," Dizdar said, "it is inscribed slowly and painstakingly."[7] The fame of *Stone Sleeper* is therefore a public validation of an accumulated social and cultural experience, of the poet "finding himself" in the tapestry of his overall work and, indirectly, in its reception with the reader. Dizdar's emphasis on the links between individual and collective participation in his poetic career bears didactic dimensions, as it engages the reader not only in the inner workings of the final product – *Stone Sleeper* – but in the ritual of collective formation as well.

Stone Sleeper was originally organized around four main thematic cycles – "A Word on Man," "A Word on Heaven/Sky," "A Word on Earth/Land," and "A Word on the Word" – but the final edition features only the first three cycles.[8] Framed by "Roads" and "Message," two poems that function as a prologue and epilogue respectively, *Stone Sleeper,* much like Northrop Frye's theory of mythos, rotates around cyclical symbols that predicate each other's meaning and function, sustaining the internal dialectic of the collection.

The predominant theme is epistemological and can be summed up as, "who are we, the Bosnians? Where did we begin and where do we go?" To address these questions, Dizdar begins a journey of self-discovery, locating the historical/aesthetic point of departure in the medieval burial sites of rural Bosnia-Herzegovina. "Stone sleeper" is thus a reference to the rugged lime tombstones – the stećak (standing stone) – clustered in the mountainous regions of Bosnia-Herzegovina, whose history is not only barely understood but also contested. Dizdar's reading gravitates toward the conventional historical interpretation: the stećak belongs to the Bogomils, a community of medieval neo-Manicheans clustered in the pockets of Southeastern Europe. After several crusades waged against them by both Catholic and Eastern Orthodox forces, the Bogomils are said to have abandoned dualist teachings and begun to convert. While some accepted mainstream Christianity (both Catholic and Orthodox), most embraced Islam following the consolidation of Ottoman rule in the region in the late fifteenth century.[9]

In inviting the collective imagination to focus on the sacred ground of medieval Bosnia, Dizdar refashions the common attitude to Bosnian landscape and history. Distilling this medieval sacred ground through his poetic voice, he brings it closer to the cultural sensibility of contemporary Bosnians. Thus, although not original, Dizdar's rendering of medieval history is probably the first systematic attempt to posit the medieval landscape as the cradle of what Benedict Anderson calls an "imagined community." Dizdar saturates the theory of Bogomil heresy with poetic power, giving it a new geographical and historical relevance. He grants a voice to the mute subjects, imbuing them with gnomic wisdom conveyed to the reader through archaic diction and aphoristic eloquence. The vernacular language – a crucial ingredient in the rise and dissemination of national sentiments[10] – assumes a double function: one, it promotes a feeling of cultural authenticity and homogeneity, and two, it blurs the line between direct and indirect speech. When reading Dizdar's verses, spatial and temporal boundaries collapse, generating a sense of cultural immediacy. Here Dizdar removes, as it were, the need for exegetical mediation: his topographic and literary representations of "stone sleepers" entice us as the very acts of self-representation.[11]

The interplay between different forms of discourse is highly effective. More than a simple poetic exercise, it is a strategy of reconnection, of erasing the gap in cultural memory. As suggested earlier, the cognitive and aesthetic link between contemporary and medieval Bosnian culture has never been a linear one. Centuries of external domination dispossessed Bosnian culture of its medieval anchor and experience, creating a rupture in cultural selfhood despite the stećak's presence in the landscape. It was only in the late nineteenth century that a systematic attempt to understand the stećak's historical function and lapidary symbolism commenced. Ironically, the initiative came from outside, originating with the Austro-Hungarian colonizer, whose project in Bosnia-Herzegovina emphasized the process of cultural and political convalescence: a decade after their occupation of Bosnia-Herzegovina in 1878, the Habsburgs erected the National Museum in Sarajevo with the intention of excavating local culture from the seeming obscurity it had endured under the Ottomans. Moreover, in an effort to steer Bosnian cultural sensibilities away from those of the Croats (with whom the Bosnians had much in common, including now the colonial ruler), the Austro-Hungarians promoted a search for local identity through local heritage, emphasizing the aspects of culture and history that were singularly Bosnian. The stećak, presented as an enduring witness to Bogomil non conformity, simplicity, and purity, provided the focal point in the colonial reconstruction of the Bosnian past.

By the early and mid-twentieth century, the stećak had become important subject matter in foreign and local studies on Bosnian ethnohistory. Accepting the position that medieval Bosnians were dualist Bogomils (locally also referred to as "Patareni" and "Krstjani"), these works perpetuated the image of medieval Bosnia as a land situated between, and torn apart by, Catholicism and Orthodoxy. Frequently employing dualist metaphors of evil and good, loss and redemption, and visible and hidden practices, scholarly studies as well as travel narratives fostered the popular imagining of the stećak as a symbol of resistance and purity. As a matter of fact, Alojz Benac argues that the first far-reaching publicity given the "Bogomil question" originated with the 1875 travel memoirs of the English historian Arthur Evans, *Through Bosnia-Herzegovina on Foot*, which dedicates a large section to the hidden purity of medieval Bosnia that then yearned to be discovered.[12]

Though a subject in its own right, the colonial imagining of Bosnia-Herzegovina of which Evans is a fine example deserves some attention here as well. Evans's motivations for "discovering" Bosnia are clearly more complex than a simple admiration of "picturesque costumes and stupendous forest scenery."[13] As post-colonial theories postulate, the colonial imaginings of the other are discursive constructions indicative not just of perceptions of the other, but of colonial self-formation and self-definition as well. In that dialectic, as Irvin Schick suggests, "the other plays a determining role as the antithesis, an embodiment of characteristics disavowed by the self that thereby paradoxically mirrors the self."[14] Evans's

book serves as a fine example of that dialectic insofar as he didac-
tically establishes a moral link between the fate of medieval Bosnia
and the political atmosphere of Europe at the turn of the century.
Eager to end the Ottoman presence in Europe, Evans and the bulk
of the Western intelligentsia looked for ways to redeem the territories still ruled by the "Sick Man." Writes Evans: "If this book
should do anything to interest Englishmen in a land and people
among the most interesting in Europe, and to open people's eyes
to the evils of the government under which the Bosniacs suffer, its
objects will have been fully attained."[15] But Evans's views of Bosnia
are underpinned by a critique of Europe's own malaise. Though
his rejection of the Ottomans is unquestioned, Evans sees their
ongoing presence as the responsibility, at least in part, of pre-
Renaissance Europe. He continues, "There never was a clearer
instance of the Nemesis which follows on the heels of religious
prosecution. Europe has mainly to thank the Church of Rome that
an alien civilisation and religion has been thrust in their midst,
and that Bosnia at the present remains Mahometan."[16] Thus his
dedication of a large section of his text to the medieval history of
Bosnia comes as no surprise: the Bogomil tragedy is represented
as the *momento mori* of the collective value system, so a clear sense
of urgency to recuperate Bosnia permeates Evans's entire narrative.
Rendered in similar ways by Rebecca West, Anthony Rhodes, and
other Western European "explorers" of Bosnia, this didactic con-
figuration of Bosnia as a site where aspects of the European self
were contested and configured further moralized the Bogomil
story as a cosmological struggle between evil and good.

Many Yugoslav writers have shared a similar view of the Bogomil
fate: the great Croatian essayist Miroslav Krleža speaks of it as a
reminder of the silenced voices of dissent that, in rejecting the
existing hierarchies, challenged the medieval European concept of
justice: "[These hands] express a challenge, supported by all the
righteous of the age; a refusal, far more radical than those of
Wycliffe, Huss or Luther, to recognize any moral authority."[17] Historians such as F. Sanjek, S. Ćirković, Ć. Truhelka, and others have
also favoured the dualist interpretation that would highlight the
symbolic and historical significance of the medieval past. Imbued
with such a system of representation and signification, the popular
imagination was quick to turn the mythos of the Bogomil strife
into the very foundation of cultural identity. In literary and artistic

treatments of Bogomil themes (e.g., by poets S. Kulenović and M. Dizdar, and artists Dž. Hozo and M. Berber), the aspiration was not to establish the historical truth but to present an axiological understanding of the medieval past. This was a way of resuscitating damaged memory, to which, ironically, the stećak stood as an enduring witness. Such artistic and literary endeavours can perhaps best be explained in terms of what David Price names – in the context of novel writing – "poietic history":

Rather than being held captive by the conventions of epistemology, [the novel of] poietic history provides the perfect discursive space for examining the past by presenting a series of representations of concrete particulars to universal conditions facing every generation ... In other words, to comprehend fully the reality of the past we must participate in the process whereby individuals, peoples, and entire cultures and societies *figured* their futures through imaginative projections of their wills.[18]

But unlike Price's novelists, Mak Dizdar situates his own reading of history within the dominant historical view, that is, *without* constructing a counter-history. He stabilizes the mainstream view by establishing continuity between the past and the present, intimating its relevance as a set of personal narratives buried/asleep in the land and recorded on the stećak. Dizdar's poetry is therefore an archeology of cultural memory that attempts to recover the wisdom of the past and its resonance in contemporary national culture. As Pierre Nora suggests in his study on the collective memory of France, however, the places of memory associated with a national culture are anchors for the present only insofar as they are representations through which the past has been remembered. Modernity has transformed them from being repositories of unmediated recollections to being evocations, or mirrors, in which we observe ourselves without ever having direct insight into lived experience.[19] The stećak to the contemporary Bosnian, to take a cue from Nora, is a "lieu de mémoire," a site that evokes a sense of continuity, an atmosphere of belonging, but provides no lived experience. Conversely, for the medieval Bosnian the stećak was a "milieu de mémoire," a place of memory permeating everyday life and thus a fountain of lived memories. Producing the stećak's meaning in modern times, then, assumes that memory is "always embodied in living societies and as such in permanent evolution,

subject to the dialectic of remembering and forgetting, unconscious of the distortions to which it is subject … [It] is always a
phenomenon of the present, a bond tying us to the eternal
present [whereas] history is a representation of the past."[20] This
kind of understanding is not alien to Dizdar. In reference to the
stećak, he explains: "For me, the stećak is but an inspiration to
address in poetic terms the existential questions pertinent to all
historical epochs. Hence a misconception that my poetry is a
direct representation of the mediaeval times, or any other for that
matter."[21] But if the medieval past is a well from which contemporary culture derives meaning and ingredients for identity formation, then the stećak is its stone incarnation without which the
identity is doomed to oblivion. For Dizdar, therefore, the challenge lies in reconciling the double function of the stećak as both
a site and place of memory, that is, of both lived and mediated
experiences, in an effort to ground the "eternal present" in the
workings of history. The poem "A text about a text" illustrates this
point: a medieval text is discovered, written right to left, and its
meaning is being debated by its five discoverers. The process of
producing a reading commences in an impressionistic, rather than
exegitical, fashion:

> And when we saw this script we'd never seen before
> In front of our very eyes from far-off times of yore
> A long silence fell between us.
>
> This stillness was broken by a voice that was calm but
>   outspoken –
> No scribe wrote this text for sure
> It looks like someone was trying to draw
>
> And then a second says racking his brains –
> Look at the right that might be where it begins
> And it's merrily flowing leftwards Widdershins
> Who was such writing written for
>
> Those who insist on reading from right to left
> Are wrong all along –
> A third one says half crazed
> And half Amazed

Look it's a secret text from the darkest days of old
Rising it seems from the depths of our murkiest dreams
Its signs are like writing
Seen in a mirror –
Mutters a mouth calm and cold

The fifth with clenched fists and trembling fingers tries to hold
This mirror of clear redeeming grace
But it slips to the floor

For in it that instant he recognizes
His own ancient
Forgotten face.

The past speaks to us in many cryptic ways, the poem suggests, and its signs are coded in many different domains, as is historically the case with the manuscript in the poem.[22] Therefore, in an effort to understand the contours of the "forgotten face," Dizdar makes *Stone Sleeper* a unique poietic discovery of the location in which collective self-formation took place. Sensitive to the political challenges facing the Socialist Federal Republic Yugoslavia, he underpins his poetry with extensive research on medieval texts (published in the prose collection *Old Bosnian Texts*), lapidary fragments, and the medieval Bosnian language. Involved in a highly intertextual enterprise, he draws into his poetry archeological, literary, folkloric, iconographic, and Biblical exegetical findings. Dizdar's work is thus not just a mirror of the self; it is a comprehensive *poiesis* of Bosnian culture, fashioned out of the material and immaterial authority of medieval history, the landscape of the dead, and Bogomil cosmology. The intimate links drawn between these ingredients suggest that the imagining of Bosnian identity is incomplete without a fusion of land, history, and mythology. All three are intricately woven into the construction of Bosnian national culture, thereby rendering confessional differences as entrenched in official national identities insubstantial.

In eclipsing the accepted national categories in Bosnia (Serb, Croat, and Muslim), Dizdar posits the medieval topos as a stage on which the shared cultural symbols are arrayed and a collective national drama enacted. Constructed subjectively as well as objectively, that drama is both emic and etic, insofar as it is derived from

Dizdar's participation in its performance on the one hand and from his descriptive (and inscriptive) efforts on the other. Assuming the oratorical role of the bard who poeticizes the knowledge that has been accumulated through history but silenced by its flux, Dizdar authorizes his own poetry to restore it. Through his poetry, cultural memory rolls back into itself, perpetuating the dialectic between things gone by and things to come, between things already spoken and those waiting to be said. Dizdar highlights the power of that dialectic in the following terms:

For hours, I have stood among the sceći of this land, in their cemeteries scattered at the feet of the ancient forests. Various symbols – the sun, twining plants, outstretched human hands – have entered into to me from the huge stone tombs. At night I have been assailed by notes scribbled in the margins of ancient books, whose lines scream question after question about the apocalypse. Then the sleeper beneath the stone comes to me. His lips open, limestone-pale, and his dumb tongue speaks again. In him I recognize myself, but I still do not know if I am on the way to unveiling his secret.[23]

The sense of awe experienced at the stećak's resting ground seems akin to what Michael Fischer terms "ethnic anxiety," namely, a feeling of uncertainty in the face of a lack (or loss) of cultural rootendess. "Ethnic anxiety," Fischer explains, "is relieved by establishing continuity with the past where previously there was breach, silence."[24] Re-establishing a link with the cultural past is ethically consequential insofar as it directs thinking about the self in a continuum that begins in the past but inevitably spans into the future. "The search for a self is a (re)-invention and discovery of a vision."[25] In his own quest for a Janus-faced cultural vision Dizdar posits the medieval topos as the territory of the authentic, the space-time of the numinous: in the topos are inscribed the answers to Bosnian historical and spatial identity. His enchantment with this past as the anchoring ground of identity, like an enchantment with a *mysterium tremendum*, sets a tone for his poetic quest. It invites a reinterpretation of culture through a triangular space/time/society paradigm.[26] It motivates archeological explorations, scriptural exegesis, mystical invocation, and ritual meditation. For Dizdar, the medieval cemetery is an environment laden with cultural meaning, a topos of an ever-enigmatic but deeply meaningful past. The present can make sense only if the past is filtered through a complex set of symbolic representations. *Stone Sleeper* is thus imbued with an axiological function: it is a framework in which the dead are not really dead but asleep, their suspended values to be reawakened by the apocalyptic quality of Dizdar's poetry.

Identifying historical and geographical boundaries ("cemeteries on the brink of primeval forests") with his poetic frame, Dizdar creates a zone from which the medieval voice can be resurrected to speak its truth. Spatially and temporally determined, the integrity of this zone becomes a significant trope in Dizdar's poetry. It is cleared of the forces of dispossession that have come in succession, from medieval times to the present. But access to the past from a contemporary vantage-point is broken and the texture of cultural cloth shredded by the forces of history. To compensate for that fragmentation, Dizdar takes recourse to epitaphs. An aporia insofar as they immortalize mortality, the epitaphs highlight the fact that historical meaning is sheltered in many different locations, each of which can intimate eclipsed moments of a forgotten history. They also carry a mnemonic potential, preserving experiences that have been lost to Bosnians through a series of historical displacements. Their axiological importance, however, can be restored if the (cultural) self is perceived in both diachronic and synchronic terms. Given that the epitaphs in Dizdar's texts are not assigned a deterministic function, their main value lies in descriptive multivocality: every epitaph has a story to tell, but no story can be activated without the poet's mediating role. In that sense, not only does the poet seek continuity with the experiences of the past, but he also circumvents the culture within which, and of which, he speaks. "A text on a watershed" is a good and simple illustration of such horizontal and vertical fusion as inspired by epitaphs:

> Pardon me
> that I pray that ye
> and my brethren my fellows my betters
> do come to my door do visit me
> that I pray that godmother motherlaw aunt and bride
> do speak my name keep me in mind pass at times by my side
> for once I was the same as ye
> and as I am so shall ye be.

A hope to be remembered after death is perhaps the most basic commemoration of life. Remembrance is attained in a multidirectional way: partly it is achieved through time, as a reconciliation with the inevitability of death by those of us who will once be as the sleepers are now. Equally important, however, is the persistence of memory in space, among our kin and kind. The two routes through which culture perpetuates itself predicate each other: unless we are bonded within a temporal trajectory with those from whom we descend, our spatial kinship is rendered inconsequential. In Dizdar's poetry, the epitaphs fulfil the function of establishing and/or making visible the cultural bonds in (with?) space and time. For example, the first stanza of the poem "Gorchin" introduces us to a soldier, apparently lost in a battle against a foreign intruder, rendered through the epitaph on his tombstone. What remains of Gorchin's life story is a gnomic inscription that testifies to the mortality of his body but suggests the immortality of his hope:

> Here lies
> Gorchin soldier
> In his own land
> Inherited by a stranger.

The name Gorchin is both personal and impersonal. It travels along the road of history, reappearing in one generation after another. With it, the culture establishes a genealogical tree, allowing itself to expand and move in different directions without losing its roots, in space or in history. The memory recovered from epigraphic details is culturally referential: the names of places and people are historically specific, giving a sense of intense familiarity with the experience in the poems. Direct and indirect speech overlap, allowing the reader to be drawn into the poem's double vocality. Then again, there is a subtle alienating dimension in the rhythmic and linguistic quality of the verse as well, which signals the importance of discursive and stylistic dialectic in creating a "milieu of memory." Suggestive of intricate personal destinies before the finality they snapshot, the epitaphs never paralyze the poetic imagination. In that sense, Dizdar, who through this kind of double vocality expands the epitaphic vignettes into historical narratives, turns the physical absence of the deceased into a haunting allegorical presence of soliloquies.

Thus the voice given to the sleepers is mediated, hybridized with Dizdar's own. To borrow Homi Bhabha's phrase, the two appear "almost the same but not quite."[27] Aware of the "mimicry" implied in his quest, Dizdar posits his voyage into the past as a cultural autobiography. Significantly, he avoids the danger of purifying the mediaeval voice of the workings of history and of the subjectivity of the ear that listens to it. Dizdar's thinking about the past is undeniably historical, not cosmological. Rather than essentializing the past, he places emphasis on the psychological dimensions of return. Like a mystic traveller, he is caught up in a perpetual paradox of movement: the more he ascends towards the summits of "Truth," the more deeply he descends into one's own self. In the Sufi tradition, for example, the ability of the mystic to encounter "Truth" is predicated on his/her skill and knowledge to remove the veils (kashf) from his inner self: as the Qur'anic verse 41:53 says: "And We shall show you Our signs on the horizons and in yourselves – do you not see?" The search for an authentic other, therefore, can only be successful as a backward movement and an intrinsic understanding of the self. The Sufi maxim of "polishing the mirror" is a historical necessity, expressed by Dizdar through different poetic devices. In the poem "A text about a text" cited above, the mirror metaphor is rather central. Conversely, in "Text about the spring," the search for selfhood is reworked with the help of natural imagery:

> I dissolved
> And streamed
> Streamwards
> Riverwards
> Seawards
> Now here I am
> Now here I am
> Without myself
> Bitter
> How can I go back
> To whence I sprang?

Given its rhetorical power, a word on Dizdar's employment of natural imagery is due here: in focusing on the mountainous countryside of Bosnia-Herzegovina, away from the clamorous modernity of urban centres, Dizdar grounds the national symbolic in the simplicity of a meaning-full landscape. Such space amplifies the voice of the individual, echoing it through a seemingly unbound void. The human intervention in the natural space is made visible by the interceding presence of Dizdar's verse. A sense of aesthetic harmony is rather compelling, melting away the demarcation line between the human-made cemeteries and the land in which they rest. Again, this is a relatively common poetic strategy: as Elisabeth Helsinger argues, rural life and national life are often made to appear as something fully integrated.[28] The voice does not dissolve into the polyphony of urban voices and choices, but remains singularly clear. Of course, the individual is allegorized at once as the general, absorbing in itself the totality of a culture and history. However, in *Stone Sleeper* the rural idyll is frequently disrupted since it is layered with fragmented and hidden complexities that yearn to be unveiled. "Text about time" reads:

> Long have I lain here before thee
> And after thee
> Long shall I lie
> Long
> Have the grasses my bones
> Long
> have the worms my flesh
> Long
> Have I gain a thousand names
> Long
> Have I forgot my name
> Long have I lain here before thee
> and after thee
> Long shall I lie.

While flux and mutation point to both the evanescence and singularity of historical experience, the naturalist symbolic, employed in the above poem and many others, allows that experience to be assimilated by nature. The stećak, man-made and man-narrated, becomes a fixture of the landscape, a ruin safeguarded by the natural world. In her study on the eighteenth-century English ruin poems, Anne Janowitz highlights the importance of "naturalizing the ruin," that is, the blending of the ruin into the natural environment with the intent of promoting "a feeling for, rather than an assertion of, the permanence of the nation."[29] In other words, nature and culture are frequently interrelated by virtue of aesthetic and structural synchronicity. In Dizdar one detects a similar lyrical association between the two. The poem "Lilies" is a good example:

> White lilies bloom in hill and coomb
> In forest and field lilies seem to be talking
> In hill and valley every lily
> Seems to be burning
> And while you're quietly walking
> Between the blossoming
> Flowers
> Perhaps like me you'll think of those
> Who've quietly walked here
> Before you
> Between
> These flowers blossoming white
> Wondering just like you
> What they might be
> Whether they might be cries
> Of delight
> Or fright
> Signs of those who passed here once
> Callously trampling
> This trackless land
> Of ours
> In search of white flowers.

Notably, the choice of the natural motif is not random: the lily is a symbol of the medieval Bosnian state, appearing on many a stećak, as well as on the royal insignia (common also among some other medieval kingdoms). In recent times, it reappeared as the symbol of the Bosnian state after the declaration of independence in 1992. Infusing the lilies with aesthetic ambivalence – are they burning or blossoming? – Dizdar turns to the Bogomil dialectic: a symbol of purity is at once a symbol of grief. One person's triumph is another person's loss. Going beyond the obvious, recovering the esoteric, is an act of historical and cultural self-affirmation. It grants a voice to the unheard.

In many respects, then, Dizdar teaches that the Bosnian historical experience is fundamentally tied to its landscape. Neither can the stećak be uprooted from its resting place – the place and site of memory – nor can the sleepers be relocated or completely silenced. They are signs that point to the presence of a culture that evolved in and against the shadows of history. The opening sentence of *Mediaeval Bosnian Texts* states: "By virtue of being the most remote western frontier overlooking the east, and the eastern overlooking the west, Bosnia has always been the dividing line of different interests and the meeting point of several influences."[30] It is through the metaphor of "frontier" as a place of fluid, marginalized identities seemingly detached from the centre yet always entrapped in its (political) circumference that Dizdar locates the ethos and ethnos of Bosnia. For him, the geography of Bosnia orchestrates its history and identity. The frontier is a space that gave rise to a psychology of persistence and resistance. In "Text about the land" Dizdar writes:

> Once upon a time a worthy questioner asked:
> Forgive me who is and what sir
> Where is
> Whence and
> Wither sir
> Prithee sir
> Is this Bosnia
> The questioned swiftly replied in this wise:
> Forgive me there once was a land sir called Bosnia
> A fasting a frosty a
> Footsore a drossy a
> Land forgive me
> That wakes from sleep sir
> With a defiant
> Sneer

But neither resiliency nor defiance, the two traits posited as Bosnia's defining attributes, is an inherent quality: both were acquired over the course of history. Despite their frequent glorification as the "soul" of Bosnia by Bosnians themselves, Dizdar's reading is much more historio-geographically informed: resiliency and defiance are coping mechanisms necessitated by the workings of time in the Bosnian landscape. Historically, these workings were occasioned by a struggle between the Bosnian people and the threatening Catholic and Orthodox establishments; cosmologically, by a conflict between two, divinely created and thus interchangeable, ethical principles. The Bosnian misfortune is therefore dialectically interpreted as the necessary source of their endurance. A resistance to spiritual defeat – by cosmic or earthly powers – raises the myth of Bogomil nonconformity and their denial, to recall Krleža, of moral hierarchies. In "A Text about the See," the message is sharp, unambiguous:

> What strange face do I see
> upon the holy see?
> Whose face does that face recall
> on the throne of Peter and Paul?
> That holy face is from hell –
> it's the face of Sataniel!

The interplay of evil and good, mortality and immortality, points to the re-enactment of cultural symbolism in order to ascertain continuity in space and time. In and of themselves, the mortality/immortality and evil/good polarities are only meaningful when functioning as agencies of cultural survival. Such applications render them ethically consequential. In a poem published in an anthology before *Stone Sleeper* Dizdar exclaims:

> So even if they beat me defeat me
> and toss my body to my crane to eat me
> or hang me in a valley, my valley
> on a tree, my tree
> and even if I die I still shall be alive.
> Alive, alone in the bedrock of the sea,
> invisible, in the boundless sea
> Against the evil lord's ill-will
> I, still alive, shall live on.[31]

But history never repeats itself verbatim; it refashions the modalities of experience regardless of its seeming circularity. The inward and outward movements create a circular atmosphere of ebb and flow, birth and rebirth, contraction and expansion. These are all powerful dualist motifs that successfully apply universal metaphors of mortality/immortality and continuity/discontinuity to the cultural specificity of Dizdar's medieval cemeteries. The employment of religious tropes allows Dizdar to inscribe the historical predicament as a cosmic one since the message thus conveyed guarantees the endurance of culture through generations. As Anderson suggests, religious language, unlike various "progressive" discourses, "concerns itself with the links between the dead and the yet unborn, the mystery of re-generation ... [it] responds to the obscure intimations of immortality, generally by transforming fatality into continuity."[32] But even such transtemporal tendencies make sense only if life is viewed as a progressive narrative. The poem "Death" reads:

> The earth is sown with a deathly seed
> But death is no end
> For death indeed
> Is not and has no end
> For death is just a path
> To rise from the nest to the skies with the blest

Spiritual rebirth and ascension are a form of cultural regeneration insofar as they create a sense that events gone by can be relived, albeit in different forms, and that the tradition can be re-enacted in an upward movement. The movement is also a form of abstraction, which further heightens a feeling that culture is both transient and transcendental. Spanning both levels of representation, the poetry makes a moral appeal to a collective self-reflection through a critical dialogue with the past. For example, the poem "Kolo" refers to a dance in which everyone holds hands, in temporal and spatial circularity, thus foregrounding the interplay between the centripetal and centrifugal tendencies of ethnic culture. Although the movement seems steady, monotonous, the atmosphere is rather unpredictable:

> Hand in hand
> bound in a bond
> Hand in hand
> salt on a wound
> Earth is so heavy
> heaven so high

Were I falcon
then I would fly

Similarly,

In this kolo of sorrow, not leader not lead
You're a tavern of carrion a maggot's bed
Robbed from its body the tomb acts alone
But when will this body
Be an act of its own?

Finally, in seeking continuity between modern and medieval Bosnian times, Dizdar places special emphasis on language, heavily employing Bosančica – the vernacular used by the Bosnian Church and preserved in the old scripts and epitaphs – which he remodels for the purpose of national authentication.[33] The activation of linguistic ties with the medieval culture is highly effective: the poems, especially those constructed as direct speech, appear as if they are inviting their readers to engage in dialogue. A glossary of unfamiliar terms and words appears at the end of the anthology as a reminder of yet another breach with the cultural past. Significantly, however, Dizdar is not championing a mass revival of the medieval language. He resurrects it for the purpose of a conversation between two parties that belong to different realms of history: one contemporary, the other medieval. Furthermore, insofar as Dizdar intertwines the archaic dialect with the visual imagery found on the stećak the conversation is multisensory, adding another dimension to the hermeneutic enterprise. Inspired by the enigma of the stećak's decorative language, he carries on the challenge of tying together pictorial and scriptural segments. Thus answers to the questions of meaning are encoded in the intimacy of textual and visual vocabulary. Like the Bogomil mythology in which Sataniel's false guidance can be affronted through redemption metaphorized as "sunčani stub" [the sun pillar], Dizdar refers to cultural salvation at once in gnostic and hieroglyphic terms. As Mitchell points out, language works with conventional signs that unfold in temporal succession, while images, presented in timeless spatiality and simultaneity, operate with natural signs.[34] In Mak Dizdar's poetry, language is deconventionalized through images, and images are marshalled into an unbroken narrative. Images become words, and words images. In removing "the veil of mystery" from one issue, he transfers it to another. The play is carried out as a subtle poetic travesty that confuses the "now and then," the "here and there," emphasizing that the dialogue with the past will never come to a halt. "Kolo," cited above, is an excellent example of the marriage between words and images. Another example is "Radmilja," a group of poems named after the most fascinating of the medieval cemeteries. There, the poem "Ruka" (Hand) attempts to decode, then re-encode in self-reflexive terms, the meaning of that common and highly diverse visual motif:

> This hand tells you to stand
> And think of your own hands.

In other words, "know thyself" is extracted from an iconic, as opposed to linguistic, signifier. It is given a narrative value despite the seemingly motionless image. But as Mitchell argues, images necessitate a multisensory apprehension and therefore depend on consciousness.[35] In other words, they cannot be perceived as images without the ability of consciousness to trick them into motion in order to demarcate their visible and hidden coordinates. In Dizdar's poetry that movement allows the image to move towards the reader in the form of a word/sound expressed in the forgotten medieval dialect.

Thus rendered with astonishing poetic energy, the symbols and inscriptions found on the stećak enable Dizdar to release his sleepers from the stillness of their resting ground. He delivers their poetics of silence as a vocalized journey through modern Bosnian imagination, confirming them not as passive recipients of history but as its active makers. Conceived as an archeological search for truth buried under the rugged tombstones, Dizdar's work is a complex mimetic enterprise that gives a new ethical momentum to the Bosnian search for selfhood. In order to draw attention to the Bosnian struggle against cultural dispossession, Dizdar reasserts the authority of its assumed Bogomil past. The Bogomil cosmological bifurcation of good and evil, mortality and immortality, and loss and redemption all gain historical relevance in relation to Bosnian landscape and history. The medieval cemeteries anchor the mythos of Bosnian identity as both places and sites of memory. They draw attention to the *loci* on which that identity is shaped: the margins of medieval manuscripts, the brink of primeval forests, the frontiers of Europe. Reaching out to the medieval past is thus a means of reclaiming a culture that has preserved its selfhood thanks to, not in spite of, its diversity and marginality.

NOTES

1 The aftermath of the 1992–95 war in Bosnia-Herzegovina has led to a new interest in Dizdar's poetic legacy, and to his characterization as a visionary "who best conveys common fears of the destruction of Bosnia and its people" (Idrizbegović 1996).

2 I am here referring to the fact that Bosnia-Herzegovina was the only republic that did not hold the status of a "nation republic" in Communist Yugoslavia. In other words, "Bosnian" was not an official national category due to the fact that the confessional differences in the population had emerged as a decisive factor in pre-empting the national unity of Bosnia-Herzegovina. For a comprehensive overview see Banac 1984.

3 It needs to be emphasized that Dizdar's national imagining is not politically or ideologically propelled despite its political overtones. In other words, his poetry is not nationalistic if by that one understands identification with the state or advocacy of state-formation. The distinction I am making here between nation-identification and state-identification is informed by Connor 1994.

4 For further biographical data, see Duraković 1979, 13–29.

5 Some of Dizdar's other collections include: *Vidovopoljska noć* (1936), *Okrutnost kruga* (1960), *Koljena za Madonu* (1963), *Ostrva* (1966), and *Stari bosanski tekstovi* (prose work, 1969).

6 Duraković 1979, 18.

7 Ibid., 18–19.

8 The collection underwent several compositional changes after its original publication in 1966. For a detailed discussion see ibid., 95–7.

9 See Sharenkoff 1927, Runciman 1960, and Šanjek 1976. A persuasive revisionist perspective can be found in Fine 1975.

10 Anderson 1991, 67–82.

11 I elaborate on the issue of Dizdar's sacred topography in Buturović 2001.

12 Benac and Bihalji-Merin [1963], xix.

13 Evans 1971, ix.
14 Schick 1999, 12.
15 Evans 1971, x.
16 Ibid., lv.
17 Benac and Bihalji-Merin [1963], xiii.
18 Price 1999, 3.
19 Nora 1996, 1–20.
20 Ibid., 3.
21 Cited in Duraković 1979, 120.
22 Dizdar 1999, 252.
23 Duraković 1979, 108.
24 Fischer 1986, 206.
25 Ibid., 196.
26 Soja 1989, 23–4.
27 Bhabha 1994a, 86.
28 Helsinger 1997, 17.
29 Janowitz 1990, 10.
30 Dizdar 1995, 7.
31 Duraković 1979, 115.
32 Anderson 1991, 11.
33 The importance of language for national self-formation is an exten-
    sively discussed topic. See, for example, Anderson, ibid., as well as
    Hobsbawm's opinion (1990) that the rediscovery of a people in the
    late nineteenth century went hand in hand with the rediscovery of
    their vernacular language.
34 Mitchell 1980.
35 Ibid., 14–17.

The Construction of Islam
in Serbian Religious Mythology
and Its Consequences

MICHAEL A. SELLS

Age-old and irrational antagonisms destroyed the former Yugoslavia, we are told. This cliché is both false and true. We must understand both its falsehood and its truth in order to work effectively toward peace in the Balkans. Certainly the cliché is false historically. Indeed, many nationalists resent Bosnia precisely because it represents a multireligious civilization within Europe. No one expressed this loathing (and self-loathing) more clearly than the late Franjo Tudjman, whose post-communist life was devoted to bringing Croatia into Europe, which for Tudjman meant rejecting its association with the "Balkans" and especially with Islam, which he detested as alien to everything European and Western. His problem and the problem of the Serb radical nationalists was that Muslims were an integral part of a 500-year-old shared civilization, the testimonies to which – from the National Library in Sarajevo to the great Old Bridge of Mostar – were everywhere. Of course Bosnia had had conflicts in the past, especially in WW I and WW II, but those conflicts were, precisely, global in scope. Despite its conflict, Bosnia had managed, for more than five centuries, to maintain its multireligious civilization and to flourish culturally within that civilization.

The truth within the falsehood is that Bosnia is indeed a place of special age-old antagonisms, not according to history, but as constructed in the religious mythology of those who carried out the atrocities. In that mythology, the same Muslims who built a shared

civilization with their Catholic and Orthodox neighbours, colleagues, friends, lovers, and family members are the eternal, inimical other.[1] The post-Tito revival of the nineteenth-century ideology
of eternal ethno-religious conflict began as the vision of a few. But
when it was exploited in a particular manner, it became the shared
vision of many. It shaped the actions of the militant nationalists in
ways that those ignoring the religious and cultural dimensions of
the conflict consistently failed to understand, with consequences
that are only now being recognized.

The effort to take seriously the religious mythology as a central
element in the Bosnia (and Kosovo) crisis is commonly met with
two forms of incredulity. One reaction is based on the premise that
religion is a matter of private and self-conscious belief. Yugoslavia
was not a religious society. Most of those who organized the violence had been communists and atheists. How then could religion
and religious mythology be a factor? The second reaction is the
assertion that religion and mythology are not prime agents but
superficial reflections of deeper causalities that must be social,
economic, and political. Both premises, as this paper will show, are
wrong. Religion and religious mythology act far beneath and
beyond self-conscious belief, in deeper structures of symbol, society, and psychology, and can effect the atheist every bit as much as
the self-proclaimed believer. Of course, manipulation of religious
mythology was not the sole cause of the tragedy; political, social,
and economic factors were also important. Every major event has
a plurality of causal factors that come together and in so doing
create the conditions for that event. Yet the mythology is more than
a mask for allegedly more important factors. Indeed, the record in
Bosnia demonstrates that the primary actors among the "ethnic
cleansers" chose a course of action that at times contradicted their
own political, social, and economic interests.[2]

I

I begin with three statements that might seem examples of simple
irrationality but whose interior argument (as irrational as it might
be) contains a logic of its own. It is this interior logic-of-its-own
that allows the authors of these statements to feel comfortable
making them and that allows their audience to find them not only
credible but also compelling, despite all evidence to the contrary.

In 1994 Biljana Plavšić, a genetic biologist and former director of The Academy of Natural Sciences in Sarajevo, explained why she and the other leaders of the Bosnian "Serb Republic" (Republika Srpska) were unable to negotiate with Muslims. The problem, Plavšić explained, was genetic.

It was genetically deformed material that embraced Islam. And now, of course, with each successive generation it simply becomes concentrated. It gets worse and worse. It simply expresses itself and dictates their style of thinking, which is rooted in their genes. And through the centuries, the genes degraded even further.[3]

Plavšić had been an atheist and biologist, the former dean of the Faculty of Natural Science and Mathematics in Sarajevo. Yet in 1994 she was interpreting Muslim religious affiliation as both a mark of genetic deficiency and a determinant in genetic deformity. What accounts for Plavšić's sudden betrayal of a lifetime commitment to the shared principles of the international scientific community in favour of a pseudo-scientific racial hygiene? What allows her audience, many of them highly educated, to suspend their own lifelong commitments in order to embrace such statements? What allows both Plavšić and her audience to then create a policy of "ethnic cleansing" based on the belief system to which they have suddenly converted? There were biological racists in Yugoslavia before the rise of post-Tito ethno-religious nationalism, but the existence of such attitudes at the margins cannot explain its triumph at the heart of Serbian society and throughout much of the Serbian intellectual elite – especially among a people who themselves had suffered under the Nazi designation of Slavs as *untermenschen*.[4]

A pair of writers popular both in Europe and in political circles in the us made the second statement. French theologian Jacques Ellul and Giselle Litmann (who writes under the pseudonym Bat Ye'or, "Daughter of the Nile") developed a theory that Islam is, by essence, a religion of violent aggression (jihad) and parasitic absorption (dhimmitude). When not destroying nations through direct military aggression, Islam "steals their blood"; indeed, what has been called Arabic and Islamic civilization is simply the stolen life force of the civilizations on which Islam feeds and whose pale corpses litter the field of history.[5] Bat Ye'or makes the following conclusive generalization about the Islamic community, or *umma*:

"The *umma* claims a monopoly of culture: the dhimmis languages are banned, relegated to the liturgy; their monuments, testimony to their civilizations' greatness are destroyed or Islamized."[6] Note the use of the present tense. It is not that an Islamic government or community had or has at times banned liturgy and destroyed or Islamized monuments of non-Muslims. It is something that the *umma* does, in the eternal present, always and everywhere. Any example of alleged Muslim tolerance is only a tactical truce in the ongoing effort of the parasite culture to drain the lifeblood of the host culture.

Bat Ye'or's claim that the monuments of the dhimmis, the testimony to the greatness of civilization, "are destroyed or Islamized" was influenced by Serbian nationalist claims about Ottoman rule. Contemporary Serbian nationalists have in turn adopted Bat Ye'or. She is a well-known non-Serb historian presenting Muslims as an ever-present threat. She validates, from a self-proclaimed stance of scientific and historical objectivity, the most radical claims of Serbian ideologues.

Accusations that Muslims are eternally destroying the monuments of other civilizations have been and are being made from the Serbian monasteries in Kosovo. It was in Kosovo in 1985 that Serbian Orthodox leaders began their claims that Kosovar Albanians were engaged in a systematic campaign to annihilate Serbian monasteries, a claim taken up later by the Serbian Academy of Arts and Sciences (SANU) in its famous memorandum declaring war on Tito's multi-religious Yugoslavia. It was from those very monasteries (that had survived 500 years of Ottoman rule) that these same religious and nationalist leaders claimed that the Ottomans, just as Bat Ye'or explains must be the case, had destroyed or Islamized all the great monuments of Serbia.

The cultural richness of monasteries such as Gračanica at Kosovo offers credibility and emotive force for official statements made from within them. Thus the claims that Muslims (Ottoman and post-Ottoman) by nature Islamize or destroy the sacral sites of other religions takes on a contradictory and ironic, but powerful, persuasion when made from within the monasteries that – according to the generalized claim – must have been destroyed.[7]

In 1992 the tragic dimension of the irony was revealed. In the name of preserving the monuments of Kosovo (the vast majority of which are still, thankfully, largely intact, despite serious incidents of attack from Kosovar Albanian militants) from the alleged eternal Ottoman and Islamic destruction, almost every Islamic monument in the Serb-army controlled areas of Bosnia was systematically destroyed. Almost all mosques, tekkes, libraries, medresas, tomb-stones, and even Ottoman secular architectural masterworks were dynamited. Hundreds of centuries-old monuments, including world masterworks such as the Colored Mosque in Foča, Ferhadiyya and Arnaudiyya in Banja Luka, and the fifteenth-century Ustikolina mosque, the oldest Ottoman monument in Bosnia, were dyna-mited, in some cases several times. Even the rubble was carried away and disposed of, like the bodies of Srebrenica, in secret graves. Where the Serb army could not occupy an area, it used pinpoint targeting to destroy mosques and libraries. Among its targets were the Sarajevo National Library (where over a million volumes and a hundred thousand rare books burned in the largest book burning in history) and the Oriental Institute of Sarajevo (the largest repository of Arabic, Persian, and Ottoman manu-scripts in Southeast Europe, which burned to the ground in Serb army shelling on 17 May 1992). The object was to eliminate every trace of Bosnian-Muslim civilization and every testimony to the 500 years of interreligious Bosnian culture.[8]

US president William Clinton made the third statement in 1994. When pressed on why the US and NATO nations were not respond-ing to the atrocities in Bosnia, Clinton stated that "Until these folks get tired of killing each other, bad things will continue to happen."[9] Former US secretary of state Lawrence Eagleburger found that this strange tendency of Bosnians to kill one another was not new: "They have been killing each other with a certain amount of glee in that part of the world for some time now." These statements, which reflect verbatim the phrasing used by many in the press and Congress, were based on two mutually reinforcing perspectives. The people of the Balkans have been killing one another "for cen-turies" out of age-old hatreds, and they are, in fact, "killing one another"; that is, there is no distinction to be made between victim and perpetrator. The claims of age-old antagonism and moral equivalence were maintained for three years, with increasing stri-dency, in the face of massive evidence that Bosnian Muslims as a people were being singled out for destruction on the basis of their religious identity (or the religious identity being imposed on them). The stubborn adherence to this view was most pronounced within the members of the Security Council and the United Nations peacekeeping establishment. UN general Lewis MacKenzie played a particularly important role in the development and maintenance of the moral equivalence fallacy, both during his tenure in Sarajevo and in his lobbying and speaking activities after retiring from the military. Because of his position as UN commander in Sarajevo at the beginning of the war, his constant evocation of moral equivalence influenced Western governments at the time they were formulating their policies, and once those policies were set, they became very difficult to change.[10]

In its November 1999 report on the atrocities in the UN declared "safe area" of Srebrenica, the United Nations admitted both this falsehood and the immeasurable human cost of this falsehood. The report makes a series of confessions, noting that the UN mission appeased those carrying out "ethnic cleansing," refused to make the necessary moral judgment about such a policy of extermination and expulsion, continually misread and misrepresented the situation on the ground to make it appear that all sides were equally guilty, and engaged in high-level negotiations with leaders who, even during the negotiations, were carrying out organized massacres. The report also states that "the failure to fully comprehend the extent of the Serb war aims may explain in part why the Secretariat and the Peacekeeping Mission did not react more quickly and decisively when the Serbs initiated their attack on Srebrenica."[11] Indeed, the period from 6 August 1989, when Bosnia was recognized as a sovereign nation, to 12 July 1995, the height of the Srebrenica atrocity, saw a continual, stubborn, and insistent series of statements by UN officials denying in effect those Serb [nationalist] war aims.[12]

II

To understand how such views on race, religion, Islam, and the atrocities in Bosnia could seem incontrovertible to those who made them and to their audience, we begin with the categories of sacred space and sacred time.[13] In Serbia, time collapsed on 28 June 1989, which marked Vidovdan, the anniversary of the death of the Serb prince Lazar in battle against the Ottoman Turks. This collapse involved more than ritual re-enactments of the battle of Kosovo. It brought together, into a single point of intensity, several powerful streams of memory, symbol, and history (a set of themes I will refer to as Kosovo mythology, a mythology that goes far beyond the battle story). It culminated the events that had brought Slobodan Milošević to power and Yugoslavia to dissolution. Conversely, the changes in society that culminated with the 1989 commemoration have themselves become the entrenched (though not necessarily unbreakable) determinants of contemporary attitudes among most Serbs.

Both Shiite Islam and much of Christianity are built around the passion of the founding figure. The collapse of time is most clearly illustrated in the theatrical re-enactments of a passion in the *ta'ziyya* in Shiite Islam and in the medieval European passion play. In both traditions, advice is given to the actor who kills Imam Husayn or puts the sword in Jesus' side. The actor should carry out his deed without hesitation, lest the audience rush the stage to prevent the deed. After carrying it out, he should exit with dispatch lest the audience rush the stage and attack the character in revenge. When the spectators rush the stage, there is a collapse of time; they no longer experience themselves as viewing a re-enactment, but rather as participating in the primordial event itself, and no longer experience any distinction between actor and original character or between actor and audience member. The event, however ancient, has become present. It is primordial, of undefined and illimitable antiquity, occurring in an eternal now.

When the spectators become the original actor and experience the passion as present, they are unified within the group as the Islamic community (*umma*) or as the body of Christ, and that group experiences an outpouring of emotion, a catharsis. The power generated by mass catharsis can serve differing ends. It can lead to a reactivation of communal values, as each individual shares with other members of the community a moral self-critique. When those staging the event (through direct theatrical work or through larger intellectual contexualization) cast blame on a scapegoat, a particular people, another kind of collapse occurs. Just as the audience members become one body, so all the people of the religion or ethnicity of the scapegoat are constituted as one body. In the timeless now of the event, all members of that body are guilty, regardless of whether or not they lived as individuals during the historic time of the passion. Until very recently Jews were not comfortable being on the streets in Europe after Good Friday because they were always potential victims of attack. Some militant clerics in Iran have associated the United States as a nation and the Jews as a people with the caliph Yazid, who ordered the killing of Husayn and his family.

In the case of Serbia, the centennial celebration of Vidovdan was the event of the century. By 1985 the preparations for the 1989 Vidovdan commemoration had become internationalized and had tapped into several currents of symbolic power. Each of these currents by itself would have been enough to galvanize interest in the celebration. The interconnections among the various currents created a force that overwhelmed everyone, including and especially those who were trying to manipulate the event. These "age-old" currents can be traced to the nineteenth century, when the portrayal of Prince Lazar as a Christ-figure, which had long been part of the Serbian tradition, was condensed and made more explicit. Lazar was portrayed at a "Last Supper" surrounded by twelve knight-disciples, one of whom was a traitor who gave the battle plans to the Turks. His death was entitled the Serbian Golgotha, and in his crucifixion was the crucifixion of the Serbian nation. The Lazar story was tied to a revolutionary mixture of romantic nationalism and anti-Islamic polemic. The combination resulted in the ideology I have named Christoslavism.

The first great representative of Christoslavism was Bishop Petar Petrović II, known also as Njegoš, whose writings have become a sacred text in their own right for Serbian nationalism. Njegoš's most important work, *The Mountain Wreath (Gorski Vijenac)*, published in 1857, recounts the event known as the "Extermination of the Turkifiers" (*Istraga Poturića*).[14] In this powerfully written poetic drama, the Orthodox bishop-knights of Montenegro call a council and decide that it is necessary to "cleanse" the country of the non-Christians. The leaders of the Muslim community are invited to convert for one last time and are told they can be either baptized in water or baptized in blood.

The Muslims suggest a *kum* ceremony, the ceremony by which blood feuds are ended in Montenegrin tribal society. In this ceremony, the leader of each warring tribe becomes the godfather (*kum*) to the son of the leader of the other tribe. The Christian bishops reply that both children must be baptized in such a ceremony. The Muslim delegation reply that "we are all one people" and suggest an interreligious ceremony in which the Christian child will be baptized and the Muslim child will receive a ritual hair cutting. The overture is rejected by the Serb bishops who then order the extermination of all Slavic Muslims. *The Mountain Wreath* climaxes with a graphic depiction of the killing of the Muslims – men, women, and children – and the burning of their mosques and compounds. After carrying out their cleansing, the Orthodox warriors are given communion without confession. In local Montenegrin society, any murder, even if it was considered justified, was ritually polluting and thus necessitated confession before any taking of the Eucharist. The offering of communion without confession suggests that the act of cleansing Montenegro of the "Turkifiers" also purified the souls of those doing the killing for the sacrament of the Eucharist.

The Mountain Wreath was memorized by Gavrilo Princep, who assassinated the Archduke Ferdinand on Vidovdan in 1914. According to one Serb nationalist, Njegoš's work was "resurrected" in the late 1980s in preparation for the 600th anniversary. It was republished, memorized, and became once again the major text for Serbian nationalism. Njegoš's work is grounded in the notion that by converting to Islam, the ancestors of Slavic Muslims and their descendants forfeited their identity as Slavs. They were "Turkifiers" (*Poturića*) and thus, by adopting a non-Christian religion, had necessarily transformed their ethnic and national identity. The *kum* reconciliation ceremony takes place between warring groups of the "same people," but, despite the Slavic Muslims' statement that they and their Orthodox Slavic neighbours are one people, the *kum* ceremony is rejected when they refuse to have their children baptized.

Christoslavic ideology was radicalized in later writings. In his doctoral dissertation, Ivo Andrić quotes Njegoš' famous verse describing Slavs who converted to Islam as cowards and cheats. He then states that this judgment by Njegoš is nothing other than the eternal voice "of the people," doubling the removal of Slavic Muslims from the people by making the articulation of that ostracism the eternal voice of the people itself. In the same work, Andrić dismisses, without any evidence that he has studied the matter, centuries of Bosnian-Muslim literary culture as devoid of creativity.[15] In his novels, Andrić brought race and blood more deeply into the notion of Christoslavism; the Slavic Muslims were part of the Ottoman/Islamic stealing of the blood of the Slavic Christians in which conversion racially transformed the converted from Slav to Turk.[16]

The collapse of time and the ideology of Christoslavism were, in the words of one Serbian nationalist in reference to *The Mountain*

Wreath, "resurrected" at the 1989 Vidovdan commemoration. As the preparations for the commemoration intensified, the relics of Lazar were ceremonially translated across greater Serbia and throughout Kosovo, eventually arriving at the Gracanica monastery near the battlefield of Gazimestan, where they were ceremonially viewed for the first time in history. The ceremonies accompanying the movement of the relics were surrounded with an increasingly virulent anti-Muslim rhetoric.

The power of the mythology was further compounded when the primordial time of Lazar and the historical ideology of Christoslavism were combined with the actual historical memory of World War II. At the same time as the relics of Lazar were being translated from station to station on their pilgrimage, the remains of Serb victims of World War II Nazi and Ustashe atrocities were being ritually disinterred amid the production of a pornography of atrocity. Glossy and graphic images of WWII atrocities were distributed by clergy and politicians amid suggestions that all Serbs had fought the Nazis and that all Albanians, Croats and Slavic Muslims had fought for the Ustashe, that the latter were genocidal, as peoples, by nature, and that they were preparing to carry out a new genocide against the Serbs. Serb writers such as Dobrica Ćosić and Vuk Drašković published a series of novels and stories depicting the barbarity of Croats and Slavic Muslims as groups. Many of Drašković's most hate-filled works appeared in the official journal of the Serbian Orthodox Church.[17]

In the mid 1980s the leaders of the Serbian Orthodox Church added to this already potent matrix of associations the claim that ethnic Albanians were carrying out systematic destruction of the Serbian monasteries in Kosovo, organized rape against Serbs, and genocide – with a master plan to "ethnically cleanse" all Serbs from Kosovo. The claims, first published in major Serbian Orthodox Church documents, were then picked up by Serbian intellectuals and found their way into the SANU memorandum that is now considered to have been the death knell of Yugoslavia. Serbian dissidents investigated the claims of both the bishops and the SANU memorandum and found them, without exception, to be false or grossly exaggerated.[18] Even so, the claims merged with the historical memory of WWII, the tendentious ideology of Christoslavism, and the primordial time of the Lazar story to create a symbolic complex that has become resistant to evidence or argument.

When Slobodan Milošević, with the acquiescence of some and the enthusiasm of many within the Serbian Orthodox Church leadership, mounted the stage at the Kosovo battlefield of Gazimestan, he stood in front of an enormous backdrop covered with emblems of Lazar and the Serbian Orthodox Church. He then looked out into a crowd in which his own picture was being held aloft next to images of Lazar and gave his speech on Serbia's battles of the past and battles to come. By this time the vectors of ethno-religious mythology had intersected: the primordial time of the battle of Kosovo, which had collapsed into the present through the power of ritual; historical memory, which had returned with the power of the repressed; the sacred space of the Serbian Jerusalem symbolized by the Kosovo monasteries; the fabricated allegations of genocide against Serbs in Kosovo; and the ideology of Christoslavism. At the intersection of these vectors, a force was created greater than the sum of its parts.

Yet Kosovo mythology could not act on its own. For such mythology to be turned into an ideology of genocide, it needed first to be instrumentalized through media propagation of hate and fear and through the organized violence of state-sponsored militias. Attacks on civilians were preceded by propaganda evocations of various aspects of the Kosovo mythology. Thus Serbian radio broadcasts that Muslims in Bosnia had a secret plan to capture Serb women and enslave them in "harems" were followed by the organized rape of Muslim women by Serb nationalists. As noted by one official with the Office of the United Nations High Commissioner for Refugees (UNHCR), the propaganda became reverse code, a signal to militias to carry out against Muslims the crimes that the Muslims were allegedly plotting against Serbs.[19] After the atrocities, when the Muslims had been killed or expelled, both civil and religious ceremonies were conducted to celebrate the cleansing. Those who carried out the atrocities were blessed by Serb clerics (following the pattern set in *The Mountain Wreath*). Military medals for the militia members and some streets of the cleansed town were named after heroes of the Lazar story. Death squad leaders took nicknames from the Kosovo mythology, with one infamous commander calling himself "Njegoš."[20]

Slobodan Milošević is not a religious man and is overtly contemptuous of historical mythology. The majority of the organizers of the siege of Sarajevo were lifelong atheists. The vast majority of Serbs (as well as other Yugoslavs) are not religiously observant. The issue is not one of personal sincerity (a trait notoriously difficult to judge). When the atheist professors of the University of Sarajevo suddenly turned up in Pale draped with symbols of the Serbian Orthodox Church and blessed by Serbian Orthodox priests and bishops, the issue was not sincerity but effectiveness. The Kosovo mythology operates as an alternative field of logic, history, and reality. In this alternate reality, the configurations of hate stereotypes, such as the otherwise ludicrous theory of the genetic deformation of Slavic Muslims, make sense. They fit comfortably within the ideology of Christoslavism, in which religious conversion is identified with ethnic or racial transformation. The key factor for policy is this: at some point the mass psychology generated by the Kosovo commemoration and by the intersecting streams of memory, imagination, and symbols surrounding it reached a critical mass. At this point, the Kosovo mythology became so strong that those who tried to manipulate it, such as Slobodan Milošević, found themselves slaves to the expectations and interior logic of this ideology of eternal conflict unto extermination. As a character in *The Mountain Wreath* proclaims: "Serbs and Turkifiers must fight until one group or the other is annihilated."

III

The militarized version of Kosovo myth and ritual culminating in the 1989 Vidovdan commemoration provided Plavšić with an alternative world of logic that rendered plausible, to herself and her audience, the otherwise inconceivable theory of the defective genes of Bosnian Muslims. The Muslim Slav was equated with racial transformation, participation in the killing of the Christ-prince Lazar, the stealing of the blood of Christianity, the atrocities of WWII, false allegations of genocide in Kosovo, and an alleged demographic plot to destroy Serb Christians. When all these factors were brought together, the genetic deformity of the Muslim Slav was not only plausible; it was self-evident.

No nation looks fondly upon its former colonizer, and the continued resentment of Ottoman rule among Serbs is not surprising. Yet despite Ottoman oppression, Muslim and Christian Slavs constructed a complex, shared civilization that had weathered the horrific violence of the anti-Ottoman revolution and its repression,

WWI, and WWII. The eternal and absolute nature of the conflict between Muslim and Christian was constructed through manipulation of symbols and the provocation of violence. But with the congealing of a mass psychology, symbolized by the millions of Serbs gathered at the battle plain of Kosovo in 1989, notional reality became social reality. A growing number of Serbs coalesced around the militarized version of the Serbian Golgotha. The real suffering of Serbs and the degradation of Serbian society that had resulted in large part from actions emanating from the militarized version of the Serbian Golgotha were now explained (and rendered inevitable) by that ideology, diverting responsibility for such suffering away from the religious nationalist leaders who had played a major role in instigating it. And although it is never popular to associate religious leaders with a crime as great as "ethnic cleansing," the bishops of the Serbian Orthodox Church have, with rare exceptions, supported the most extreme anti-Muslim propaganda and militia violence.[21]

The militarized Kosovo story that was used to motivate and justify genocide in Bosnia also played a role in shaping international opinion. The notion that the violence in Bosnia was an inevitable recurrence of "age-old antagonisms" was itself constructed, at least in part, through the Kosovo myth. Bat Ye'or's claim (cited above) that the *umma* or Islamic community is inherently, through jihad and dhimmitude, inimical to non-Muslim civilizations was in part grounded in the work of Serb nationalists and then used by the current generation of Serb nationalists as a justification for their actions in Bosnia. The claim of Balkan age-old hatreds was also intertwined with the wider theory of a "clash of civilizations" between the West and an essentialized Islam that is, by its very nature, at war with Western values. Bat Ye'or's claim (that it is of the unchangeable nature of Islam to aggressively attack and parasitically absorb all non-Muslim cultures) has had a specialized appeal to Islamophobe and Serb-nationalist movements in the US, as well as a more general influence on the wider public.[22]

During the NATO operation in Kosovo, the neo-Confederate and anti-immigrationist movement within the Christian-right adopted the Serbian nationalist cause during NATO's Kosovo operation, condemning NATO leaders as war criminals and referring to Kosovo as the "Serb Alamo." Numerous leaders of the Christian-right see a direct parallel between the threat that Hispanic and other immigrants pose to white Christians – what one of their leaders refers to as "The Browning of America"– and the militant Serb nationalist claim that the Kosovar Albanians are immigrants who have usurped Serb soil.[23]

If Bat Ye'or and Jacques Ellul's history shows that Islam always and everywhere entails jihad and dhimmitude, including the annihilation or Islamization of all non-Muslim monuments, the Serbian Orthodox Church has been no less categorical. Not only has it not renounced the falsifications concerning alleged Albanian genocide against Serbs in the 1980s, but it has, in the wake of the NATO operation in Kosovo, insisted that NATO is now carrying forward the genocide on behalf of the Albanians. The lavish and sophisticated Serbian Orthodox web page includes a page entitled "NATO bombing of Serb monuments," with large explosion symbols over each of the great Serbian masterworks.[24]

IV

Two major misconceptions have resulted from a refusal or inability to take seriously the cultural factors, especially the marshalling of religious nationalism, in the conflict in the former Yugoslavia. The first misconception is shown in frequent claims that the NATO operation in Kosovo harmed the widespread opposition to Milošević in Serbia. Opponents of NATO point to the Belgrade demonstrations of 1996–97 as proof of such opposition. But most demonstrators were opposed not to the policy of war, conquest, and ethno-religious purification, but to its lack of success. True dissidents, such as Mladin Zivotić, explained this phenomenon, but those in the West wishing to attack any intervention on behalf of Balkan Muslims refused to listen.[25] Symptoms of a radicalized society were everywhere in Serbia. The most popular celebrity in Serbia was Arkan, an international criminal indicted for war crimes and famous for the sadism of his militias. The most successful politician in the 1997 elections was Vojislav Šešelj, famous for what is known in Serbia as the Rusty Spoon trend in Serbian politics (Šešelj called for Croats to have their eyes gouged out with rusty spoons). The most popular member of the opposition to Milošević, Vuk Drasković, continually incited hate and fear among Serbs, associated with the brutal Serbian Guard militia, and was an open advocate, along with all major figures in Serbian politics, of the destruction of the

Kosovar Albanian-Muslim community.[26] And Vojislav Kostunica, who led the ouster of Milošević, continued to maintain a militant Kosovo ideology, denounced the war-crimes tribunal as a Western plot against Serbs, and supported the most radical proponents of ethnic cleansing in Bosnia. As one of his first acts as president, Kostunica journeyed to Foča in Southern Bosnia, the town that has become the symbol of organized rape and mass atrocity by Serb militias. Foča's name had been changed to Srbinje (Serb-Place) after the Muslim community was destroyed, and a Serbian Orthodox seminary had been dedicated to christen the change. Kostunica's trip to Srbinje, where he met with those who continue to block all efforts to allow the survivors to return home, made his sentiments crystal clear. Kostunica had also been an apologist for and supporter of the Serb army actions at Srebrenica in July 1995.[27] Some Serbian dissidents have raised controversy by speaking of the need for Serbian society to undergo a process similar to that of the denazification of Germany after WWII and have suggested that a NATO occupation of Serbia might best facilitate such a program. The point is not, of course, that Serbian society is Nazi but that it has become so radicalized and so demoralized that, even with a less despotic government, its intellectual and political elite remain attached to and invested in the most virulent anti-Muslim mythology. The German parallel is also useful in showing that radicalized societies can and do change. In the case of fascism, European societies changed when fascism was thoroughly defeated.

The second misconception permeates the statements and writings of United Nations negotiators, generals, and civil-affairs staff. The Serbs have legitimate concerns with any Bosnia that would leave them as a minority and deserve a voice in deciding the fate of Bosnia. Those concerns are indeed genuine. But within two months of UN recognition, the leaders of the Republika Srpska made it perfectly clear that, while talking about rights, protections, and maps with UN negotiators, they were pursuing a program of annihilation on the ground. That program had nothing to do with the legitimate military objectives of those fighting a "civil war"; indeed, the atrocities continually damaged support for the Serb cause and ultimately led both to NATO bombing and to a Croat-Bosnian offensive in the fall of 1995. There was nothing in particular the Bosnian Muslims could do, say, or offer that would have protected them from the genocidal aims of a program so deeply embedded in the radicalized Kosovo mythology.

Serbian nationalists have been willing to see the Serbian population of Krajina expelled, the Serbian population of Kosovo expelled, Serbia isolated culturally, economically, and politically, and Serbian religious and historical heritage desecrated by war crimes carried out in the name of Serbs. Consistently, since the tragic conflict began in 1991, the legitimate interests of Serbs have been placed beneath the ideology of ethno-religious purification. When the concentration camp system was set up around the town of Prijedor, when all the mosques and Islamic monuments in Serbian-army-controlled Bosnia were dynamited, when General Mladić took the captives away from Srebrenica for mass extermination, the legitimate interests of Serbs were the last thing taken into consideration.

In the ominous hours before the Srebrenica massacre, UN special representative Yasushi Akashi and UN general Bertrand Janvier insisted that the Serb forces would not commit a war-crime in Srebrenica if the UN turned it over to them. Their arguments ignored three years of atrocity by Mladić and the clear ideology of ethno-religious cleansing advocated by Serb nationalists.[28] And although the Bosnian Serb leaders betrayed every legitimate interest of Serbs, they remained popular even among those whose lives were devastated by their ambitions. Both General Mladić's atrocity at Srebrenica and his attack on Bihać had disastrous consequences for Serbs. In addition, after persuading the Krajina Serb army to attack the safe area of Bihać from across an international border, thus giving the Croatian government a pretext to launch its operation against the Krajina Serb Republic, Mladić refused to help the Krajina Serbs – even though both parties had signed a mutual defense agreement. Despite his desecration of Serbian heritage, his military defeat, and his betrayal of hundreds of thousands of Serb refugees, General Ratko Mladić remains a hero among a disturbingly large proportion of Serbs.[29] NATO's many critics fault its leaders for not taking more seriously the allegedly good-faith proposals of the Serbian delegation at Rambouillet, especially the Milošević proposal that any force in Kosovo be run by the United Nations. These critics need to take into consideration what Bosnia teaches us about the character and record of Serb nationalism and the negotiating tactics of Serb leaders, who for three years treated every negotiation as an opportunity to stall for more time to carry out ethnic cleansing. They also need to consider the UN's own devastating evaluation of its performance in Bosnia.

POSTSCRIPT

There is a final irony to this construction of Balkan Islam. In addition to regarding Bosnian Muslims as "Turkifiers" within the framework of Christoslavic hatred of Turks, Serbian nationalists repeatedly claimed that they were allied with fundamentalist states like Saudi Arabia or radical states like Libya and Iraq, citing as evidence the fact that many Bosnians (such as former prime minister Haris Silajdžić) had studied in Libya when Yugoslavia and Libya considered themselves brother third-world nations. The first irony is that Saudi Arabia did very little to help Bosnian Muslims during the genocide and that Libya and Iraq in fact supported the Milosevic regime unequivocally throughout the period of atrocities. The second irony is that a new campaign of cultural destruction is now being waged against Balkan Muslims, orchestrated by Saudi aid groups acting under the ideology of the radical Wahhabi sect of Islam and operating under the guise of architectural restoration. The Saudi groups and local agents have destroyed the interior of the grand sixteenth-century Begova Džamija, one of the most important Islamic monuments in Europe, and numerous other mosques and religious structures in Kosovo.[30] In the spring of 2001, they arranged the destruction of the 200-year-old central mosque in Rahovec (Orahovac), which had escaped destruction by Serb militias. In each case the modus operandi has been the same: the Saudi aid groups promise officials of a town major funding for reconstruction, but to obtain the funds, the town officials must grant the Saudi group blank-cheque permission to demolish buildings or parts of buildings. The groups then construct a huge, out of scale mosque in what has been called the "modern-gym" or "airport-terminal" style. In Rahovec, the Saudi Joint Relief Committee pressured the local imam into demolishing the historic seventeenth-century Çarshi Mosque in favour of a huge new Saudi-style mosque that would dominate the landscape and tower over two Sufi tekkes – one motive for the destruction being the effort to seize control of local Islamic institutions and drive out Sufi and other non-Wahhabi Muslim influence.[31] As Kosovar Muslims who are attempting to resist such destruction have pointed out, massive out-of-scale projects imitate exactly what Serb nationalists did in Kosovo during the 1980s: construct massive edifices to demonstrate dominance and control. The Wahhabi attack on Bosnian and Kosovar heritage is particularly venal, coming on the heels of such massive devastation. Wahhabism is only two centuries old, yet its representatives presume to dictate the meaning of Islam to a rich and deep Bosnian and Kosovar Muslim culture that stretches back to the fifteenth century.

What is it about Balkan Islam in general and Bosnian Islam in particular that, within a period of one decade, has caused it to be attacked so methodically by Croat Catholic, Serb Orthodox, and Saudi-Wahhabi groups? Perhaps one answer can be found in the writings of Bosnian-Muslim writers such as Rusmir Mahmutćehajić. In *Bosnia the Good*, Mahmutćehajić attempts a reconstruction of Bosnian history that is grounded in a view of Bosnia as a multi-religious society and in a view of Islam that embraces multi-religious culture. Mahmutćehajić considers Balkan Islam to be just as rooted in the Bosnian homeland as are Orthodoxy and Catholicism and argues his case in part through an appeal to distinctive Balkan-Muslim architectural patterns that are anathema to Wahhabism.[32] For those who use violence to create and project back into history their vision of enclosed, isolated, and pure religious identities, the monuments of Balkan Islam are a natural first target.[33]

NOTES

1 The Islam in Bosnia-Herzegovina presented in this essay is the caricature constructed by Serb religious nationalists in post-Tito Yugoslavia. For a glimpse of rural Bosnian Muslims at the end of the Tito era and up until the war in Bosnia, the best source is Bringa 1995. For a view of Bosnian urban culture, see Kurspahić 1997 and Mehmedinović 1998. For a superb overview of Bosnian literary culture, see Agee 1998. Other central works include Buturović 1995 and other articles in the same issue of *Cultural Survival*, Buturović 1996, and Sijarić 1996. For historical perspective, see Donia and Fine 1994, Malcolm 1994, Pinson 1993, and Norris 1993. The latter work, though disorganized at times, is a mine of information on Bosnian Islam not found anywhere else in non-Slavic writings.

2 Two caveats are needed. In stating that the myth of age-old hatreds
was the belief of the few that became the belief of the many, I am
speaking of dominant beliefs. Human beings commonly maintain
contradictory beliefs, often at different levels of intensity. As the
black consciousness movement showed in the United States, to the
surprise of many whites, many who think of themselves as (and are)
well-motivated believers in racial harmony and equality can hold
(usually in ways invisible to themselves) prejudices that are glaring
to the oppressed group. Similarly, many Croats and Serbs may have
been influenced by the patterns discussed below, even as they lived
on another level with Slavic Muslims and considered them to be of
the same people. It is when an exclusivist belief comes to dominate
a person or group that the road to ethnic cleansing is paved. To
maintain that post-WWII Yugoslavia was a functioning multicultural
nation or that Bosnia represents a 500-year-old multi-religious civilization does not necessitate a romanticizing of the past or a denial
of either its open conflicts or its interior tensions. Similarly, to stress
the importance of cultural and religious paradigms is not to deny
the political, economic, and social aspects of conflict. (The question is not whether the conflict in Bosnia was a "religious war"; such
a term is far too crude to be either affirmed or denied.) Rather, it
is to affirm that the conflict cannot be fully understood without
taking into consideration cultural and religious dimensions and that
any policy based upon ignorance of those dimensions is unlikely
to succeed.
3 Biljana Plavšić, *Svet*, Novi Sad, September 1993, cited and translated by Slobodan Inić, in "Biljana Plavšić: Geneticist in the Service
of a Great Crime," *Bosnia Report: Newsletter of the Alliance to Defend
Bosnia-Herzegovina* 19 (June–August 1997), translated from *Helsinška
povelja* (Helsinki Charter), Belgrade, November 1996.
4 Here I focus on Serbian religious mythology. Those acting in the
name of Croatian religious mythology have been no less ruthless,
but their field of myth and ideology is structured in a different
manner and needs a separate treatment.
   The village of Medjugorje is a particular centre of Croatian religious nationalism. An estimated 20 million pilgrims from around
the world have journeyed to hear the six young Croats who allegedly began seeing and receiving messages from the Virgin Mary in
1981. The messages themselves speak of love and tolerance, but the
small group of Franciscans who control the pilgrimage trade are

avid supporters of the most violent wing of the Croatian ruling party, the Croatian Democratic Union (HDZ). It was in a circle around Medjugorje that the five most infamous Croat concentration camps were constructed in 1993, even as pilgrims continued to travel to the sight that, according to the Medjugorje supporters, was the one miraculous place of peace in all of Bosnia-Herzegovina.

Throughout the war in Bosnia, Croat and Serb forces collaborated with one another in a joint effort to destroy Bosnian Muslims in accordance with agreements made between Tudjman and Milošević at Karadjordjevo in 1991 and between Radovan Karadžić and the extremist Croat warlord Mate Boban at Graz in 1993.

5 See Bat Ye'or, *The Decline of Eastern Christianity under Islam: from Jihad to Dhimmitude, Seventh–Twentieth Century*, with a foreword by Jacques Ellul, translated from the French by Miriam Kochan and David Littman, Madison: Farleigh Dickinson University Press, 1996, 115, 128 (where Islamic civilization is characterized as "feeding off their [the subject peoples'] vigor and on the dying, bloodless body of dhimmitude"), and 165. Bat Ye'or's characterizations were taken up with enthusiasm by Father Richard John Neuhaus in an article entitled "Approaching the Century of Religion," *First Things*, October 1997. Father Neuhaus also explains that the nature of Islam as jihad as formulated by Bat Ye'or can be seen in Bosnia. The article is available online at http://www.firstthings.com/ftissues/ft9710/public.html. *First Things* is published by The Institute on Religion and Public Life. For Bat Ye'or's influential testimony before the US Congress, see "Past is Prologue: The Challenge of Islamism Today," US Congressional Briefing, Human Rights Caucus, "The Persecution of Christians Worldwide," Tuesday, 29 April 1997.

6 See Bat Ye'or, *Decline*, 258–9. In opposing the essentialism of Bat Ye'or and Jacques Ellul, I am not opposing criticism of the actions of militant or intolerant Muslims. On the contrary, only when the essentialist myth of the eternal malevolence of a group (religious, ethnic, or racial) is dismantled is it possible to formulate cogent criticism of particular groups or subgroups acting in the name of that larger entity. As long as Bat Ye'or and Jacques Ellul, and their followers, perceive all of Islam and all Muslims as agents of jihad and dhimmitude, it is hard to see how they can criticize any particular behaviour or action, since whatever is being done is in accordance with the timeless and essential order. The only rational response to such an essentialist and timeless enemy is constant warfare.

7 For a glimpse into the rich heritage of classical Serbian architecture in Kosovo, see Peić 1994 and Subotić 1998.
8 See Pašić 1994, Društvo arhitekata Sarajevo 1994, and Riedlmayer
   1994, 2001, and "Testimony Presented at a Hearing of the Commission on Security and Cooperation in Europe, US Congress, April 4,
   1995," available online at http://www.haverford.edu/relg/sells/
   killing.html.
9 President Bill Clinton, 14 May 1993, cited by Rosin Sullivan, *The
   New Republic*, 14. This statement culminated a long series of progres-
   sively stronger affirmations of the fallacy of moral equivalence and
   age-old hatreds. Earlier, for example, Secretary of State Warren
   Christopher had educated congress on "ancient antagonisms" and
   spoken of the Bosnian catastrophe as a "problem from hell," as
   quoted in the Associated Press report by Barry Schweid, *Philadelphia
   Inquirer*, 19 May 1993: A3. For Eagleburger's statement, see the transcript of Charlie Rose's televised interview of Eagleburger: Charlie
   Rose Transcript no. 1420 (1995, Thirteen/WNET), 5.
10 The tenacity with which MacKenzie propounded the doctrine of moral
   equivalence and opposed efforts at more forceful intervention against
   "ethnic cleansing" and genocide is documented in Off 2000, 123–234.
11 "Report of the Secretary-General Pursuant to General Assembly
   Resolution 53/35: The Fall of Srebrenica," Fifty-fourth session,
   Agenda item 42, The situation in Bosnia and Herzegovina
   (15 November 1999), paragraph 476. The full report is online at
   http://www.haverford.edu/relg/sells/reports/Unsrebrenicareport.htm.
   The phrase "Serb war aims" used in the United Nations report is
   misleading. The war aims of Serbian religious nationalists entailed
   the killing of many Bosnian Muslims, expulsion of the survivors, and
   systematic annihilation of every trace that they ever existed or
   shared a civilization with Serbs. Tragically, in part through the
   manipulation of the Kosovo mythology, those war aims were shared
   by an increasing majority of Serbs in both Bosnia and Serbia proper.
   But generic terms like "Serb war aims" are insidious: they work to
   create the sense of unanimity that the militants claim while denying
   and marginalizing the dissidents who are waging a difficult and cou-
   rageous struggle against such aims. Of particular importance on the
   question of moral equivalence is the following admission from the
   UN Srebrenica report, from paragraph 496 (emphasis mine):

   The failure to fully comprehend the extent of the Serb war aims may
   explain in part why the Secretariat and the Peacekeeping Mission did not

react more quickly and decisively when the Serbs initiated their attack on Srebrenica. In fact, rather than attempting to mobilize the international community to support the enclave's defense we gave the Security Council the impression that the situation was under control, and many of us believed that to be the case. The day before Srebrenica fell we reported that the Serbs were not attacking when they were. We reported that the Bosniacs had fired on an UNPROFOR blocking position when it was the Serbs. We failed to mention urgent requests for air power. In some instances in which incomplete and inaccurate information was given to the Council, this can be attributed to problems with reporting from the field. *In other instances, however, the reporting may have been illustrative of a more general tendency to assume that the parties were equally responsible for the transgressions that occurred.*

12 A major exception to this pattern is the UNHCR, whose officials were clear and devastating in their description of what was occurring and what the UN response had been.

13 The discussion below of the Kosovo mythology in Serbian religious nationalism is a summary and update of the more detailed presentation in Sells 1996. In that book I offer full documentation and numerous examples for each element in Kosovo mythology. In this paper, rather than demonstrating in full the existence and operation of this mythology, I attempt to offer a clear summary of it and its implications for policy toward the Balkans (and toward other situations where religious nationalism is a factor in conflict). See also Anzulović 1999 and Judah 1997.

14 Bishop Petar Petrović II (Njegoš), *The Mountain Wreath (Gorski vijenac)*, translated and edited by Vasa Mihailovich, Irvine, Ca.: 1986.

15 Andrić 1990, 20, a translation of the dissertation presented to the dean of the Faculty of Philosophy at Karl Franz University in Graz, Austria, on 14 May 1924 under the title *Die Entwicklung des geistigen Lebens in Bosnien unter der Einwirkung der türkischen Herrschaft.* Contrast Andrić's portrayal of Bosnian-Muslim literary culture with its depiction by a nineteenth-century Bosnian-Muslim scholar in Edin Hajdarpasic's introduction to and translation of Safvet Beg Basagic Redzepasić, *Herceg-Bosnia and Eastern Scholarship, translated by Edin Hajdarpasic from the appendix of Kratka Uputa u Proslost Bosne I Hercegovine* [*A Short Instruction in the Past of Bosnia-Hercegovina, 1463– 1850*], Sarajevo: Vlastita Naklada, 1900. Hajdarpasic's essay and translation can be found outline at http://virtu.sar.usf.edu/~ehajdarp/ safvet.html. An intimate view into Bosnian-Muslim literary culture is given by Muhammad al-Khanji al-Busnavi in his *al-jawhar al-asnā' fī*

tarājim 'ulamā' wa shu'arā' busnā [*The Shining Jewel: Portraits of Scholars and Poets of Bosnia*], Cairo: 1930. Al-Khanji's biographies frequently focus on religious jurists who were also poets. Many of them took poetic pen names in the Persian style and composed poetry in Ottoman Turkish, Persian, Arabic, and/or South Slavic Aljamiado, and sometimes in all of the above languages. To be considered cultured, one was expected not only to have mastered several major language systems, but also to compose outstanding poetry in them.

16 For further discussion of Christoslavism in Andrić, particularly in his famous 1942 novel *The Bridge on the Drina*, see Sells 1996, 45–50. Of special importance is the motif of "blood stealing." Through the devçirme system the Ottomans are said to steal the blood of Christian Serbs; Muslim Slavs are nothing other than Christian souls trapped inside the Turk body. *The Bridge on the Drina* also includes a graphic description of the impaling of the Serbian revolutionary who is trying to destroy the bridge. Many people have said that this is one of the most powerful passages they have ever read in literature and that, after reading it, they were trembling. Not only is it a classic example of the passion scene, in which every aspect of the crucifixion and killing is gone over in detail, but the description of the impaling has sexual overtones as an implied, mythic version of anal rape. For a discussion of racism and sexual fear, see Young-Bruehl 1996. Of special relevance to the ideology and atrocities of "ethnic cleansing" is the section on the "obsessive" pattern found in anal ideologies of purification. See Andrić 1977.

17 See Cigar 1995.

18 Leaders of the Serbian Orthodox Church continue to refer to this alleged genocide as if it were a fact (see below), and these allegations are absolutely central to the Serbian religious nationalist program.

A key work on this issue is Popović, Janca, and Petrovar 1990. In regard to the Telegraphic Agency of the New Yugoslavia (TANJUG) and journalist reports alleging massive rape of Serb women by Albanians, Natasha Kandić carried out thorough investigations in the police stations where the crimes were alleged to have been reported. What she found was that from 1986 to 1989 there had been only three cases of international rape, two of those involving Serbs who had raped Albanian women, as opposed to the more than 200 cases of Serbs raped by Albanians reported in the media. Svetlana Slapsak analyzed the column "Echoes and Reactions"

("Odjeci i reagovanja") in the popular daily "Politika," a forum for letters attributed to "angry common people." The stylistic regularity of the letters and the constant allegations of Albanian depravities committed against Serb women, children, and cultural heritage allowed her to conclude that they had been fabricated by a handful of journalists in Belgrade. I am indebted to Zoran Mutić for the above information. Mutić attempted to promote the book but found that the other former Yugoslav republics no longer were concerned with Serbian "interior" politics, that the Albanians already knew the facts, that most Serbs would not be willing to read it, and that most Bosnians were too preoccupied with their own problems to take an active interest. The book, unfortunately, has never been translated.

19 See the comments by Jose Maria Mendiluce quoted in *Vreme News Digest* 170 (24 December 1994) concerning the atrocities he witnessed in the northeast Bosnian town of Zvornik.

20 See Branko Perić, "Belgrade Implicated in Banja Luka Assassination Attempt," IWPR (Institute for War and Peace Reporting) Crisis Report 87 (26 October 1999): www.iwpr.net. In explaining the theories regarding the attempted assassination of dissident Serbian journalist Željko Kopanje, Perić refers to a number of exposés conducted by his newspaper, *Nezavisne Novine*, that pointed to links between Belgrade and specific atrocities in Bosnia. One story detailed the activities of a paramilitary group from Doboj called The Mice in the Teslić municipality during June 1992:

> It seems, according to *Nezavisne Novine*'s articles, that a group of 16 civilian and military police who made up Mice executed 38 Bosniaks and Croats from Teslić in the night between 12 and 13 June 1992 and then buried them in two mass graves. In mid-September international investigators opened one of these mass graves, on Mount Borje, at the time when *Nezavisne Novine* ran a story about that case. Mice came to Teslić under the auspices of a certain "Njegoš", who took over command of the town' crisis headquarters, in the beginning of June 1992. Njegoš was a conspiratorial name for the instructor of Red Berets, a special unit that had been dispatched as "instructors" to Mount Ozren by Serbia's state security service.

21 See Sells 1996, chapters 3 and 4, and note 24 below.

22 Bat Ye'or is an authority for the movement that seeks a special law in the US to protect Christians from "global persecution," a movement dominated by virulently Islamophobic ideologues. See "Past is Prologue: The Challenge of Islamism Today," *U.S. Congressional*

Briefing, Human Rights Caucus, "The Persecution of Christians World-
wide," Tuesday, 29 April 1997 (2:00–4:00 P.M.); and the review of
Bat Ye'or's work by Richard John Neuhaus, "The Public Square,"
First Things 76 (October 1997), 75–93. Bat Ye'or's lecture, "Myths
and Politics: Origin of the Myth of a Tolerant Pluralistic Islamic
Society," 31 August 1995, was delivered at a Symposium on the
Balkan War (Chicago, Illinois) under the auspices of the Lord
Byron Foundation (see the following note on the Lord Byron Foundation) and the International Strategic Studies Association. The lec-
ture was delivered less than a month after the Srebrenica massacre,
of which Bat Ye'or made no mention.

23 The three principle figures in the neo-Confederate connection to
Serb militancy are: Thomas Fleming, a writer for the neo-Confederate
League of the South, president of The Rockfort Institute, and editor
of *Chronicles: A Magazine of American Culture*; Sir Alfred Sherman, co-
founder and chairman of The Lord Byron Foundation; and Srdja
Trifkovic, executive director of The Lord Byron Foundation and foreign editor of *Chronicles: A Magazine of American Culture.* The Rockfort Institute and its journal, *Chronicles,* are central vehicles for the
anti-immigrationist elements within the Christian right. For further
details, with examples of the extreme positions taken by the Rockfort Institute and the web of associations it has with Serbian nationalist and other groups, see M. Sells, "The GOP-Right, Belgrade
Lobby, and Neo-Confederacy, Multiple Connections," at
http://www.haverford.edu/relg/sells/reports/gopbelgrade.htm, and
"'Mutt America': the Racio-Religious Right and Genocide in the
Balkans" at http://www.haverford.edu/relg/sells/reports/
muttamericabelgrade.htm.

24 See "The Bombing of Serbian Shrines" page at http://spc.org.yu/
Svetinje/svetinje_e.html. Father Sava Janjić and Artemije
Radosavljević, bishop of Raška and Prizren, have distinguished
themselves among the other Serbian Orthodox religious leaders by
their willingness to show concern for both Albanians and Serbs and
to criticize specific crimes committed by Serbs. Yet even they have
recently reverted to the mythology of alleged genocide in the
1980s, showing how very strong the currents of religious nationalism can be, and Bishop Artemije has attacked the War Crimes
Tribunal in The Hague as an anti-Serb plot. On the other hand,
they have remained vocal critics of the Belgrade regime. When the
head of the Serbian Orthodox Church, Patriarch Pavle, attended a

reception hosted by Milošević, Artemije sent a vigorous letter of objection. A major power in the circle of Pavle is the recently appointed episcope (bishop) of Mileševa, Filaret. Filaret was one of the leaders of the Serbian Orthodox clergy who supported extremist nationalism. He once held a skull in his hands, which he claimed belonged to a child killed by Croats, and posed in his priestly vestments with a rifle. He is an associate of Vojislav Šešelj. See Vlado Mares, "Rift in the Serbian Orthodox Church," IPWR Report 101 (10 December 1999): info@iwpr.net.

25 See Laura Secor, "Testaments Betrayed, Yugoslavian Intellectuals and the Road to War," Lingua Franca 9.6 (1999), online text available at: http://www.linguafranca.com/9909/testbet.html.

26 For an explicit statement of the plan to destroy Kosovar Albanians, see the program of Vojislav Šešelj's Serbian Radical Party, which is a central part of the Milošević governing coalition. The Šešelj program not only calls for the removal of 360,000 Kosovar Albanians claimed to have emigrated from Albania after World War II, as well as the removal of their descendants (which would leave almost no Kosovars), but offers specific steps: Kosovars would be fired from all employment, evicted from all housing, and required to compensate Serbia for fifty years of back rent, etc. Šešelj's program differs from the programs of Drašković and The Serbian-American lobby known as "The Serbian Unity Congress" only in its willingness to spell out the implications of the demand for mass expulsion by all of these groups. The language and the sadistic set of steps to be taken are eerily reminiscent of the Ustashe program against Croatian Jews drawn up by the interior minister, Andrije Artuković. Point twenty-five of Šešelj's Serbian Radical Party program of 1991 calls for the following:

25. The suppression of the Albanian separatist insurgence in Kosovo and Metohija by all available means, and in order to make the relapse of that insurgence impossible, we are pledged to an immediate implementation of the following measures:

— to efficiently preclude the establishment of any form of the Kosovo-Metohija political territorial autonomy,

— to expel without delay all 360 thousand Albanian emigrants and their descendants,

— to prevent any state financial subsidies of the Albanian national minority, and to divert the funds formerly allotted for the purpose, to the exclusive financing of the Serb return to Kosovo and Metohija,

- to proclaim the state of war in Kosovo and Metohija and institute military government for not less than ten years,
- to immediately disband the local agencies of civilian authority and institutions financed from the state budget, which operate in the Albanian language, such as the University, The Academy of Sciences and Arts, book and newspaper publishers and the like,
- to immediately shut down and conserve all factories and other production units, which operate uneconomically because of the systematic sabotage of employed Shiptars,
- to issue emigration passports to all Shiptars, who express such a wish,
- as it has transpired that Albania is a state lastingly hostile to Serbia, a belt 20 to 50 km wide as the crow flies along the Albanian border is to be proclaimed an area of strategic importance for our country, and all members of the Shiptar national minority are to be moved from it, with a fair financial compensation,
- all Shiptars, who hold Serbian citizenship and reside abroad, acting from separatist positions there, must be immediately deprived of the Serbian citizenship and forbidden to return,
- all Shiptar social benefits, notably those stimulating an excessive birth rate, must be abolished immediately,
- forcible collection of outstanding communal dues must be undertaken without delay, and tenants, defaulting on their rent, while living in flats owned by the state, must be evicted,
- the real property of Kosovo-Metohija Serbs, which was seized from them by the fascist occupier or the Titoist communist regime, is to be returned immediately to its legitimate owners or their heirs,
- to hold no parliamentary elections in that territory until the ethnic structure of the population is restored to the ratio which existed in April 1941,

Point twenty-five then moves on to plans to give seized Kosovar land to Serbs and Serb police and military, and to proclamations of support for the Bosnian Serbian Democratic Party (SDS) of Radovan Karadžić and the equally radical Serbian nationalist party in Krajina.

For more on the 1991 Programme Declaration of the Serbian Radical Party, see http://www.haverford.edu/relg/sells/reports/srpclean1.htm. For the position of the Serbian Unity Congress (SUC), see http://www.haverford.edu/relg/sells/reports/suckos.htm.

27 See Naša Borba, quoted in V. Koštunica, 1995, "Koštunica on Srebrenica," *OMRI Daily Digest* 2, no. 135 (13 July), online at http://www.bosnet.org/archive/bosnet.w3archive/9507/msg00115.html. "The International community failed the test." This, Naša Borba

reported on 13 July, is how Vesna Pešić, president of the Citizen's Union of Serbia, described the developments in Srebrenica, sharply criticizing the Bosnian Serbs. But Vojislav Kostunica, leader of the Democratic Party of Serbia, said the Bosnian-Serb army's latest move was an "act of self-defense." He claimed that NATO air strikes had provoked the annexation of the enclave, adding that the peace mediators were trying to "extinguish fire with fuel."

See also Prpa 2000, available online at http://www.nacional.hr/htm/249043.en.htm, in which Koštunica's militancy is depicted in detail.

28 Akashi and Janvier decided Srebrenica's fate at a meeting on 9 June 1995 in which they refused General Rupert Smith's repeated warnings. In response to Smith, Janvier made the following statement:

> The Serbs need two things: international recognition, and a softening of the blockade on the Drina. I hope that these conditions will be met quickly, given the urgent situation. I think the Serbs are aware of how favorable the situation is to them – I don't think that they want to go to an extreme crisis. On the contrary, they want to modify their behavior, be good interlocutors. It is for this that we must speak to them – not negotiate, but to show them how important it is to have a normal attitude.

For the full transcript, in which this statement appears, see http://www.haverford.edu/relg/sells/srebrenica/splitjune9.html.

29 Phillip Corwin, an assistant and advisor to Yasushi Akashi, shows just how self-contradictory the effort to maintain moral neutrality and good-faith negotiations during attempted genocide had become. See Corwin 1999. Corwin explains that the Bosnian-Serb army only attacked civilians or small units but refused to fight an equally armed foe (202–3), yet he praises the ability of the Serb soldiers (70) and suggests that they could withstand a NATO attack, while elsewhere he suggests that such force might be successful against the Serb army (35). He also admits that Akashi, and Janvier misjudged the Serb army attack on Srebrenica, yet he continually holds up both Akashi and Janvier as unfairly criticized. Finally, he concedes the horror of Srebrenica and admits that it followed a pattern of atrocities committed by Mladić, but throughout his account of Srebrenica he directs his outrage not against the Serb army but against the Bosnian government. At the heart of these contradictions is the stubborn insistence that it was possible to carry out good-faith negotiations with the likes of Radovan Karadžić and Ratko Mladić and a stubborn refusal to admit that they were not

defending (however poorly) legitimate Serb interests but acting out of an ideology of ethno-religious purification.

For a discussion of those in academia who obscured the moral situation during the genocide and a fine philosophical perspective on the tragedy, see Campbell 1998.

One recent example of the criticism levelled against NATO's intervention in Kosovo can be found in Said 1999, available online at http://www.ahram.org.eg. Said assumes that had NATO just agreed to negotiate more, the NATO air strikes in Kosovo would have been avoided and the threat to the Kosovars ended. Yet he gives no evidence that such a negotiation could have succeeded. Said writes that those supporting the NATO operation showed "no memory of what happened in Rwanda four years ago, or in Bosnia, or the displacement of 350,000 Serbs at the hands of Tudjman, or the continuing atrocities against the Kurds, the killing of over 560,000 Iraqi civilians, or – to bring it back where it all started – Israel's ethnic cleansing of Palestine in 1948." He also writes the following: "If diplomacy is always to be preferred over military means, then diplomacy must be used at all costs." Only someone who himself had not remembered Bosnia or ever really looked at it seriously could make such a statement. Diplomacy was tried right up to and through the exterminations at Srebrenica. For three years, the Milošević and Karadžić regimes used diplomacy to stall for more time to carry out more ethnic cleansing. Reverting to the 1992–5 paradigm of diplomacy at all costs would have certainly led to a similar fate for Kosovars: mass killings inside Kosovo and hundreds of thousands of survivors living on the borders of Serbia, Macedonia, and Montenegro in Gaza-like refugee camps, for generations, with each generation more radicalized and more determined to return home.

30 For before and after pictures of the now gutted masterwork, see Michael A. Sells, "Wahhabi Destruction of the Begova," posted online at http://www.haverford.edu/relg/sells/reports.html, and Denison 2001, 33. Destroyed were the rich textures of the classic interior, with its ceramic tiles, detailed mural frescoes, and other decoration. In place of this masterwork of Ottoman design, there is now a soulless interior described of hospital-white plaster.

31 See Saïd Zulficar, "Paper Presented to the International Symposium on Cultural Heritage and Diversity held 18–21 December 2000, Tokyo," and idem, "Alerte Aux Iconoclastes!" *Al-Ahram Hebdo*, 28 February 2001, available online at http://www.ahram.org.eg/ Hebdo/arab/ahram/2001/2/28/Nullo.htm. For a view of central

Orahovac before its destruction at the hands of the Saudi aid committee, see *People Property: The Human Voice of Housing*, at http://www.ppmagazine.co.uk/mayfeat1.html. For documentation of the effort to bring authenticity to Kosovo restoration and to resist the destruction of heritage under the guise of restoration, see the web site of Patrimoine sans Frontières, the organization founded by Saïd Zulficar after he left his position at the United Nations Educational, Scientific, and Cultural Organization (UNESCO), at http://www.axelibre.org/psf1.htm. See also "Alerte aux Iconoclastes!" Zulficar discusses the Saudi-directed destruction of 150 Balkan-Muslim edifices before the 1999 war in Kosovo. After the war, the Saudi groups destroyed or damaged the classic Hadum library, madrasah, and cemetery in Gjakova (Djakovica), the seventeenth-century Bula-Zade Mosque in Peje (Peć), the seventeenth-century Rogovo Mosque, and the seventeenth-century Katër Lule Mosque in Prishtina. In Bosnia, in addition to its destruction of the Begova interior, the Saudi group seriously damaged the Careva Mosque under the guise of renovation. It has been noted by those who have attempted to resist the Saudi-Wahhabi campaign of cultural cleansing in Bosnia-Herzegovina and Kosovo that much of the destruction occurred during the same period as the Afghan Taliban's destruction of ancient Buddhist sculptures and other artifacts. The Taliban are heavily influenced by Saudi Wahhabism, and Saudi Arabia is their most important ally and financier. Wahhabism is named after its eighteenth-century founder, Ibn 'Abd al-Wahhab. The sect has seized and maintained power by aligning itself with the Saudi monarchy.

32 Mahmutćehajić 2000a, 2000b.

33 The depredations carried out by Saudi-Wahhabi aid groups against Balkan Muslims and their culture mirror a larger irony, particularly given that these depredations followed on Serb and Croat nationalist attacks against Balkan Muslims based in part on portraying them as Saudi-style fundamentalists. Due to its enormous wealth and strategic geographical position, the Saudi-Wahhabi establishment plays a dominant role in forming the image of Islam in the West, an image of despotism, intolerance, inequality, and misogyny. The vast majority of Muslims who are not Wahhabis thus suffer a double blow: their own culture is attacked by Saudi-sponsored missionaries and aid groups with enormous wealth and resources, even as they are subjected to prejudice based on a Western image of Muslims that is itself based on the behaviour of Saudi Wahhabis. See Mernissi 1996.

Bosnia-Herzegovina: Chosen Trauma and Its Transgenerational Transmission

VAMIK D. VOLKAN

The term "chosen trauma" refers to the shared image of an event that causes a large group (i.e., ethnic group) to feel helpless, victimized, and humiliated by another group. Of course, no group intends to be victimized, but it can "choose" to psychologize and to mythologize the event. When this occurs, the group carries the image of the event – along with associated shared feelings of hurt and shame, as well as the defenses against perceived shared conflicts that these feelings initiate – from generation to generation. During this transgenerational transmission, the image of the event emerges as a significant large-group marker; the group draws the shared image of the traumatic event into its very identity (Volkan 1997, 1999a, 1999b). In order to illustrate these two concepts, chosen trauma and transgenerational transmission, I turn my attention to Bosnia-Herzegovina after the collapse of communist Yugoslavia. Of course, what I present in this chapter is not a complete psychopolitical analysis of the situation in the former Yugoslavia; here I will focus only on a Serbian shared trauma that took place 600 years ago and on some of its consequences in Bosnia in the early 1990s.

THE HISTORICAL AND PSYCHOLOGICAL BACKGROUND TO 1992

After becoming independent from Byzantium in the twelfth century, the Kingdom of Serbia thrived for almost 200 years under the leadership of the Nemanjić dynasty, reaching its peak under the beloved Emperor Stefan Dušan. By the end of his twenty-four-year reign, Serbia's territory reached from the Croatian border in the north to the Aegean Sea in the south, from the Adriatic Sea in the west to Constantinople in the east. Dušan died in 1355, and the Nemanjić dynasty came to an end a short time thereafter. In 1371, Serbian feudal lords elected Lazar Hrebeljanović leader of Serbia, though he assumed the title of prince or duke rather than king or emperor. The decline of Serbia that followed is primarily attributed to the expansion of the Ottoman Empire into Serbian territory, culminating in the Battle of Kosovo on 28 June 1389 at the Kosovo Polje (the Field of the Black Birds). Despite a gap of some seventy years between the Battle of Kosovo and the total occupation of Serbia by the Ottoman Turks, the belief that the two events were coterminous gradually developed.

Thanks to recent works such as Emmert's (1990), we now have, in English, various versions of the historical "truth" of the Battle of Kosovo. We know that the Turkish sultan Murad I was fatally wounded by a Serbian assassin during or after the battle. We also know that either the wounded sultan or his son Bayezid ordered the execution of Prince Lazar, the leader of the Serbian forces and their allies, who had been captured during the battle. Ottoman forces apparently returned to Adrianople (Edirne) after the Battle of Kosovo, and Lazar was succeeded by his son, Stefan Lazarević, who reportedly became a close ally of Murad's successor. With heavy losses on both sides and the deaths of both leaders, many historians now consider the battle to have been essentially indecisive.

What is important in this case, however, as in others, is not the historical truth, but the impact of the shared mental image of the "chosen trauma" on a large group's identity. By the time the Turks gained substantial control over Serbia – fully seventy years after Kosovo – the battle had slowly begun to evolve into a "chosen trauma" for the Serbian people. There is ample evidence that the interpretation of events at the Battle of Kosovo has gone through a number of transformations. For example, though early chronicles of the battle did not specify the name of Sultan Murad's assassin, a later version asserts that one of a small group of Lazar's soldiers slipped through Turkish defenses and was able to stab Murad, another affirms that Lazar himself led this group, and still another account identifies Miloš Kobila (or Kobilić or Obravitch), one of Lazar's sons-in-law, who had been accused of being a traitor prior to the battle, as the heroic assassin. (After some time, Miloš was generally accepted as the actual assassin.) Perhaps most importantly, the disunity of the Balkan Slavs (even that of Lazar's own family) and the continued existence of Serbia for many decades after the battle were substantially forgotten. As a result, as Marković (1983) has written, the memory of Kosovo came to function as a "sacred grief"; "mere mention of that name suffices to shake a Serb to the depths of his soul" (111) because it is associated with Serbia's subjugation to the Ottoman Empire.

Mythologized tales of the battle were transmitted from generation to generation through a strong oral and religious tradition in Serbia, perpetuating and reinforcing Serbians' traumatized self-representations. Because Lazar had become a shared image of Serbians' traumatized self-representation – passed down through generations – he initially had to be absolved for sealing the fate of Serbia. According to legend, Saint Ilya, in the shape of a gray falcon, appeared before Lazar on the eve of the battle with a message from the Virgin Mary. Lazar was given two choices: he could win the battle and find a kingdom on earth, or he could lose the battle, die a martyr's death, and find a kingdom in heaven. The following is a version of a Serbian folk song on Lazar's dilemma:

> Dear God, what shall I do and
> Which kingdom should I choose?
> Should I choose the Kingdom of Heaven
> Or the kingdom of earth?
> If I choose the kingdom,
> The kingdom of the earth,
> The earthly kingdom is of short duration
> And the Heavenly is from now to eternity.
> (qtd in Marković 1983, 114)

Naturally, the legend affirms that, being a devoutly religious person, Lazar chose defeat and death. As the myth of Lazar as religious martyr spread, icons in which he was depicted as a Christ-like figure began to appear in Serbian churches and monasteries.

By propagating this legend, Serbians collectively tried to deny the shame and humiliation of the defeat at Kosovo. But, under Ottoman control, Serbians' helplessness and victimization could not be denied, for they had no power to bring back their glorious past. So they clung to – and identified with – the martyrdom of the legend. In fact, that sense of martyrdom fit well with their pre-Ottoman perception of themselves. Even during the Nemanjić period, Serbians believed that they had sacrificed themselves for the other Christians of Europe since they had served as a "buffer" against the advancing Muslim Turks. The Greek Orthodox Serbians, however, felt that they had received no appreciation from their Roman Catholic neighbours in Europe for their "sacrifice."

The Ottomans did not directly force the Serbians to convert to Islam en masse – except for the youngsters they collected to go through the *devşirme*, a process through which a Christian youth was taken away from his family to become a Muslim and educated so as to serve the sultan. After the Ottomans moved into Balkan territory, "The Orthodox Patriarch himself testified in a letter to the Pope in 1385 that the Sultan left to his church complete liberty of action" (Kinross 1977, 59), and even during the reign of Murad I, the seeds of a multicultural, multi-religious, and multilingual Ottoman Empire had been sown. It is nevertheless true that "in the Ottoman Empire everyone was equal, but the Muslims were more equal" (Volkan and Itzkowitz 1994, 64), and some Slavs did become Muslims over the course of the first two centuries of Ottoman rule – especially in Bosnia, a "gray area" between Orthodox and Roman Catholic influence. During the Ottoman period these ancestors of today's Bosnian Muslims became middle- and upper-middle-class city dwellers in Bosnia-Herzegovina, while peasants in Serbia and Croatia remained Orthodox and Roman Catholic. By the middle of the sixteenth century, half of the population of Bosnia was Muslim, and Sarajevo was nearly all Muslim.

Among those who remained Christian, the idea that Prince Lazar – and by extension the Serbians as a group – had chosen a kingdom in heaven rather than a kingdom on earth remained alive in a rather covert fashion, except during some rebellions such as the one in 1804–15. Embracing their identity as victims, Serbs glorified their supposed persecution in songs such as this one:

> Drink, Serbs, of God's glory
> And fulfill the Christian law;
> And even though we have lost our kingdom,
> Let us not lose our souls.
> (qtd in Marković 1983, 116)

As a result of sharing traumatized self-images pertaining to the same "chosen trauma," then, Serbians held onto an identity of victimhood and became "perennial mourners" (Volkan and Zintl 1993) of the loss at Kosovo. Of course, the reality that their territory was occupied by the Ottomans supported this shared perception, and the church and folk singers effectively kept the chosen trauma in public awareness. The day of the Battle of Kosovo, 28 June, was commemorated as St Vitus' Day and through the centuries became the subject of other legends that strengthened the victimized group identity. One folk story that sprang up, for example, asserted that the flowers on the mountainous plain of the Kosovo battlefield were "crying" – in reference to their stems being bent, which makes the flowers appear to be bowing their heads in grief.

In the latter part of the nineteenth century, however, as the decline of the Ottoman Empire coincided with the awakening of nationalism in Europe, other aspects of the Lazar and Kosovo legends became more readily observable. Lazar had been transformed from an ineffective leader into a saint and martyr, but now Lazar's and Miloš's images gradually changed from those of victims and tragic figures to those of heroes and, ultimately, of avengers. Whereas paintings and icons of Lazar and Miloš from the Renaissance typically depicted them as saintly or Christ-like, for example, some from the late nineteenth and early twentieth century increasingly featured them as strong and warrior-like figures. Whether Serbians share a sense of victimization or a sense of revenge, however, there would be no collective Serbian identity without the context of the symbol of Kosovo. Mothers began to greet their children as the "avengers of Kosovo." The direct and indirect message was this: reverse not only the shame and humiliation, but also the grief and helplessness within the shared self-representation.

In 1878, after much political scheming and many wars, the Serbians (as well as Montenegrins) were declared independent from the Ottoman Empire by the Treaty of Berlin. The treaty, however, placed them under the control of Austria-Hungary, which in turn tried to suppress Serbia's "Kosovo spirit." Serbia soon found itself embroiled in the Balkan Wars of 1912–13 but was finally able to "liberate" Kosovo after more than 500 years. A young soldier later recalled this event:

The single sound of that word – Kosovo – caused an indescribable excitement. This one word pointed to the black past-five centuries. In it exists the whole of our sad past – the tragedy of Prince Lazar and the entire Serbian people.

Each of us created for himself a picture of Kosovo while we were still in the cradle. Our mothers lulled us to sleep with the songs of Kosovo, and in our schools our teachers never ceased in their stories of Lazar and Miloš.

My God, what awaited us! To see a liberated Kosovo. When we arrived in Kosovo ... the spirits of Lazar, Miloš and all the Kosovo martyrs gazed on us. (Vojincki Glasnik, 28 June 1932, qtd in Emmert 1990, 133–4).

Cvijic (1986) supports the idea that such identification with the martyrs of Kosovo was an attempt to reverse felt humiliation and helplessness: for a soldier "to kill many Turks means not only to avenge his ancestors but also to ease the pains which he himself feels" (Emmert 1990, 135).

Less than two years after Kosovo's liberation, on St Vitus' Day 1914, a Bosnian Serb named Gavrilo Princip assassinated Archduke Francis Ferdinand and his pregnant wife in Sarajevo, precipitating the start of World War I. What is known about Princip is that as a teenager he was filled with the transformed images of Lazar and Miloš as avengers – as were most other Serbian youngsters (Emmert 1990). Although Serbia was "free," the Austro-Hungarian Empire exerted significant influence over much of the region after the Ottomans left. In Princip's mind, it appears that the old and new "oppressors" were condensed, and the desire for revenge was trans-ferred to the Austro-Hungarian heir apparent.

After World War I, the attempt to bring all southern Slavs into one kingdom finally succeeded, and the kingdom of the Serbs, Croats, and Slovenes was founded, known later as Yugoslavia ("land of the Southern Slavs," distinguishing these peoples from northern Slavs such as Poles, Slovakians, and Romanians). Yugoslavia was formed of five "lands": Serbia, Montenegro, Slovenia, Croatia, and Bosnia. As one might expect, the kingdom was fragmented by fre-quent quarrels. After World War II (what happened in the Nazi period is another story that reveals much about the present day Serbian-Croat-Muslim enmities, but beyond my scope here), Yugo-slavia was reorganized as a communist state with Marshall Josip Broz Tito as its head. The new Yugoslavia included the original five "lands," now called republics, plus Macedonia. Kosovo and Vojvod-ina, in southern and northern Serbia, respectively, remained "auton-omous" republics. Under the communist regime in Yugoslavia,

Serbs, Croats, Muslims, Slovenes, Montenegrins, and others lived together in relative, though not constant, peace; in the late 1960s and early 70s, for instance, Croat nationalists demanded the formation of an independent Croatia. To combat such problems, the communists attempted to create a "Yugoslav man" similar to the Soviet ideal of "Soviet man" in which all peoples were considered equal and connected through the higher objectives of communist ideology. Prince Lazar's representation was officially degraded as a "symbol of reactionary nationalism" (Kaplan 1993, 39); in Bosnia-Herzegovina, more than one-fourth of all marriages were mixed, and less than 3 per cent of all Muslims attended prayers in a mosque (Vulliamy 1994). But, as we now know, each group in Yugoslavia strongly held onto its own identity rather than becoming a single "Yugoslavian" people. After Mikhail Gorbachev's 1987 introduction of *glasnost* and *perestroika* in the USSR, the Socialist Republic of Yugoslavia began to destabilize as each group began to ask "Who are we now?" and "How are we different from others?"

THE REACTIVATION OF
A CHOSEN TRAUMA

In April 1987, Slobodan Milošević, then a communist bureaucrat, was attending a meeting of 300 party delegates in Kosovo. At the time, only 10 per cent of the population in Kosovo was Serbian; the majority, as is the case today, were Albanian Muslims. During the meeting a crowd of Serbs and Montenegrins tried to force their way into the hall. They wanted to express their grievances about hardships they were experiencing in Kosovo, but the local police blocked and prohibited the crowd's entry. At that moment, Milošević stepped forward and said: "Nobody, either now or in the future, has the right to beat you." The crowd responded in a frenzy, spontaneously singing "Hej Sloveni" (the national anthem) and shouting "We want freedom! We will not give up Kosovo!" In turn, Milošević was excited; he stayed in the building until dawn – thirteen hours later – listening to their tales of victimization and their desire to reverse shame, humiliation, and helplessness.

Milošević apparently came out of this experience a transformed person, clad in the "armour" of Serbian nationalism; he would later declare in a speech that Serbs in Kosovo are not a minority since "Kosovo is Serbia and will always be Serbia." I do not have sufficient data to make a sophisticated attempt at understanding Milošević's inner world or to know whether this transformation occurred suddenly. The information that is available, however, does offer some insight into Milošević, the second son born to an Orthodox priest during the Nazi occupation of 1941. A loner, aloof, humourless, and self-centred, he comes from a severely dysfunctional family. When he was seven, his favorite uncle killed himself with a bullet to the head. When he was twenty-one his father did the same. When he was in his early thirties, his mother hung herself in the family sitting room (Vulliamy 1994). Those who know him describe him as alternately angry and depressed. He married his teenage sweetheart but is not known to have many other lasting and trusting relationships. When Milošević became president of Serbia in 1992, a saying in Belgrade went something like this: "Have pity on the person whom Milošević has called a friend."

It was this Milošević who, with his allies and minions, unleashed Serbian nationalism in the last decade of the twentieth century; one episode in particular demonstrates how he did so. According to historians, about one year after Lazar's execution, a tomb was completed for him in the Ravanica monastery, and he was declared a saint. When Ottoman rule reached Ravanica, Lazar's remains were moved to Frushka Gora, northwest of Belgrade. In 1889, the 500th anniversary of Kosovo, plans for moving Lazar's mummified body back to Ravanica were discussed, but never materialized. As the 600th anniversary approached, however, Milošević and others in his circle were determined to bring Lazar's body out of "exile." Lazar's mummified body was placed in a coffin and taken "on tour" to every Serbian village and town, where he was received by huge crowds of mourners dressed in black (Kaplan 1993). As a result, Serbs began to feel the defeat in Kosovo as if it had occurred only yesterday (a "time collapse" initiated by Serbian leadership), an outcome facilitated by the fact that the "chosen trauma" had been kept alive throughout the centuries in legend and folk belief. As Serbs greeted Lazar's body, they cried and wailed and gave speeches declaring that they would never allow such a defeat to occur again; sharing the affects associated with traumatized self-images invisibly connected all Serbs more closely to each other. Although it is unclear precisely what Milošević (with the help of the Serbian Church and certain academics) consciously intended to achieve, he apparently reactivated Lazar's images in Serbs' minds, thus ensuring that grieving his defeat at the Battle of Kosovo could at last be accomplished and that reversing the helplessness, humiliation, and shame created by the 600-year-old trauma could finally be completed. Serbs began, as a result of his actions, to develop similar self-images that incorporated a new sense of entitlement to revenge.

As the 600th anniversary of the Battle of Kosovo approached, Milošević ordered the building of a huge monument on a hill overlooking the battlefield. Made of red stone representing blood (Kaplan 1993), it stands 100 feet over the "grieving" flowers and is surrounded by artillery-shell-shaped cement pillars inscribed with a sword and the dates 1389–1989. On the tower are written Lazar's words before the battle calling every Serbian man to fight the Turks. If a Serb fails to respond to this call, Lazar's words warn: "He will not have a child, neither male or female, and he will not have fertile land where crops grow"; as some photographs reveal, this call to battle was reprinted on the T-shirts of many of those present at the Field of the Black Birds on the anniversary itself. By building the monument linking 1389 with 1989, Milošević was "resending" Lazar's ancient message in the present. The message to the Serbian men was clear: "Either fight 'the Turks' – Muslims – or lose your manliness!" At the celebration, Milošević "took the podium from dancing maidens in traditional folk costume and transported the crowd to heights of frenzied adoration with a simple message: 'never again would Islam subjugate the Serbs'" (Vulliamy 1994, 51).

Riding this wave of nationalism, Milošević grew in prominence. In 1990 the six Yugoslav republics held elections, and communists were defeated everywhere except in Serbia and Montenegro. In Serbia, Milošević was elected head of the communists, now called the Serbian Socialist Party. In 1991 Milošević summoned Radovan Karadzić, the Bosnian Serbs' leader, and others to meet with him to discuss the future of the republics. In June 1992, after disposing of his "friend" and mentor Ivan Stambolić, then state president, whom he had accused of betraying the Serbs in Kosovo, Milošević was elected president of the third "Yugoslavia" (the Serb-Montenegrin federation).

Meanwhile, Turks once more became the "clear and present" enemy. Hasan Aygün, who ran the Turkish embassy in Belgrade, has described how he was considered "public enemy number one" in the Serbian capital city. Everywhere he went Serbs asked him "Why are you [Turks] planning to invade us?" Mr Aygün thinks that almost every Serb believed that a Turkish invasion was imminent, and he feared for his physical safety because of the time collapse during this period. One of his observations particularly interested me: he said that many Serbian youngsters had developed a new game – playing Russian roulette with pistols loaded with live ammunition. Unsurprisingly, many of these teenagers had to be taken to the hospital dead or with head wounds. To me, this shared new "game" suggests an identification or attempted identification with Lazar's image carried through generations. Like the Lazar of legend, these youngsters were experiencing two choices: death/ martyrdom or life/revenge on Turks.

Serbs now experienced Bosnian Muslims as an extension of the Ottoman Empire and often referred to them as "Turks." There is, of course, a certain truth to this perception since Bosnian Muslims played a significant role in Ottoman Turkish history; one of the most famous Ottoman grand viziers was a Serbian raised in the *devşirme*, and many Bosnian-Muslim epic songs refer to their glories under the Ottomans (Butler 1993). Within the emotional atmosphere resulting from a time collapse, however, the Serbs, especially those living in Bosnia-Herzegovina, began to feel entitled to do to Bosnian Muslims what they believed the Ottoman Turks had done to them.

Before the ethnic cleansing and systematic rape of Bosnian-Muslim women began, Serbian propaganda increasingly focused on inflaming the idea that the Ottomans, now symbolized by the Bosnian Muslims, would return. One piece of propaganda against Bosnian Muslims read:

By order of the Islamic fundamentalists from Sarajevo, healthy Serbian women from 17 to 40 years of age are being separated out and subjected to special treatment. According to their sick plans going back many years, these women have to be impregnated by orthodox Islamic seeds in order to raise a generation of janissaries [Ottoman troops] on the territory they surely consider to be theirs, the Islamic republic. In other words, a fourfold crime is to be committed against the Serbian woman: to remove her from her own family, to impregnate her by undesirable seeds, to make her bear a stranger and then to take even him away from her (Gutman 1993).

This propaganda aimed to create fear among Serbs that the Bosnian Muslims intended to resurrect the *devşirme* and to create a new janissary army. Though there is a kernel of truth in this idea – Bosnian-Muslim leader Alija Izetbegovic had alluded in speeches and in print to the possibility of an Islamic enterprise in Bosnia for which he sought the help of other fundamentalist elements in Muslim countries (whether he was referring to a theoretical position or a wish is unclear) – the fear equating Bosnian Muslims with Ottoman Turks was mostly based on fantasy, for the former had virtually no military power.

Yet the massive projection of the Serbs' aggression onto Bosnian Muslims was so great that it began to "boomerang"; based on the past trauma and time collapse, Serbs perceived a threat when one did not actually exist and felt compelled to act against it. Thus the collective idea that Muslims had to be exterminated slowly began to develop. The Serbs emotionally prepared themselves to "purify" their identity of any possibility of contamination by the Ottoman Turks/Bosnian Muslims. For example, Sarajevo contained many buildings, works of art, and manuscripts that reflected the city's past under the Ottomans. A precious Koran, given by the grand vizier Mehmet Pasha, was featured in the city's famous Gazi Hosrev library. Through the siege of Sarajevo, the Serbs attempted to erase these monuments of the Bosnian Muslims' cultural and religious heritage. Interestingly, many Bosnian Serbs who bombarded the Bosnian capital were natives of the city (Butler 1993); in their collective regression and response to time collapse, they bombed their own city because it "needed" to be purged of any Muslim connection.

Alongside the shared fantasy that Muslims must be cleansed or exterminated was another – that the *devşirme* must be reversed and the number of Serbs increased to carry on the battle. Hence a conscious strategy of intimidation was condensed with an unconscious one, resulting in the systematic rape of thousands of Muslim women by Serbian soldiers. The assumption was that the child produced by the rape of a non-Serb woman would be a Serb and not carry any of the traits of the mother. Serbs thus sought to truly reverse their victimhood both by killing young Muslim men and by replacing them with new "Serb" children. Although, as Beverly Allen (1996) notes, "Enforced pregnancy as a method of genocide makes sense only if you are ignorant about genetics. No baby born from such a crime will be only Serb. It will receive half its genetic material from its mother" (80), the "psychological truth" is more important than biological reality in conditions of inflamed ethnic animosities. Fact and fantasy, past and present were intimately and violently intermingled.

FINAL WORDS

I do not wish to reduce what happened in Bosnia-Herzegovina to the reactivation of a transgenerationally transmitted "chosen trauma" alone. But I do want to emphasize that knowing about psychological processes, especially unconscious ones, can enlarge our understanding about how they may become the fuel to ignite the most horrible human dramas and/or to feed the fire once hostilities start. Psychoanalytic research into the transgenerational transmission of shared trauma, its activation in leader-follower relationships, and the associated phenomenon of "time collapse" can illuminate many hidden aspects of ethnic or other large-group conflicts and show us how internal and external world issues become intertwined.

From the Ashes:
The Past and Future of
Bosnia's Cultural Heritage

ANDRÁS RIEDLMAYER

Barely a decade ago, in March 1992, the people of Bosnia, a small and ancient country in the heart of Europe, voted for independence. In a national plebiscite, with more than 63.4 per cent of the electorate participating, voters cast their ballots almost unanimously in favour of an independent, democratic, and pluralistic Bosnia. As Bosnia's National Assembly met in the capital city of Sarajevo after the vote, more than 100,000 citizens – Muslims, Christians, and others – rallied in front of the Parliament building, holding signs and shouting in unison: "Mi smo za mir!" – "We are for peace!"

The shouts for peace were silenced by gunshots, as Serb nationalist gunmen, concealed on the upper floors of the Holiday Inn across the street, opened fire on the crowd, killing and wounding dozens of people as they ran for cover.

The date was 6 April 1992. In the days and months that followed, the Serb-led Yugoslav National Army systematically bombarded Sarajevo from prepared positions on the mountains overlooking the city. Snipers with telescopic sights picked off civilians as they ran down the streets of the capital in search of food, water, and shelter.[1]

Thus began the assault on Bosnia-Herzegovina. From the beginning, it was characterized by two features that had little to do with military objectives:

- The mass expulsion of civilians driven from their homes, robbed, raped, and murdered for being of the "wrong" ethnicity and religion, and
- The deliberate targeting and destruction of cultural, religious, and historic landmarks by nationalist extremists.

Their targets have included: the National Library in Sarajevo, the Regional Archives in Mostar, local and national museums, the Academy of Music, the National Gallery, entire historic districts, Muslim and Jewish cemeteries, and, above all, the places of worship of the ethnic and religious groups that were singled out for what was euphemistically called "ethnic cleansing."

Three and a half years of war and "ethnic cleansing" in Bosnia, allowed to proceed unchecked by the international community, turned more than half of the country's four million people into refugees and cost the lives of more than 200,000 men, women, and children. The cultural casualties were no less staggering. More than one thousand of Bosnia's mosques, hundreds of Catholic churches, and scores of Orthodox churches, monasteries, private and public libraries, archives, and museums were shelled, burned, and dynamited, and in many cases even the ruins were removed by nationalist extremists in order to complete the cultural and religious "cleansing" of the land they had seized.[2]

Table 1
Destruction of Islamic religious buildings in Bosnia 1992–95

Building type	Total no. before the war	Total no. destroyed or damaged	Percentage destroyed or damaged
Congregational mosques (*Džamije*)	1,149	927	80.68
Small neighbourhood mosques (*Mesdžidi*)	557	259	46.50
Total no. of mosques	1,706	1,186	69.52
Qur'an schools (*Mektebi*)	954	87	9.12
Dervish lodges (*Tekije*)	15	9	60.00
Mausolea, shrines (*Turbe*)	90	44	48.89
Bldgs of religious endowments (*Vakuf*)	1,425	554	38.88

Based on data from the Institute for Protection of Cultural, Historical and Natural Heritage of Bosnia and Herzegovina, *A Report on the Devastation of Cultural, Historical and Natural Heritage of the Republic/Federation of Bosnia and Herzegovina from April 5, 1992 until September 5, 1995* (Sarajevo, 1995), supplemented with information from the database of the State Commission for the Documentation of War Crimes on the Territory of Bosnia and Herzegovina (Državna komisija za prikupljanje činjenica o ratnim zločinima na području Republike Bosne i Hercegovine), the Islamic Community of Bosnia-Herzegovina, and other sources.

Table 2
Destruction of Islamic religious buildings in Bosnia 1992–95

Building type	Total no. before the war	No. damaged/ destroyed by Serb extremists		No. damaged/ destroyed by Croat extremists	
		damaged/ destroyed	total	damaged/ destroyed	total
Congregational mosques (*Džamije*)	1,149	540/249	789	80/58	138
Small neighbourhood mosques (*Mesdžidi*)	557	175/21	196	43/20	63
Total no. of mosques	1,706	715/270	985	123/78	201
Qur'an schools (*Mektebi*)	954	55/14	69	14/4	18
Dervish lodges (*Tekije*)	15	3/4	7	1/1	2
Mausolea, shrines (*Turbe*)	90	34/6	40	3/1	4
Bldgs of religious endowments (*Vakuf*)	1,425	345/125	470	60/24	84

Although we have been told that it was "ancient hatreds" that fuelled this destruction, it is not true. The history that has been destroyed, the buildings, the books, and the historical documents, all spoke eloquently of centuries of pluralism and tolerance in Bosnia. It is this evidence of a successfully shared past that exclusive nationalists have sought to erase.

Since the Middle Ages, Bosnia has been a complex and multi-faceted society, where cultural and religious influences from East and West have met and interacted, both with each other and with a rich indigenous tradition.

Alone in medieval Europe, the Kingdom of Bosnia was a place where not one but three Christian churches – Roman Catholicism, Eastern Orthodoxy, and a schismatic local Bosnian Church – existed side by side. While the leaders of all three churches were called upon by medieval Bosnian rulers to witness acts of state, the state did not regularly favour one church over the others. Religious tolerance, or perhaps one might term it a relative detachment from religious affairs, was characteristic of Bosnia for most of the medieval period. As a result, none of the three churches could rely on the steady and exclusive patronage of either the ruling dynasty or the nobility, and all three remained organizationally weak, their clergy largely uneducated (these factors later contributed to the decision by a large proportion of the Bosnian people to abandon

Medieval Bosnian gravestones (stećci) at Radimlja, near Stolac in Herzegovina. Photo: András Riedlmayer

Christianity for Islam). Poorly endowed, the churches in medieval Bosnia were in no position to build great cathedrals or impressive monastic establishments.

The kings of Bosnia and the powerful local nobles, on the other hand, built as many as 300 castles to guard their mountainous domains and grew prosperous from the revenue of trading caravans and from the precious metals extracted from Bosnia's mines. Aside from a few precious manuscripts and art objects, however, little remains of the rich material culture of the medieval period. What has survived in relative abundance are examples of a distinctively Bosnian art form, the *stećci* (singular: *stećak*): massive medieval gravestones, some in the shape of solid

Traditional Bosnian Muslim gravestones at Jakir, near Glamoč in western Bosnia. The very large headstone in the centre marks the grave of Omer Aga Bašić, an eighteenth-century local notable. Photo: András Riedlmayer

stone sarcophagi, others vertically oriented. Many of the *stećci* are beautifully decorated with figural carvings and incised geometric patterns; often they are grouped in spectacular locations over-looking the countryside.[3]

Islam arrived in Bosnia more than 500 years ago, when the armies of the Ottoman sultans swept across the Balkans and onwards into Hungary. Their advance appeared unstoppable, and many at the time felt it was directed by the hand of God. Through-out Europe, this was an age of religious ferment, and preachers everywhere, among them Martin Luther, saw in the coming of the Ottomans a sign of divine judgment. In Bosnia, many people from all social and religious backgrounds – more than half the popula-tion by the 1700s – adopted the triumphant faith of the Islamic conquerors. A distinctive Bosnian-Muslim culture took form, with its own architecture, literature, social customs, and folklore.[4]

Although most of the new Muslim converts were and remained poor farmers, many Bosnians rose to join the ranks of the Ottoman ruling elite as soldiers, statesmen, Islamic jurists, and scholars. Among the most famous of these Bosnian converts was Mehmed

Pasha Sokolović (1505–79), who served as grand vizier (chief minister) to three Ottoman sultans, among them the greatest ruler of the age, Sultan Süleyman the Magnificent.

Mehmed Pasha administered an empire that stretched across three continents, from Yemen to Algiers, from Baghdad to the gates of Vienna, and he married Princess Esmahan, Sultan Süleyman's granddaughter. In addition to his accomplishments as a soldier and statesman, Mehmed Pasha was also a generous patron of architecture. Among his many endowments were two great mosques in Istanbul, the imperial capital, designed by the court architect Sinan, and the famous bridge over the Drina that he commissioned as a benefaction for his home town of Višegrad.

In turn, the Ottoman sultans and their local governors also embellished Bosnia's towns with splendid mosques and established endowments to build and support libraries, schools, charity soup-kitchens, and other pious foundations around which markets, neighbourhoods, and entire new towns grew.[5]

Among these new Ottoman towns in Bosnia were Sarajevo, Banja Luka, and Mostar. Located at strategic river crossings and the intersections of trade routes, they became cultural and commercial centres, thanks to newly built bridges, bazaars, inns for merchants and travellers, and other social service institutions.

The history here is reflected in the buildings: Muslim, Christian, and Jewish townspeople lived, worked, and worshipped side by side. Standing in the centre of Sarajevo's old bazaar is the Gazi Husrev Beg Mosque, founded in 1531 by Bosnia's first native Muslim governor. Within sight of the great mosque stands the old Orthodox church, built in the same period (before 1539) to attract tradesmen of that faith to the city's newly laid-out bazaars.[6] Another Ottoman governor, Siyavuş Pasha, endowed an Islamic pious foundation (*waqf*) in 1580–81 to erect a large apartment building (*han*) for the poorer members of Sarajevo's Jewish community and granted permission for the construction of the city's first synagogue next to the *han*.[7] A bit to the west is Sarajevo's Roman Catholic cathedral, built in 1889 on the site of an older church in a part of the old city known in Ottoman times as Latinluk, the Latin (i.e., Roman Catholic) quarter.[8] The mosque, the synagogue, and the Orthodox and Catholic churches are all located close to each other in the city centre, within an area of less than half a square kilometre.

South of Sarajevo lies the city of Mostar, which owes its name ("Bridge-keeper") and prosperity to the graceful Ottoman bridge that joins the banks of the Neretva River. When the Ottomans conquered the region in the late 1400s, Mostar was a modest set-tlement of twenty households grouped around a medieval tower that guarded a shaky bridge of wooden planks suspended on chains. After the administrative centre of Herzegovina was moved to Mostar in 1522, the Ottoman provincial governors, most of them Bosnian Muslims, and other prominent local Muslim families made pious endowments that built more than a dozen mosques, as well as schools, markets, and inns, around which the city's new neigh-bourhoods developed. The addition of the soaring stone arch of the Ottoman bridge in 1566 gave the city its defining landmark. By the end of the sixteenth century, Mostar had grown into the third largest town in Bosnia, a thriving centre of commerce and culture. At the height of its prosperity in the late 1600s, the city had thirty mosques and seven madrasas (theological schools); the craftsmen in its bazaars were organized into thirty different guilds according to their specialties. As in Sarajevo, the look in Mostar also bespeaks a long history of intermingled public life, with the Islamic minaret, the Catholic campanile, and the steeple of the Orthodox cathedral reaching up from one skyline.[9]

The placement of architecture is an intentional, thoughtful, political act. People who cannot abide the sight of each other will not build their houses and the most important monuments of their religious and communal life in the shadows of those of the others. Those who commissioned these buildings and works of art, as well as those who made them, represented a variety of religious tradi-tions and artistic influences. The resulting monuments, manu-scripts, and art objects demonstrate the degree to which cultures transformed and acted upon each other in Bosnia.

Thus a number of mosques in Bosnia, among them one built in the sixteenth century by the powerful Predojević family in the village of Plana, near Mostar, have the look of medieval churches, with minarets that resemble rustic Romanesque church steeples. We see another example of cross-cultural influence in a splendid sixteenth-century cope, a Roman Catholic liturgical vestment in the treasury of a Bosnian-Franciscan monastery. The cope is made of a silk brocade that is immediately recognizable as a luxury textile in the high-Ottoman court style. A Church Slavonic Gospel manuscript,

Mostar skyline before the war, including a clock tower
endowed by a seventeenth-century Muslim lady benefactor,
a minaret (eighteenth century), and the Serbian Orthodox
Cathedral (nineteenth century) on the ridge overlooking
the old city. Photo: Documentation Center, Aga Khan
Program, Fine Arts Library, Harvard University.

Mosque of Hasan Pasha Predojević (sixteenth century) at Plana, near Bileća in Herzegovina. Photo: Documentation Center, Aga Khan Program, Fine Arts Library, Harvard University.

produced in the scriptorium of a Serbian Orthodox monastery at the beginning of the seventeenth century, has the Cyrillic text of the Christian scriptures framed by bands of illumination that are unmistakably Ottoman and Islamic in inspiration. The illuminator of this manuscript, presumably a Christian monk, was familiar with and must have had access to Islamic books as models.

Finally, we have the example of two little churches in the village of Ljubinje in Herzegovina, one of them Roman Catholic the other Serbian Orthodox, both looking almost exactly alike. One could say that their uncanny resemblance stems from the fact that the area probably had only one master stonemason, who probably knew only one way to build a church. But more important is the fact that these two churches stood within sight of each other in the same small community for a hundred years or more and that this apparently did not bother either the Orthodox or the Roman Catholic parishioners.

Roman Catholic liturgical vestment made from an
Ottoman silk brocade textile, in the treasury of the
Bosnian Franciscan monastery of Zaostrog. Pious
legend has it that the vestment was made from a
mantle donated to the monastery by the last Bosnian
king, Stjepan Tomašević (d. 1463), but the textile
dates from at least a century after his death.
Photo: Documentation Center, Aga Khan Program,
Fine Arts Library, Harvard University.

Slavonic gospel manuscript with Islamic-style illumination, produced in an Orthodox monastic scriptorium of the early seventeenth century. Photo: Documentation Center, Aga Khan Program, Fine Arts Library, Harvard University.

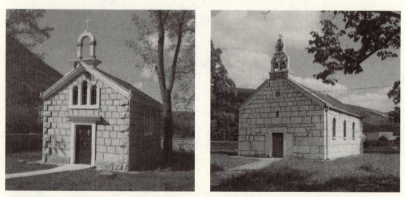

The Roman Catholic (left) and Serbian Orthodox (right) parish churches in the village of Ljubinje, Herzegovina. Photo: Documentation Center, Aga Khan Program, Fine Arts Library, Harvard University.

The remarkable thing about all of the above examples is that they involve items made for religious purposes, items in which the symbolic content matters more than it would in objects intended for mundane uses. Yet those who commissioned these objects, those who made them, and those who used them deliberately chose to reach across religious and cultural boundaries and evidently did not perceive such choices as problematic.

Of course, the fact that different religions and cultural traditions managed to coexist and engage in fruitful interactions in Bosnia should not be taken to imply an absence of hierarchies of status or of periodic frictions and rivalries between individuals and groups. Like other regions of Europe in the early modern era, Ottoman Bosnia had its share of corrupt officials, oppressive land-lords, and rebellious peasants, bandits, blood-feuds, and other sources of social discord. However, the fact of pluralism itself was considered a given. Over the *longue durée*, Bosnians of different religious traditions found ways to live, work, and build together.

The "ancient hatreds," then, are for the most part of recent vintage – not the inevitable outcome of a history marked by endless conflict, but conscious creations of the essentialist ideologies of our own troubled times. Before the Gazi Husrev Beg Mosque in Sarajevo was deliberately targeted for shelling by Bosnian-Serb artillery in 1992, it had stood unmolested for 461 years.

Bosnia's Ottoman centuries came to an abrupt end in the year 1878, when a conference of the European powers met in Berlin and placed the province under Austro-Hungarian administration. The new rulers brought a Viennese taste for the eclectic to their efforts to modernize Bosnia's cities. Erecting new schools, museums, and civic institutions, they sought to bring their newly acquired territory into the modern age. The buildings and cityscapes that are the most enduring legacy of four decades of Habsburg rule in Bosnia-Herzegovina display a characteristically Bosnian blend of cultural influences.[10]

Among the most handsome monuments of this eclectic era is Sarajevo's beloved Town Hall (Vijećnica in Bosnian), a Moorish Revival-style building erected on the bank of the Miljacka river in the old town centre in the 1890s. In addition to housing the municipal administration, Vijećnica was also where Bosnia's first national parliament held its meetings on the eve of World War I. After 1918, when Bosnia was absorbed into the newly created Yugoslav state,

The first Bosnian parliament, meeting in the Vijećnica (Town Hall) of Sarajevo in 1910. Historic postcard in the collection of the Documentation Center, Aga Khan Program, Fine Arts Library, Harvard University.

the building continued to serve as Sarajevo's city hall until the end of World War II. In 1945, the mayor's office was moved out, and for the next half century the historic Town Hall became the home of Bosnia's National Library.

An hour after sunset on the evening of 25 August 1992, the National Library was bombarded and set ablaze by a tightly targeted barrage of incendiary shells fired from Serb nationalist positions on the heights overlooking the building. The library is located in the centre of Sarajevo's old town, at the bottom of a deep valley. According to eyewitnesses, the phosphorus shells – which start burning as soon as they leave the muzzle and leave a distinctive, white-smoke trail – came from seven different Bosnian-Serb army firing positions on the mountains facing the old town on the east and south sides of the valley. Only the library was hit – surrounding buildings stand intact to this day. Once the library was fully ablaze, the shelling ceased. However, Bosnian-Serb army troops swept the surroundings with heavy machine-gun and anti-aircraft cannon fire aimed at street level, in order to keep away the Sarajevo firemen and volunteers trying to save books from the burning building. As the flames started to die down around daybreak, the shelling with incendiary munitions resumed and the

The same room in the Vijećnica (old Town Hall) being
used as the main reading room of the National and
University Library of Bosnia-Herzegovina in the 1980s.
Photo: Documentation Center, Aga Khan Program, Fine
Arts Library, Harvard University.

building continued to burn for some fifteen hours; it smoldered
for days thereafter. An estimated 1.5 million volumes were con-
sumed by the flames in this, the largest single incident of deliberate
book-burning in modern history.

A librarian who was there described the scene: "The fire lasted
for days. The sun was obscured by the smoke of books, and all over
the city sheets of burned paper, fragile pages of grey ashes, floated
down like a dirty black snow. Catching a page you could feel its
heat, and for a moment read a fragment of text in a strange kind
of black and grey negative, until, as the heat dissipated, the page
melted to dust in your hand."[11]

The inferno left the library a gutted shell, its interior filled with rubble and the carbonized remains of more than a million books. Before it was burned, the National Library held 155,000 rare books, unique special collections and archives, 478 manuscript codices, more than 600 runs of periodicals, the national collection of record of all the books, newspapers, and journals published in Bosnia since the mid-nineteenth century, as well as the main research collections of the University of Sarajevo. The books and archives destroyed by the fire included many items recorded nowhere else – irreplaceable documents of centuries of Bosnia's social, cultural, and political life. One of the Sarajevo citizens who risked their lives to pass books out of the burning library building told a television camera crew filming the smoldering ruins: "We managed to save just a few, very precious books. Everything else burned down. And a lot of our heritage, national history, lay down there in ashes."[12]

Three months earlier, the Serbian gunners' target had been Sarajevo's Oriental Institute, which housed the country's largest collection of Islamic manuscript texts and the former Ottoman provincial archives. It was shelled and burned with all of its contents on 17 May 1992. Once again, the Institute was targeted with incendiary munitions, while the surrounding buildings were left untouched. In addition to more than 5,200 manuscript codices in Arabic, Persian, Ottoman Turkish, and *alhamijado* (Bosnian Slavic written in Arabic script), the Oriental Institute's destroyed collection included the Ottoman-era provincial archives and a set of nineteenth-century cadastral registers recording the ownership of land in Bosnia at the end of Ottoman rule. There was widespread speculation at the time that the Oriental Institute had been targeted in order to destroy the land records.

We have evidence that these attacks were not isolated cases of "collateral damage," incidental to the general mayhem of warfare, but part of a deliberate and systematic effort to target cultural heritage. In September 1992, BBC reporter Kate Adie interviewed Serbian gunners on the hillsides overlooking Sarajevo and asked them why they had been shelling the Holiday Inn, the hotel where all of the foreign correspondents were known to stay. The Serbian officer commanding the guns apologized to Ms. Adie, explaining that his men had not meant to hit the hotel but had been aiming at the roof of the National Museum behind it.

View of the burned-out interior of the National and
University Library (Vijećnica) at the end of the war.
Photo: Matej Vipotnik (1996). Documentation Center,
Aga Khan Program, Fine Arts Library, Harvard
University.

The museum was badly damaged during the 3½-year siege.
Shells crashed through the roof and the skylights, and all of its 300
windows were shot out; shell holes penetrated the walls of several
galleries. Parts of the National Museum's collection that could not
be moved to safe storage remained inside the building, exposed
to damage from artillery attacks and to decay from exposure to the

elements. Dr Rizo Sijarić, the museum's director, was killed by a shell burst during Sarajevo's second winter under siege (10 December 1993) while trying to arrange for plastic sheeting from UN relief agencies to cover some of the holes in the building.[13]

The catalogue of losses does not stop there. One could mention the destroyed and looted monastery, church, and library of the Franciscan Theological Seminary in the Sarajevo suburb of Nedžarići; the shelling and partial destruction of the Regional Archives of Herzegovina in Mostar; the 50,000 volumes lost when the library of the Roman Catholic bishopric of Mostar was set ablaze by the Serb-led Yugoslav army; the burning and bulldozing of the sixteenth-century Serbian Orthodox monastery of Žitomislić, south of Mostar, by Croat extremists; and similar acts of destruction in hundreds of other Bosnian communities subjected to "ethnic cleansing" by Serb and Croat nationalist forces.

This systematic assault on culture can be explained as an attempt to eliminate the material evidence – books, documents, and works of art – that could remind future generations that people of different ethnic and religious traditions once shared a common heritage and common space in Bosnia. The goal of nationalist extremists is to create a religiously and ethnically "pure" future, based on the premise that coexistence is – and always was – impossible. The continued existence of a heritage that speaks of a history characterized by pluralism and tolerance contradicts this premise, which is why, amidst an ongoing armed conflict, such efforts were invested in destroying the relics of Bosnia's "impure" past.

In addition to transforming the landscape to better accord with the demands of ideology, there is also a practical aspect to the war on culture. While the destruction of a community's cultural and religious institutions and records is, first of all, part of a strategy of intimidation aimed at driving out members of the targeted group, it also serves a long-term goal. These records were proof that others once lived in that place, that they had historical roots there. By burning the documents, by razing houses of worship and bulldozing graveyards, the nationalists who overran and "cleansed" hundreds of towns and villages in Bosnia were trying to insure themselves against any possibility that the people they had expelled and dispossessed might one day return to reclaim their homes and property.

In a context in which ethnic identity is defined by the religious choices made by one's ancestors, it is religious buildings – mosques, churches, monasteries – that serve as the most potent markers of a community's presence. Thus it is not surprising that the destruction of houses of worship became one of the hallmarks of "ethnic cleansing" in Bosnia.[14]

At the conclusion of hostilities at the end of 1995, in the territory seized by Bosnian Serb forces during the war, more than 95 per cent of all non-Serb residents had been killed or expelled, and out of many hundreds of mosques only one had escaped destruction. According to UN officials, the sole surviving mosque in what is now the Republika Srpska (Bosnia's Serb entity) is the one "in the village of Baljvina near Mrkonjićgrad. Although the Bosnian Serbs had expelled Muslims from the village early in the war, when a Serb gang later came to destroy the mosque, the local Serb inhabitants persuaded them to leave the mosque alone, saying it was part of the 'local color.'"[15]

More typical is what happened in Trebinje in eastern Herzegovina on the night of 27 January 1993, where Serb nationalist militiamen celebrated the feast of St Sava, the medieval founder of the Serbian Orthodox Church, by burning down the town's oldest mosque and expelling thousands of Trebinje's Bosnian-Muslim residents:

It burned all night as drunken men in paramilitary uniforms fired machine guns in the air. By morning Trebinje's 500-year-old mosque was ashes and a dark-eyed young man, Kemal Bubić, 29, joined thousands of numbed people moving eastward. "At that moment everything I had was burned down," he said. "It's not that my family was burned down, but it's my foundation that burned. I was destroyed."[16]

Another small town in Bosnia is Foča on the Drina, east of Sarajevo. In April 1992, Foča was overrun by Serb nationalist militia, who killed or expelled the town's majority Bosnian-Muslim population, set up a rape camp for Muslim women in the local sports arena, and set about blowing up Foča's sixteen ancient mosques. Among them was the Aladža Mosque, built in 1557, once one of the loveliest examples of Islamic religious architecture in the Balkans. Hardly a trace remains of it today; the blasted walls were levelled by bulldozer and dumped into the nearby river. Only the faint outlines of the mosque's foundation and a small circle of white marble splinters, the shattered remnants of the ablution fountain, poke through the weeds. "Cleansed" of its mosques and Muslims, Foča has been renamed Srbinje ("Serb Town") to celebrate its new ethnically pure identity.[17]

View of the sixteenth-century Aladza Mosque
in Foča, before the war. Photo: Documentation
Center, Aga Khan Program, Fine Arts Library,
Harvard University.

On 13 March 1993, six mosques were blown up in a single night
in the Serb-occupied town of Bijeljina in eastern Bosnia. The next
day, bulldozers were clearing away the rubble, and a long line of
trucks and buses stood ready to take away the town's terrified
Muslim residents. Two months later, in May 1993, Western reporters visiting the town found grass and trees planted on the levelled
sites; it was as if the mosques and the town's 30,000 Muslims had
never been there.[18]
   In the northern Bosnian city of Banja Luka, which had been
under the control of Serb nationalists since before the beginning
of the war, and where there was no fighting, all sixteen of the city's
mosques were blown up between April and September 1993. In

Razed site of the sixteenth-century Aladža Mosque in Foča after the war.
The circle of stones in the foreground is what remains of the ablution fountain;
the outlines of the mosque's foundation can still be seen in the grass growing
on the site. Photo: Lucas Kello (1996). Documentation Center, Aga Khan
Program, Fine Arts Library, Harvard University.

the centre of the city stood the Ferhadija Mosque, built in 1583
by Ferhad Pasha Sokolović, the Ottoman governor of Banja Luka
and a cousin of Sultan Süleyman's famous Bosnian grand vizier. In
the same way that Gazi Husrev Beg's benefactions had made Sarajevo flourish, it was the endowments founded by Ferhad Pasha and
his successors that helped turn Banja Luka from a sleepy village
into Bosnia's second city.

On the evening of 6 May 1993, as the city's Serbs were cele-
brating Djurdjevdan (the Orthodox feast of Saint George), Banja
Luka's remaining Muslim residents huddled in their houses, apprehensive that, as on other such occasions since the start of the war,
the celebrations would turn into a pogrom. At around 11 P.M.,
witnesses looking out their windows saw Bosnian-Serb army troops
blocking off the streets around two old mosques near the city
centre, the 410-year-old Ferhadija and the seventeenth-century
Arnaudija Mosques. A short while later, they heard military trucks
pulling up in front of the two mosques. After midnight, powerful
explosions were heard, and by morning both mosques were gone.
Of the lovely Arnaudija, nothing remained but a pile of rubble.
Next to the empty site of the Ferhadija, the stump of the minaret

The sixteenth-century. Ferhadija Mosque in Banja Luka, the day after it was reduced to rubble by Bosnian Serb sappers in May 1993. The stump of the toppled minaret in the foreground and the mausoleum of Ferhad Pasha Sokolović to the right were subsequently also blown up and the rubble removed by the Serb municipal authorities. The mufti's office in the background is the only Islamic community building in Banja Luka that still stands.
Photo: Aleksandar Aco Ravlić (1993). Documentation Center, Aga Khan Program, Fine Arts Library, Harvard University.

still stood, but not for long. Despite pleas from the Muslim community to spare the remains, Banja Luka's Bosnian-Serb mayor, Predrag Radić, declared the minaret a "hazard to passersby" and ordered the municipal roads department to remove it. Using more explosives and pneumatic drills, the remaining fragments of the ancient stonework were broken up into gravel, which was trucked off to a secret dump site outside the city limits to prevent it from ever being used in rebuilding the mosque.[19]

By the end of that year, all of the city mosques and eleven Roman Catholic churches in the Banja Luka area had been destroyed. As elsewhere, the destruction of the monuments was also a signal for the expulsion of the people who cherished them – an estimated 550,000 Bosnian Muslims, Roman Catholic Croats, Gypsies, and other non-Serbs who lived in this area before the war were killed or forced into exile.

In Višegrad, site of the famous old Ottoman bridge on the Drina, they came for the Muslims in August 1992. A British reporter passed through town at the end of the month and interviewed refugees huddled in sheds outside the city limits. "We are ready to run if they come for us again," one Muslim refugee said, as he described how the great bridge had been used night after night as a killing ground by drunken Serb militiamen. "They bulldozed the two mosques in the main street in Višegrad so we wouldn't come back," he said.[20]

In 1993, emboldened by the Western powers' endorsement of ethnic partition, Croat nationalists launched an all-out war to carve an ethnically pure "homeland" out of Herzegovina and parts of central Bosnia. There had been ominous signs the year before, in the first months of the war, following the devastating April–June 1992 siege of Mostar by the Serb-led Yugoslav National Army (JNA), in which most of the city's historic monuments – including seventeen of its nineteen mosques and all three of Mostar's Catholic churches – had been damaged or destroyed by JNA shelling.[21]

On a high ridge overlooking the old town of Mostar is the great Serbian Orthodox cathedral (*Saborna crkva*). The cathedral was built in 1863–73, during the last years of Ottoman rule; Sultan Abdul Aziz himself selected the site for the church and donated 100,000 silver coins for its construction, while the Russian czar sent money for the interior decoration. For more than a century the tall, Serbian Baroque steeple of the Orthodox cathedral had been part of Mostar's skyline – surviving even the horrors of World War II, when Croat fascists had first turned on their Serb neighbours.

At the beginning of June 1992, the Serb forces besieging Mostar were driven out of artillery range. Withing days, the city's Serbian Orthodox cathedral was destroyed in a single, enormous explosion in the middle of the night of 15 June 1992. Those responsible clearly wanted no stone left on stone: more than a hundred nearby houses were also damaged in the blast. While no group openly claimed responsibility for the attack, it was widely understood to have been the work of Croat extremists taking vengeance for the destruction of the city's Catholic churches.

During the same month, Croat militias rounded up and expelled or imprisoned many Bosnian-Serb civilians living in the areas under their control. By summer's end, Croat nationalist forces had begun the process of expelling all non-Croats from their self-styled

The blasted ruins of the Serbian Orthodox Cathedral in Mostar, blown up by Croat nationalist extremists in June 1992.
Photo: András Riedlmayer

Croatian Republic of Herceg-Bosna. First to be "cleansed" was the small town of Prozor, where in October 1992 Croat nationalists shelled the mosque and the surrounding neighbourhood, robbed and terrorized the town's 5,000 Muslim inhabitants, and sent them fleeing into the mountains as night fell.[22]

By the spring and summer of 1993, "ethnic cleansing" was in full swing throughout the areas designated for Croat nationalist control under the proposed Vance-Owen partition plan for Bosnia, and the old town of Mostar was once again being shelled, this time by Croat forces.

The following is an excerpt from a report issued by the Office of the United Nations High Commissioner for Refugees (UNHCR) on 23 August 1993:

In early July [1993], hundreds of draft-age men in Stolac, a predominantly Muslim town, [southeast of Mostar] were reportedly rounded up [by the Bosnian-Croat authorities] and detained, probably in [the concentration camps at] Dretelj and Gabela. The total number of detained civilians from Stolac is believed to be about 1,350 ... On 1 August, four mosques in Stolac were blown up. That night, witnesses said, military trucks carrying soldiers firing their weapons in the air went through the town terrorizing and rounding up all Muslim women, children and elderly. The cries and screams of women and children could be heard throughout the town as the soldiers looted and destroyed Muslim homes. The soldiers, who wore handkerchiefs, stockings or paint to hide their faces, took the civilians to Blagaj, an area of heavy fighting northwest of Stolac.[23]

The four mosques mentioned in the report are (or were) charming examples of regional architecture, three of them dating from the 1730s and one from the 1600s, built by local craftsmen to the taste of the patrons, well-to-do Muslim-Slav families from nearby Mostar. These were not what art historians call great works of art. But for the Muslim residents of Stolac, they embodied their hometown's Islamic past. The extremists who destroyed these monuments are well aware of the vital connection between a community of people and its cultural heritage.

More than a year after the end of the war, in January 1997, United Nations police monitors escorted two busloads of Bosnian-Muslim refugees seeking to return to their homes in Stolac. They were turned back on the outskirts of town by a stone-throwing mob organized by the Croat nationalist mayor of Stolac. As the refugees and their UN escorts retreated under a hail of eggs and stones, the mob chanted: "No more Muslims, no more mosques, no more bowing prayers."[24]

A Croat nationalist militiaman, interviewed in Mostar in September 1993, explained to a British reporter why he was trying to destroy the 427-year-old Ottoman bridge: "It is not enough to clean Mostar of the Muslims," he said, "the relics must also be removed."[25]

A Muslim resident of Mostar, interviewed during that summer, was asked why he had stayed on, despite the shelling, the hunger, and the other dangers of life under siege: "I'm fighting for the bridge," he said, as if that explained it all. Less than two months later, on 9 November 1993, after hours of concentrated bombardment by a Croatian army tank firing its cannon at point-blank range, the bridge at Mostar finally collapsed into the river. By an eerie coincidence, the bridge was felled on the fifty-fifth anniversary of Kristallnacht, the night when Jewish synagogues and institutions were smashed and burned throughout Hitler's Great German Reich – that, too, was an integral part of what today is euphemistically called "ethnic cleansing."

Like German Jews in the 1930s, most Bosnian Muslims today are in fact highly secularized. But a people's identity is inextricably linked with the visible symbols of their culture. Once those anchors are gone, the past, like the future, can be recreated by the victors.

In the Drina river town of Zvornik there were once a dozen mosques; in the 1991 census, 60 per cent of its residents called themselves Muslim Slavs. By the end of 1992, the town was 100 per cent Serb, and Branko Grujić, the new Serb-appointed mayor, was telling foreign visitors: "There never were any mosques in Zvornik."[26]

The historian Eric Hobsbawm has written: "History is the raw material for nationalist or ethnic or fundamentalist ideologies, as poppies are the raw material for heroin addiction ... If there is no suitable past, it can always be invented. The past legitimizes. The past gives a more glorious background to a present that doesn't have that much to show for itself."[27] To this, one should also add: before inventing a new past, the old one must first be erased.

In Bosnia, this erasure took a quite literal form. Consider, as an example, the city of Banja Luka, where in early 1994, only months after the last of the city's sixteen mosques and eleven Roman Catholic churches had been blown up, the city fathers presided over the opening of an exhibition marking the sixty-fifth anniversary of Banja Luka's designation as the regional capital. The exhibition was organized by the regional museum, which had been renamed "The Museum of the Republika Srpska," and featured historical photographs of Banja Luka from the 1920s and 30s and documents of the period. Of the dozens of old photographs displayed in the exhibition, not one showed any trace of a mosque or minaret. Like the "vanishing commissars" airbrushed out of photographs in Stalin's Russia, these major landmarks of Banja Luka's urban landscape had vanished from the photos on display. In the new, "ethnically pure" construction of the past, they had never existed. In fact, they could not have existed – since according to the newly promulgated version of local history, Banja Luka was and always had been a purely Serb city.[28]

In the world-view of those who organized this exhibition, pluralism is anathema, and coexistence is declared an impossibility. The past, with its evidence of cultural intermingling and synthesis, has to be refashioned to conform to the nationalist paradigm of an apartheid future. That which contradicts the paradigm – people, buildings, works of art, or the written word – has to be removed along with the memory of its existence.

Early twentieth-century postcard showing the main market street in Banja Luka, with the Ferhadija Mosque towering in the background. Postcard in the collection of the Documentation Center, Aga Khan Program, Fine Arts Library, Harvard University.

In an effort to fight this assault on memory and to resurrect lost collections of original manuscripts and documents from the ashes, a group of scholars from Bosnia, Canada, and the United States, myself included, have established the Bosnian Manuscript Ingathering Project. We were prompted by the realization that, although the Oriental Institute and many other manuscript collections in Bosnia are now ashes, a number of the destroyed originals probably still exist in the form of microfilms, photocopies, or other facsimiles taken by foreign scholars as part of research projects or sent abroad as part of exchanges between Bosnian libraries and foreign institutions. By collecting copies of these copies of lost originals, we hope to help our Bosnian colleagues to resurrect at least part of their burned collections in facsimile.

We collect data by a variety of means, including an interactive website, announcements in scholarly conferences and journals, and directly approaching individuals. Our first successful recovery, a haul of approximately 700 pages of copies of manuscipts, came from a retired professor at the University of Toronto, who had brought the copies back from a research trip to Sarajevo nearly twenty years ago. We scanned these and other recovered photo-copies onto a CD-ROM, which we delivered to the Oriental Institute in Sarajevo in November 1998. While that represents a mere frac-tion of what was lost, we are determined to continue. Each item we uncover is one bit of light rescued from the darkness of oblivion and one more way to frustrate the aims of those who tried to destroy Bosnia, its people, and their cultural heritage.[29]

Unfortunately, cultural heritage and cultural institutions tend to rank low on the international community's list of priorities for postwar reconstruction. For the United Nations and for most non-governmental organizations (NGOs) and intergovernmental agen-cies operating in the usual crisis-response mode, the aftermath of genocide in the Balkans is just another "humanitarian crisis," which, paradoxically, reduces those most immediately affected from full human beings to "victims." Stripped of all local specificity (a personal or collective past, cultural characteristics – let alone cultural values or needs), they become indistinguishable from all the other nameless victims of floods, wars, and other calamities around the world. What the international agencies, quite rightly, focus on first is people's elemental requirements: shelter, food, and medical care. Usually ignored in the process are questions such as who these people (specifically) are as individuals or as a commu-nity, what in fact happened to them, or what they (specifically) might want or need.

What is particularly striking in all of this is the reversal of per-spectives – the "ethnic cleansers" show a keen understanding of cultural and religious factors: these are the main criteria by which they select their targets (both human and material) for attacks and destruction. The people who have been "cleansed" because of their cultural and religious identity also understand this all too well, which is why, amidst the devastation, they express such concern for the rebuilding of houses of worship and cultural and educational facilities. Paradoxically, it is those engaged in the "humanitarian response" who prefer to set aside such considerations as "inappropriate to the first phase of reconstruction."

Long after the end of the war, international officials have continued to mostly pay lip service to the need for the reconstruction and protection of Bosnia's war-ravaged cultural and religious heritage. One of the features of the 1995 Dayton Peace Agreement is a clause (Annex 8) establishing a Commission to Preserve National Monuments, which, along with the Commission on Human Rights (consisting of the Office of the Ombudsman and the Human Rights Chamber), is among the few governmental bodies granted jurisdiction in both the Federation and the Republika Srpska, the two entities that together comprise postwar Bosnia-Herzegovina. However, more than five years after Dayton, the Commission to Preserve National Monuments remains mired in disputes about procedural issues and has yet to undertake any meaningful measures for the protection of Bosnia's cultural heritage.

Among the commission's meager accomplishments so far has been a tentative agreement on a list of buildings and sites to be designated "national monuments" (although there is no consensus on what obligations such a designation might impose on the local authorities). One of these "national monuments" is the Ferhadija Mosque in Banja Luka, a historic building that no longer exists and whose reconstruction has been persistently blocked by the Serb nationalists who remain in control of the Republika Srpska. The municipal authorities in Banja Luka have not only removed the rubble of the Ferhadija and the other demolished mosques, but they have also deleted the mosques from the city's master plan. The sites where the mosques once stood have been reserved for public parks and other uses according to the bureau of urban planning, which has declared reconstruction of the mosques to be out of the question.

In frustration, the Islamic Community of Bosnia, acting on behalf of the few thousand Muslims who still remain in Banja Luka and the tens of thousands of exiled Banja Lukan Muslims who want to return, turned to the Human Rights Chamber for redress. In July 1999, the Human Rights Chamber ruled that the Government of the Republika Srpska had denied the right of the Islamic community to freedom of religion by refusing to allow the reconstruction of mosques destroyed in the war. The chamber specifically established that the Islamic community had property rights to fifteen sites of destroyed mosques and the right to enclose the properties. According to the decision, the Government of the Republika Srpska may not allow other construction on these sites and must issue any construction permits necessary to rebuild mosques on seven of the sites.[30]

Following another year and a half of obstruction by the Bosnian-Serb authorities, threats of further legal action, and a great deal of earnest exhortation and cajoling on the part of international officials, on 19 March 2001 the urban planning department of the Banja Luka municipality finally issued the necessary construction permit authorizing the rebuilding of the Ferhadija Mosque.

Although the funds and the plans for the reconstruction were not yet ready, a cornerstone laying ceremony was set for 7 May 2001, the eighth anniversary of the mosque's destruction. The Republika Srpska Ministry of the Interior and Banja Luka's police chief promised to provide security for the event, the police chief assuring reporters that he expected no problems. However, the ceremony, which was supposed to mark the beginning of reconciliation in Banja Luka, turned into a pogrom instead. As one wire service report described the event,

Up to 2,000 nationalist Serbs rioted Monday to prevent a groundbreaking ceremony for reconstruction of a 16th-century mosque in the Serb-run city of Banja Luka. The mob broke through a police cordon protecting international diplomats and some 1,000 former Muslim residents of Banja Luka who arrived to attend the ceremony. The visitors were stoned and beaten, their prayer rugs stolen and burned, the Muslim flag ripped down from the Islamic community building, burned and replaced by a Bosnian Serb flag.

To further insult the Muslims, the mob chased a pig into the park where the mosque once stood, slaughtered it, and hung its head in front of the Islamic community building, where about 250 people, including the diplomatic corps and former Muslim residents, hid from the mob.[31]

The mob surrounded the building for six hours, breaking all the windows and screaming "Kill the Turks [i.e., the Muslims]." Among those trapped inside were the US, Canadian, British, and Swedish ambassadors to Bosnia, and Jacques-Paul Klein, head of the UN mission in Bosnia. To their credit, the diplomats refused offers of safe passage until all of the Bosnian Muslims in the building had been evacuated to safety. More than thirty people were injured in the Banja Luka pogrom; Murat Badić, a sixty-one-year-old Bosnian Muslim who had come to pray at the ceremony, was beaten unconscious and subsequently died of his injuries.

In the days after the incident, it became clear that the riot in Banja Luka, and a similar anti-Muslim mob action to stop the reconstruction of a mosque in Trebinje two days earlier, had been carefully prepared. The Banja Luka municipal public works department had reportedly dumped truckloads of rocks near the site of the mosque the night before the event as ammunition for the rioters. In an effort to placate international officials after the riot, the Republika Srpska minister of education sacked the principals of six secondary schools in Banja Luka who had released their pupils from classes to allow them to take part in the "protest."[32]

After the initial wave of expressions of outrage, some officials suggested that projects for the rebuilding of mosques and churches that were destroyed during the war ought to be postponed – perhaps indefinitely – because such buildings may be perceived as "provocative" (presumably by those who destroyed them in the first place).

However, after many years of pandering to such sensitivities, the time has come for the international community to face reality. There has to be a recognition among policy makers that cultural rights, religious freedom, and the right of refugees to return to their prewar homes are inextricably linked with each other. The protection and reconstruction of religious and cultural heritage damaged or destroyed in the 1992–95 "ethnic cleansing" of Bosnia is not a frill to be dispensed with or a "sensitive matter" better left untouched. It is central to the issue of restoring multiculturalism and a civil society in postwar Bosnia. Without guarantees of cultural security, including the rebuilding of destroyed houses of worship and cultural institutions, hundreds of thousands of Bosnians will never have the confidence to return to the communities from which they were expelled.

How can and should we respond to these attacks against culture? First, we have to reassert and act on our own belief that there are principles of decency and international legality that are worth defending. This means doing everything in our power to make sure that those who have violated international laws protecting cultural property are indeed punished and not rewarded for their deeds. In addition to supporting criminal prosecutions of those responsible, the international community should make a concerted effort to ensure some measure of restitution. In Bosnia, Kosovo, and other post-conflict situations, it is vital that effective steps be taken to make certain that reconstruction projects will not be held hostage by bureaucratic obstruction or mob violence.

The restoration of damaged or destroyed cultural heritage is not a matter that can be safely ignored, left to the victims to sort out, or hopefully put up for adoption by interested NGOs. As the post-war experience in the Balkans has amply demonstrated, most of the NGOs active in the aftermath of war and "ethnic cleansing" are neither interested in nor well qualified for undertaking such projects. The NGOs' lack of experience in dealing with heritage, combined in some cases with aggressive sectarian agendas, can do more harm than good, compounding and completing the destruction wrought by the "ethnic cleansers" and causing further divisions in the community.[33]

Unfortunately, most international aid agencies and other non-sectarian organizations concerned with reconstruction have tended to shy away from projects that involve religious monuments, in the mistaken belief that the rebuilding of houses of worship is a sensitive issue best avoided for the sake of postwar reconciliation. In this, they ignore the key role that such projects can play in promoting the return of minority refugees, one of the principal goals of the international community in post-Dayton Bosnia. By avoiding such projects, the secular organizations leave the field open to sectarian sponsors, such as Islamic fundamentalist aid agencies from the Arab world that have their own agendas and little interest in furthering interreligious and intercommunal harmony in Bosnia.

The fragmented political arrangements in post-Dayton Bosnia do not favour institutions that used to be supported at the national level, including those involved in the protection of cultural heritage before 1992. At the local level, where most authority now resides, there is a serious shortage of expertise and resources for dealing with the cultural catastrophe wrought by the war. In addition to funding for specific projects, there is an urgent need for training in proper methods of assessment and in current techniques and approaches used in the conservation of historic buildings and sites.

Perhaps even more crucial is the drafting and enforcement of standards and regulations in order to stop the ongoing destruction of important buildings and heritage sites that survived the war only to fall victim to uncontrolled postwar development.

One of the most important ways in which governmental and international agencies can support the work of cultural reconstruction is through sponsoring programs for training and technical and material assistance that can help bolster the capability of the local institutions in Bosnia. For some years to come, the need for an international presence and for international assistance will continue. But ultimately it will be these institutions and the new generation of Bosnian heritage experts who will be responsible for ensuring that their country's rich multicultural past remains a legacy and a lesson for future generations of Bosnians.

NOTES

1 On the vote for independence, see Kofman 2001. For a day-by-day account and analysis of the siege of Sarajevo through 29 February 1994, see *Final Report of the United Nations Commission of Experts Established Pursuant to Security Council Resolution 780 (1992), Annex VI, Part 1: Study of the Battle and Siege of Sarajevo*, United Nations Security Council Doc. S/1994/674/Add.2 (Vol. II), 27 May 1994; also available online at http://www.ess.uwe.ac.uk/comexpert/ANX/VI-01.htm et seq. For the impact on the Bosnian capital's cultural heritage and institutions as of 1994, see Čengić and Duraković 1994 and the catalogue of a 1993–94 exhibition organized by the Society of Architects of Sarajevo to document the destruction of their city, *Urbicide–Sarajevo = Sarajevo, une ville blessée*, Bordeaux: Arc en rêve, Centre d'architecture; Paris: Centre Georges Pompidou, [1994].

2 Council of Europe, Committee on Culture and Education, *Information Reports on the Destruction by War of the Cultural Heritage in Croatia and Bosnia-Herzegovina*, Strasbourg: Council of Europe, Parliamentary Assembly, 1993–97, nos 1–10 = Assembly Documents nos 6756, 6869, 6904, 6989 + addendum, 6999, 7070, 7133, 7308, 7341, 7674, 7740; Riedlmayer 1995; Blažina 1996; and Lefèvre 1996.

3 On medieval Bosnian art and its deployment in support of modern discourses on Bosnian identity, see Wenzel 1965, 1993. The complex history of Bosnia's cultural heritage is presented in a

fascinating recent study in Lovrenović 1998; Lovrenović's argument is summed up by Milenko Jergović in a review article in *Bosnia Report* (London) n.s. 4 (June/July 1998), available online at http://www.bosnia.org.uk/bosrep/junjul98/survival.htm: "Bosnia's cultural and civilizational identity forms a unity in its meanings, but its image is expressly that of a mosaic. No element of the mosaic was formed on its own or can today represent the whole." An English translation of Lovrenović's book is about to be released by New York University Press under the title *Bosnia: A Cultural History.*

4 The best survey in English of Bosnian society and culture in the Ottoman era is Malcolm 1996, chapters 4–10. The richness and complexity of the artistic heritage produced in this period is well illustrated in Filipović 1987.

5 On the the the great Islamic foundations that built Sarajevo, see Kostović 1995 and Pašić 1994.

6 Boris Nilević, "O postanku stare pravoslavne crkve u Sarajevu" ["On the origin of the Old Orthodox Church in Sarajevo"], *Prilozi historiji Sarajeva: radovi sa Znanstvenog simpozija "Pola milenija Sarajeva," održanog 19. do 21. marta 1993. godine,* ed. Dževad Juzbašić, Sarajevo: Institut za istoriju, Orijentalni institut, 1997, 61–5. On Orthodox Christian art of the Ottoman period in Bosnia, see also Rakić 2000.

7 For the early history of Sarajevo's Spanish-Jewish community and of the city's first synagogue, see Moritz Levy, *Die Sephardim in Bosnien: Ein Beitrag zur Geschichte der Juden auf der Balkanhalbinsel,* Sarajevo, 1911; reprt Graz: Wieser Verlag, 1996, 11–22, 134. Siyavuş Pasha's grant of permission for the building of a synagogue next to the *han* was, technically, a violation of Islamic law – which allows the repair and reconstruction of pre-existing non-Muslim houses of worship but not the erection of new ones where none had stood before. What makes this bending of the law all the more remarkable is that the property was entangled with not one but two Islamic pious foundations: the *waqf* of Gazi Husrev Beg, which owned the land underneath the buildings, and that of Siyavuş Pasha. For the history of Siyavuş Pasha's foundation and of the great *han* he built for the Jews of Sarajevo (which they called El Cortijo, the "Great Courtyard," in Judaeo-Spanish), see Alija Bejtić, "Sijavuš-pašina daira," *Prilozi za proučavanje istorije Sarajeva,* 2 (1966): 61–102.

8 For the history of the Catholic community in sixteenth-century Sarajevo, see Fra Ljubo Lučić, "Franjevačka prisutnost u Sarajevu"

["The Franciscan presence in Sarajevo"], *Prilozi historiji Sarajeva: radovi sa Znanstvenog simpozija "Pola milenija Sarajeva," održanog 19. do 21. marta 1993. godine*, ed. Dževad Juzbašić, Sarajevo: Institut za istoriju, Orijentalni institut, 1997, 239–60. On Catholic art and culture in Bosnia under Ottoman rule, see Sorić, Avdagić, et al. 1988.

9   Pašić 1995.

10 Krzović 1987 and Spasojević 1999.

11 Eyewitness account by Kemal Bakaršić, chief librarian of Bosnia's National Museum, in "The Libraries of Sarajevo and the Book That Saved Our Lives," *The New Combat: A Journal of Reason and Resistance* 3 (Autumn 1994): 13–15. On the burning of the National Library, the Oriental Institute, and other libraries and archives and the role these attacks played in the process of "ethnic cleansing," see also Riedlmayer 2001.

12 Account of the attack on the library and the ensuing fire based on: reports filed from the scene by Kurt Schork, "Sarajevo's Much-loved Old Town Hall Ablaze," Reuters Library Report, 26 August 1992, and by John Pomfret, "Battles for Sarajevo Intensify as Bosnian Peace Conference Opens," Associated Press, 26 August 1992; personal interviews with library workers, fire fighters, and other eyewitnesses; unedited footage from TV BiH; quote from volunteer rescue worker aired on ABC News, 13 January 1993.

13 Kate Adie's interview cited in "Bosnia's Written History in Flames? The Major Libraries and Archives Reported Destroyed," *The Art Newspaper* (London), 3, no. 21 (October 1992): 1; for damage to the National Museum, see Rizo Sijarić, "Update on the Zemaljski Muzej, Sarajevo," *Museum Management and Curatorship* 12 (1993): 195–9; Marian Wenzel, "Obituary: Dr. Rizo Sijarić, Director of the Zemaljski Muzej, Sarajevo. Killed in Sarajevo, 10 December 1993," *Museum Management and Curatorship* 13 (1994): 79–80.

14 On the connections between ethnicity, religion, and genocide, see Sells 1998.

15 Jolyon Naegele, "Banja Luka's Mufti Tells Of 'Four Years Of Horror,'" *RFE/RL Weekday Magazine*, 6 September 1996, available online at http://www.rferl.org/nca/features/1996/09/ F.RU.960906165722638.html.

16 Duško Doder, "On Serb Holy Day, Hellfire for Foes," *The Boston Globe*, 10 February 1993.

17 On the destruction of Foča's Bosnian-Muslim community and of the monuments that testified to more than 600 years of Muslim culture

in Foča, see Faruk Mutić, *Foča: 1470–1996*, Sarajevo: Šahinpasic, 1997; Šemso Tucaković, *Aladža dzamija: ubijeni monument* [*The Aladža Mosque: murdered monument*], Sarajevo: Institut za istraživanje zločina protiv čovječnosti i medjunarodnog prava, 1998; "History, Culture and Destruction of Foča" (website), http://www.haverford.edu/relg/sells/reports.html#Foca.

18 US Department of State. *Supplemental United States Submission of Information to The United Nations Security Council In Accordance with Paragraph 5 of Resolution 771 (1992) and Paragraph 1 of Resolution 780 (1992): [Eighth Report] June 16, 1993*, online at http://www.haverford.edu/relg/sells/reports/8thC.html. The expulsion of Bosnian Muslim civilians from Bijeljina during the war and the continued abuses returnees have met with since Dayton are described in the May 2000 Human Rights Watch report, *Unfinished Business: The Return of Refugees and Displaced Persons to Bijeljina*, http://www.hrw.org/reports/2000/bosnia/.

19 Based on eyewitness accounts of the destruction, including that of Bedrudin Gušić, who had the unenviable task of serving as the elected chairman of the Committee of the Islamic Community in Banja Luka from May 1992 until November 1994. Mr Gušić's account was published in Bosnian in the Sarajevo daily *Oslobodjenje*, 16–23 March 1995; an English translation is posted online at http://www.haverford.edu/relg/sells/banjaluka/gusic1.html and http://www.haverford.edu/relg/sells/banjaluka/gusic2.html. The removal of the remains of the mosques was witnessed by Frank Westerman, who reported on the Bosnian war for the Amsterdam daily *NRC Handelsblad*; his account of the destruction and his interview with Banja Luka's Serb nationalist mayor, Predrag Radić, appears in Westerman's book, *De Brug over de Tara*, Amsterdam: Uitgeverij Atlas, 1994, 7–13; my English translation is posted online at http://www.haverford.edu/relg/sells/banjaluka/banjaluka.html.

20 Maggie O'Kane, "Then they set the house on fire and everyone inside was screaming ... I was the only one who got out," *The Guardian* (London), 20 August 1992; Alec Russell, "Serbs pursue survivors of 'ethnic cleansing,'" *The Daily Telegraph* (London), 20 August 1992.

21 The destruction of Mostar and its architectural monuments in the April–June 1992 JNA siege was documented by the Mostar Society of Architects (Društvo arhitekata Mostar) in an illustrated exhibition

catalogue, *Mostar '92: urbicid,* ed. Ivanka Ribarević-Nikolić and Željko Jurić, Mostar: Hrvatsko vijeće obrane općine Mostar, 1992.

22 Vulliamy 1994, 221–34; John Burns, "Croats Wield the Guns in 'Cleansed' Town," *New York Times,* 30 October 1993.

23 UNHCR Press Release REF/1034. On the destruction of cultural heritage in Stolac, see also Matej Vipotnik, "Searching for Bosnia's Lost Cultural Treasures," *Berserkistan* (online newspaper), 30 July 1996, posted at http://www.haverford.edu/relg/sells/stolac/stolac.html, and the documentation compiled by the presidency-in-exile of the Municipality of Stolac, *Crimes in Stolac Municipality, 1992–1994,* Mostar: Zid, 1996, 45–54; the text of the latter is also available online at http://www.haverford.edu/relg/sells/Stolac/StolacCrimes.html.

24 "Bosnian Croats Block Return of Muslims," Reuters, 2 February 1997; four years later, an investigation revealed that little had changed in Stolac: Nick Thorpe, "Croat Town Now a Criminal Haven: SAS Investigator Asks Why Gangsters And Ethnic Warriors Live Freely in Stolac, Bosnia," *The Guardian* (London), 2 May 2001, online at http://www.guardian.co.uk/international/story/0,3604,481599,00.html.

25 Robert Block, "Croatian Death Squad Talks Tough around the Pooltable," *The Independent* (London), 6 September 1993. Since the end of the war, the stones of the historic bridge have been recovered from the riverbed – it will be rebuilt; Jerrilynn Dodds, "Bridge over the Neretva," *Archaeology* 51 i (January–February 1998): 48–53.

26 Branko Grujić interviewed by Carol J. Williams, "Serbs Stay Their Ground on Muslim Lands: Conquering Warlords Bend History and Reality in an Attempt to Justify Their Spoils," *Los Angeles Times,* 28 March 1993; Laura Silber, "Serb Mayor Confident in Bosnian Town Where Mosques Are Rubble: Voters Go to Polls in Referendum on Peace Plan," *Financial Times* (London), 17 May 1993; Roger Cohen, "In a Town Cleansed of Muslims, Serb Church Will Crown the Deed," *New York Times,* 7 March 1994.

27 Eric Hobsbawm, "Debunking Ethnic Myths," *Open Society News* (Winter 1994): 1, 10–11, p. 10, condensed from a lecture delivered at Central European University, Budapest, at the opening of the 1993–94 academic year; a longer version was published under the title "Outside and Inside History," in Hobsbawm's collection of essays *On History,* London: Weidenfeld and Nicolson, 1997.

28 The 1994 exhibition is described by the Banja Luka historian Aleksander Aco Ravlić, himself a Bosnian Serb but outraged at what was being done to his city, in his book *Banjalučka Ferhadija: ljepotica koji su ubili* [*The Ferhadija of Banja Luka: A Murdered Beauty*], Rijeka: AARiS, 1996, 57, English summary 172. For the use of retouched photographs to "correct" an ideologically unacceptable past, see David King, *The Commissar Vanishes: The Falsification of Photographs and Art in Stalin's Russia*, New York: Metropolitan Books, 1997.

29 The Bosnian Manuscript Ingathering Project was established in 1994 by Amila Buturović (York University), András Riedlmayer (Harvard University), and İrvin Cemil Schick (Massachusetts Institute of Technology and Harvard University); for further information, see the project's home page at http://www.applicom.com/manu/ingather.htm.

30 The Human Rights Chamber's decision in the Banja Luka case, delivered on 11 June 1999, is available online at http://www.gwdg.de/~ujvr/hrch/0000-0999/0029admmer.htm. Sites of destroyed mosques in towns throughout the Bosnian-Serb entity have also been rezoned for other uses in order to prevent reconstruction. In Bijeljina, the sites of the town's levelled mosques have been used as flea markets, parking lots, and sites for shops and kiosks. In a letter dated 7 July 1999, the Serb-controlled municipality refused permission for the rebuilding of the Atik mosque in the old town centre. The reason cited was that the urban plan for that part of the town had changed and that a theatre is now planned for that site. François Perez, the Office of the High Representative's special envoy in Bijeljina, backed the municipal authorities, terming the request to rebuild the mosque "too extreme" and suggesting that "maybe in time, a mosque could be built in the periphery of town." (Human Rights Watch interview with François Perez, Bijeljina, 28 September 1999, cited online at http://www.hrw.org/reports/2000/bosnia/Bosn005-06.htm#P649_138143).

31 Aida Čerkez-Robinson, "Muslim leader urges restraint following attack," *Associated Press*, 8 May 2001.

32 For a report on the mob attack in Trebinje, in which one international official was beaten severely enough to require hospitalization, see "Serbs Block Bosnia Mosque Ceremony," BBC News, 6 May 2001, online at http://news.bbc.co.uk/hi/english/world/europe/newsid_1315000/1315262.stm. On the advance preparations for the anti-Muslim riot in Banja Luka, see "Erupcija ubiljačkog šovinizma

u BiH" [Eruption of murderous chauvinism in Bosnia], *Feral Tribute* (Split) no. 817, 14 May 2001, article available online at http://search.feral.hr/arhiva/tmp/2001/817/erup.html, English summary at http://www.ohr.int/ohr-dept/presso/bh-media-rep/round-ups/default.asp?content_id=498#6. The Croat extremists who run Stolac have also blocked efforts by Muslim returnees to rebuild even one of the town's four destroyed mosques, reportedly telling the mufti of Mostar, "If you start building a mosque, we will build a [Catholic] church on its cornerstone"; reported in *Ljiljan* (Sarajevo), 27 May 2001, English translation available online at http://www.tfeagle.army.mil/tfeno/Feature_Story.asp?Article=12638.

33 All but a handful of the 156 mosques that have been repaired, rebuilt, or newly constructed in Bosnia since the war have been sponsored by Islamic relief agencies from Saudi Arabia, which have used their financial clout in order to promote the intolerant Islamic fundamentalist missionary agenda of the Saudi-based Wahhabi sect. Stephen Schwartz, "Islamic Fundamentalism in the Balkans," *Partisan Review* (July 2000): 421–6; Saïd Zulficar, "Alerte aux iconoclastes!" *Al-Ahram Hebdo*, 28 February 2001, online at http://www.ahram.org.eg/Hebdo; Jolyon Naegele, "Saudi Wahhabi Aid Workers Bulldoze Balkan Monuments," *RFE/RL Weekday Magazine*, 4 August 2000, online at http://www.rferl.org/nca/features/2000/08/F.RU.000804130919.html.

Turning Points:
Key Decisions in Making Peace
in Bosnia-Herzegovina
and Croatia[1]

PETER W. GALBRAITH

The Dayton Peace Accords have been criticized as a prelude to partition. Certainly Dayton is not an ideal settlement. The central government has few powers, and the constitution is structured to make the exercise of those powers difficult. It is ,of course, absurd for a state to have two armies that are mutually hostile, as now exists in Bosnia under the Dayton Treaty.

Now that the balance of power has shifted within Bosnia against the Republika Srpska and within the region very much against Serbia, I believe it is time to consider revising the Dayton Accords, not to complete the partition as some have suggested, but rather to strengthen the common institutions. The Dayton Treaty itself should be judged both by the circumstances that prevailed and by the resources available to the diplomats at the time that it was negotiated. It is not, as John Fine suggests a settlement imposed by the Western powers reflecting Western views. Rather the Dayton Treaty was the most to which the parties could agree in order to achieve the minimum of ending the war. I think the verdict that President Izetbegovic rendered when he signed the Dayton Accords was probably the right one. He said "this is not a just peace, but it would be more unjust to continue the war."

In *To End a War*, Richard Holbrooke provides a superb account – both as history and as literature – of the negotiations leading up to Dayton. He begins more or less with Operation Storm, the

Croatian offensive that retook the Krajina in August 1995 and, by changing the situation on the ground, opened the door to peace.

Even before Operation Storm, the United States pursued a strategy that helped create the opportunities we exploited. I would like to describe the strategy and how it evolved. As US ambassador to Croatia I had a ringside seat from which to view all that happened and participated in a part of it. Inevitably a first hand account emphasizes what the speaker saw and did, and this history will be no exception.

As ambassador to Croatia during the war I dealt with a series of interlocutors. These included the government of Croatia, with which I was charged with conducting US relations; rebel Serbs, who occupied 27 per cent of the country and with whom I tried to negotiate a political settlement; the United Nations, which was headquartered in Zagreb; and, sometimes, Bosnia-Herzegovina, where we had no functioning embassy and a mostly absent ambassador.

THE WASHINGTON AGREEMENT

When I arrived at post in June 1993, there was a three-way fight in Bosnia among the Bosnian Serbs, the Bosnian Croats, and the Muslim-led Bosnian government. To be blunt, the situation looked completely hopeless. To visitors, I said this part of the Balkans risked becoming a Lebanon(Bosnia) next to a Cyprus (Croatia), a country of battling warlords next to a land permanently partitioned between hostile camps.

Not only did the situation look hopeless in 1993, but we also had no road map out. During the 1992 presidential campaign Bill Clinton had advocated "lift and strike," that is, lifting the arms embargo on the Bosnian government combined with air strikes at Serb positions that were attacking Sarajevo and other Bosnian towns. By 1993 neither course was possible. The Muslim-Croat war made it physically impossible to get arms to the Bosnians even if the US administration had been inclined to contemplate a unilateral lifting of the embargo, which it was not. With peacekeeping troops on the ground, neither Britain nor France was prepared to support a multilateral initiative to lift the arms embargo, and our NATO allies deployed in the former Yugoslavia, Canada included, opposed air strikes as likely to put their people at risk.

Warren Christopher, I think, early on concluded that Bosnia could not be solved and instead devoted his attention to other more promising areas of the world (in his view) such as the Middle East. Further, Christopher's first assistant secretary of state for European and Canadian Affairs, Steve Oxman, seemed disengaged from the issue, never once visiting Bosnia or Croatia. This was a source of considerable frustration for me – I used to call the European Bureau "the Home Alone" Bureau for its lack of meaningful guidance – but it also left me a certain latitude to pursue our policy goals without a lot people looking over my shoulder.

In my view, the situation was hopeless as long as the Muslim-Croat War continued. Ending that conflict became my top diplomatic priority. Ending that war not only would save lives, but could open the door to cooperation between two sides – the Bosnians and the Croats – that were victims of Belgrade/Pale aggression. And even if we could not persuade the United Nations Security Council to lift the arms embargo, a Bosnia-Croatia alliance would better enable both sides to arm themselves: the Bosnians would gain access to Croatia's existing network for acquiring black market arms, the Croats would benefit from the several Islamic countries that wanted to arm the Bosnians.

I had two immediate objectives: first, to persuade the Croatian government that the United States could be a reliable partner in pursuit of a settlement that ended the Serb occupation of Croatia and, second, to persuade Croatian president Franjo Tudjman that he had to choose between our support and his ambition for a greater Croatia carved out of Bosnia. Of course, the goal was not just to frame the choice but to make sure he made the right one.

In my policy messages back to Washington, I urged that we reward Croatia's cooperation by (1) linking sanctions relief for Serbia not just to a settlement in Bosnia, but also to one in Croatia, (2) looking the other way in the face of Croatian (and Bosnian) violations of the arms embargo, (3) engaging diplomatically to end the partition of Croatia by trying to find a peaceful settlement in the Krajina, and (4) supporting Croatia's desire for closer relations with the West. If Croatia persisted in its support for Bosnian-Croat forces fighting against the Bosnian government, I felt sanctions of some form against Croatia were inevitable. Eventually all elements of this approach were adopted by the Clinton Administration, although not in any single decision or strategy paper.

Many of my initial forays were in the realm of public diplomacy. I travelled to all the towns along the confrontation line, stressing

US support for Croatia's territorial integrity. In my first trip as ambassador, I went to Vukovar, the Serb-occupied Danubian city that had become the symbol of Croatia's independence struggle after holding out for several months against a vicious artillery assault by the Yugoslav Army that had left the city in ruins. These forays captured the public imagination but more importantly gave me a vehicle to make a second point: the United States would only support Croatia's territorial integrity to the extent that Croatia accorded the same respect to Bosnia's unity and borders.

Croatian president Franjo Tudjman tended to hear what he wanted to hear, so it was hard to get through to him even after many hours of pointed discussion. But the message did get through to others in his government, notably Foreign Minister Mate Granic. Equally important, the opposition began to make Tudjman's Bosnia policy a political issue. Drazen Budisa, the liberal leader, spoke eloquently at his party's 1993 fall convention on Bosnia, saying boldly that Croatia deserved the sanctions the international community threatened over Tudjman's policy.

Tudjman's ambitions for greater Croatia were only one obstacle to our goal of forging a Muslim/Croat/Croatia alliance. A more immediate problem was the atrocities perpetrated daily by the Bosnian-Croat military (the Croatian Defense Council or HVO). These included the shelling of East Mostar, the blocking of humanitarian aid convoys to Central Bosnia, and the holding of Muslim prisoners, many of whom had been HVO soldiers, in brutal conditions in prison camps. We had an obvious humanitarian interest in ending these atrocities, but also a strong political interest, as they made it extremely difficult to negotiate peace between the two sides. From my point of view, it was hard to persuade Washington that the negotiation track offered much hope in the face of daily reports of unspeakable acts.

Many of these reports came from our embassy. I focused our political reporting on Bosnian-Croat conduct in Herzegovina and western Bosnia, knowing that Croatia would ensure American diplomats access (because of its desire for US help) that no one else could get. Some of these diplomats took huge, but ultimately worthwhile, risks to document the mistreatment of Muslims in HVO camps.

I used our reporting in my meetings with Tudjman, Granic, and Defense Minister Gojko Susak. Granic, who had already played a key role in 1992 in persuading Tudjman to open Croatia's borders to Bosnian refugees, found our protests useful, I think, to his own agenda, which was to reverse Croatia's growing diplomatic isolation. Unlike Tudjman, who believed the West would ultimately support Croatia as a Catholic bastion against Russian-led Orthodox Christianity and Islamic fundamentalism, Granic understood that most Americans (including the administration) saw Bosnia as a case of aggression against a sovereign state. Croatia, he saw, was rapidly moving from the category of victim to that of aggressor.

After a month on the ground, I came to the conclusion that the Bosnian-Croat leader, Mate Boban, would never follow through on promises to end the atrocities. It was also clear to me that the Muslims would never trust a peace deal involving Boban. Getting rid of Boban became, in my view, a necessary precondition to ending the Muslim-Croat war.

Although he never said so directly, I sensed that Granic shared this assessment and was prepared to bring Tudjman along. I decided to give Granic the necessary ammunition. In a BBC interview in September 1993, I compared the behaviour of the HVO leadership to that of the Bosnian Serbs, a none-too-subtle suggestion that they were committing war crimes. These comments received prominent attention in the Croatian media, evidence that some in Zagreb were prepared to jettison Boban. In my almost daily meetings with Tudjman and Granic on the Muslim-Croat war, I began to link the demands in our demarches that the atrocities stop to the removal of Boban. We also began to suggest that Croatia itself could face sanctions, an action that would not only be devastating for Croatia, but also involve many risks for the international community that depended on Croatia as a base for humanitarian activity in Bosnia and as a host to more than 500,000 Bosnian refugees.

In January 1994 Granic called me into the Foreign Ministry to advise me that Boban would be taking "a long vacation." He was replaced by a low-key lawyer from the Posavina, Kresimir Zubak, who proved a reliable negotiating partner and later became the Croat member of Bosnia's post-Dayton tripartite presidency.

On 17 February 1994 US special envoy for the former Yugoslavia, Charles Redman, and I called on President Tudjman. Redman laid out a proposal , inspired by Ivo Komsic and other moderate Bosnian Croats, for a joint Muslim-Croat Federation to replace the proposed separate Muslim and Croat republics of the moribund Owen-Stoltenberg plan. Under the American plan power would be devolved, to the extent possible, to ethnically defined cantons, with power-sharing arrangements among Croats and Muslims at the federation level. We told Tudjman that if Croatia accepted this proposal, the United States would work diplomatically to bring about the recovery of Croatia's own territory and would support Croatia's desire for closer relations with the West.

Tudjman's initial response was not encouraging. He said, "I accept your proposal but if the Serbs have their own republic than so must the Croats." In short, he was prepared to accept American support but not pay the price of giving up on a separate Croat republic.

Redman and I left the meeting discouraged. I went on to deliver a previously scheduled speech at Zagreb's Lisinski concert hall using the occasion to warn that non-cooperation could lead to sanctions against Croatia. The next day, Granic called me in to deliver a protest from Tudjman over my speech. When I began to explain, Granic cut me off, saying that he understood my point and that I would have a better answer to our proposal after the weekend. The following Monday (21 February), Redman and I again saw Tudjman, who this time accepted our proposal. Within days we had Granic, Zubak, and the Bosnian foreign minister, Haris Silajdzic, in Washington, where we worked out an agreement to create the Federation of Bosnia and Herzegovina. Immediately, the Muslim-Croat war ended. The federation proved, as Holbrooke writes in his book, the foundation of us efforts to end the entire war.

ARMS FOR BOSNIA

In April of 1994 the Bosnian government approached the Croatians to ask that Croatia permit arms to transit its territory for the Bosnian army. The Croatians then asked the United States how it should respond to the Bosnian request. Our answer became one of the most controversial elements of us policy in the Balkans, as congressional Republicans tried (unsuccessfully) to make the response a political issue in the 1996 presidential election.

The Croatian government was not asking our view on whether they should enforce a United Nations arms embargo. In fact Croatia had successfully circumvented the embargo and was continuing to arm itself. Ostensibly, they were asking whether they should also permit Bosnia to violate the embargo. However, this was not the real issue.

Tudjman only reluctantly agreed to the federation and never fully gave up on his dream of creating a greater Croatia at Bosnia's expense. I believe that he hoped we would tell him (as the Bush administration had in September 1992 when an Iranian cargo plane loaded with Bosnia-bound arms landed in Zagreb) that he should enforce the embargo. At a minimum, this would have provided a pretext to keep the Bosnian army weak. He may also have hoped that blocking arms would destroy the federation in such a way that Croatia would not be blamed.

President Clinton decided that I would tell Tudjman that I had "no instructions" on how to answer his question. The answer was diplomatic code for saying we did not object if Croatia facilitated the flow of arms to Bosnia. This was the right decision. The us did not itself unilaterally violate the arms embargo, an action that would have seriously jeopardized relations with allies that had peacekeeping troops in Bosnia and that would have undermined other UN sanctions such as those in place against Serbia-Montenegro and Iraq. On the other hand, Clinton's decision enabled the Bosnians to acquire desperately needed weapons to defend themselves and contributed to the military changes in 1995 that made Dayton possible.

SEEKING A POLITICAL SETTLEMENT IN THE KRAJINA

The 1991 war had left Belgrade-backed Serbs in control of 27 per cent of Croatia's territory in three geographically distinct areas: (1) the Krajina, a sparsely populated Serb-majority region in the west extending from Dalmatia to the outskirts of Karlovac; (2) ethnically mixed western Slavonia around Pakrac; and (3) a predominantly Croat, ethnically mixed sliver of land along Croatia's Danube border with Serbia comprising parts of eastern Slavonia, Baranja, and western Srijem and commonly referred to as Eastern Slavonia. In 1991, the Yugoslav army and Serb paramilitaries brutally expelled ethnic Croats from all these territories, creating a vociferous domestic lobby for a speedy solution. Since January 1993, there had been a low-intensity conflict over the demarcation line between the Serb-held territories and the rest of Croatia.

With the signing of the Washington Agreement, the United States became much more engaged in the Croatia peace process, as we had promised President Tudjman we would. I became the designated

American negotiator. My first task was to co-sponsor ceasefire talks initiated by Russian deputy foreign minister Vitaly Churkin at the Russian Embassy in Zagreb. Two all night negotiating sessions produced an agreement in the early hours of 30 March 1994.

Following this success, the talk's co-sponsors (which also included the European Union (EU) and the United Nations) decided to pursue in the same format a second round aimed at confidence building and economic cooperation between the two sides with the ultimate view of proceeding to a third stage on a political settlement. Because the four-party sponsorship had begun in Zagreb, the talks became known as the Zagreb-4, or Z-4, talks. While an economic and confidence building agreement was concluded on 2 December 1994, the process of getting there proved frustrating both to the Croatian government and to the international mediators. While both sides played elaborate games, often cancelling negotiations for the most trivial reasons, it became clear that the Serbs were not prepared to engage on the core issues and that Croatia might soon opt for a military solution.

Long before the economic agreement was finished, I came to the conclusion that time for peaceful settlement was running out. Therefore, in early fall 1994 EU envoy Gert Ahrens, Russian ambassador Leonid Kerestedzhiyants, and I decided to jump to the final stage of the process and put forward a proposed political settlement.

Ahrens, Kerestedzhiyants, and I prepared a comprehensive thirty-page proposal that provided extensive self-government for Serbs living in those parts of the Krajina where they had been a majority in the 1991 census. Under the plan (which the Croatian press promptly dubbed the Z-4 Plan) the Krajina would have its own parliament and president, would control its local police, would have exclusive jurisdiction over domestic issues such as education, culture, the environment, and the local economy, and would have exclusive power to raise and spend revenues within the self-governing area. (The political autonomy provisions for Kosovo proposed at Rambouillet were almost a carbon copy of the Z-4 plan.) Our idea was to demonstrate in detail just how much self-government was possible for Serbs within Croatia and thus to induce their leaders to engage in serious negotiations.

Unfortunately, the Serb leadership refused even to receive the plan. When the sponsoring ambassadors travelled to the Serb capital, Knin, on 30 January 1995 to present the plan to the Krajina-

Serb leadership, the self-styled president, Milan Martic, refused to touch the document. President Tudjman, who intensely disliked the plan for giving too much autonomy to the Serbs, was shrewd enough to agree to negotiate on the basis of the document.

THE BIHAC CRISIS

The next critical turning point was the Bihac crisis of 1995. Bihac was a Muslim-held enclave bordered to its north and west by the Serb-held Krajina region and to its east and south by Bosnian-Serb territory. Its population, including Muslim refugees from surrounding towns, was about 160,000.

In September 1994 Bihac's defender, Bosnian Fifth Corps commander Dudakovic, launched an offensive that seized significant Serb territory. Unfortunately, he over extended his lines and, without the ability to resupply, fell victim to a ferocious Bosnian-Serb counterattack. In these attacks, the Bosnian Serbs were supported by the Krajina Serbs, who crossed the international border to aid the Bosnian Serbs. By mid-November, there was a real danger that Bihac might fall. On 10 November Granic and Susak summoned me to a meeting to pose a simple question: if Croatia took military action through the Krajina to save Bihac, would the United States block possible UN sanctions against it for widening the war? I phoned and cabled for instructions.

We never answered the Croatians' question. However, I did present a strong demarche to Tudjman warning of the risks to Croatia of a wider war. Tudjman turned to Granic and Susak, telling them "that's exactly what I think." In November 1994 neither Croatia nor the United States was ready for a wider war. Fortunately, Bihac's defenses held.

Seven months later, the Bosnian and Krajina Serbs renewed their attacks on Bihac. This time the response was very different. Unwilling to allow the Serbs to shift the strategic balance of power by creating a consolidated western Serb territory, Croatia mobilized not only to relieve Bihac but to retake the entire Krajina. Four days before the Croatians initiated military action, I told Tudjman he could not count on US support if his forces ran into trouble. I also warned him that harming civilians or UN peacekeepers would have disastrous consequences for Croatia's relations with the United States. I pointedly did not tell him not to go forward. On 4 August

1995 Croatia launched Operation Storm, taking the Krajina in four days and dramatically altering the military balance in the war.

There were many reasons the second Bihac crisis turned out so differently from the first. In light of Martic's refusal even to discuss a possible political settlement, both Croatia and the international mediators saw little prospect for a negotiated resolution to the Krajina question. Croatia had retaken western Slavonia in a two-day military operation in May, meeting almost no resistance. More significantly neither Milosevic nor the Bosnian Serbs had made any effort to aid their Croatian cousins. By the time he launched Operation Storm, Tudjman could be quite sure that neither Milosevic nor Mladic would intervene.

Events had also changed the equation for the United States. Two weeks before, Bosnian-Serb general Ratko Mladic had overrun the Srebrenica safe area and systematically murdered more than 7,000 men and boys. The attack on Bihac appeared to be part of a campaign aimed at eliminating the enclaves and their people. If Bihac fell, the killings would certainly be many times greater than in Srebrenica. NATO had neither the will nor the means to prevent the fall of Bihac. The Croatian army did.

Even up to the last minute, the United States tried to find a peaceful solution. Two days before Operation Storm began, with Croatian preparations well-advanced, I travelled to Belgrade for a meeting with Milan Babic, the "prime minister" of the Krajina-Serb para-state and the one leader who seemed to have considered the interests of the Serb population as some part of his political calculus. We met alone in the office of the American charge in our embassy in Belgrade. I outlined the dire circumstances facing the Serbs and Tudjman's conditions for not going forward with an attack. Babic apologized for the behaviour of the Krajina-Serb leadership both in attacking Bihac and in refusing negotiations, rightly suggesting that it was incredibly stupid. He readily agreed to Tudjman's terms for a settlement (as I understood them), but in the end it was too late. By the time I met Tudjman the next day to report on Babic's concessions, he had already made the decision to launch Operation Storm at dawn the next day. Further, he doubted Babic could actually bring along Martic and the other Krajina leaders, and here he may well have been right.

As I wrote in a cable to Washington at the time, the attack on Krajina would be devastating for its civilian population, most of whom would flee. However, in the hierarchy of evil, the fall of Bihac would be even worse. The Croatian army behaved in an appalling manner after retaking Krajina. All Serb homes were looted and a large proportion torched. Several hundred isolated stragglers, often elderly Serbs too frail to flee, were murdered. We protested these acts and ultimately imposed sanctions on Croatia forcing it to agree to the return of Serb refugees and to the restoration of their property. However, I believe we made the right decision not to block Operation Storm. Unfortunately, in some situations there are only bad choices, and we chose the least bad.

THE BANJA LUKA DECISION

The final turning point I would like to cover is our message to Tudjman in September 1995 that he should not take Banja Luka. Here, I am not sure we made the right decision. I believe that Richard Holbrooke, who delivered the message, shares my doubts.

After Operation Storm, the Croatian army swept across western Bosnia. By the middle of the month they were nearing Banja Luka, by far the largest town in Serb hands. Holbrooke and I met Tudjman alone in his Pantovcak office in the hills above Zagreb. Holbrooke had instructions to tell Tudjman to stop the offensive but was uncertain as to whether to go ahead with the instructions. I shared his doubts, and we went over the issue in detail before the meeting, as we both understood that this conversation could determine the entire future of Bonia-Herzegovina, not to mention the us peace initiative. In the end Holbrooke told Tudjman not to take Banja Luka, while explicitly inviting the Croatians to help the Bosnians take Sanski Most (as they did) and Prijedor (which they did not).

Several factors influenced our thinking. Foremost, we were concerned about the 400,000 Serb civilians in the Banja Luka area (both residents and refugees from areas already taken by the Croatians), who certainly would face a chaotic and terrifying flight through the Posavina corridor. Croatia's conduct in the Krajina and western Bosnia provided no reason to believe its armies would treat these civilians in a humane way. I was also concerned that if Tudjman actually took Banja Luka, long the cornerstone of his plan for greater Croatia, he would never surrender it to the federation. Holbrooke had been persuaded by Milosevic that, in a postwar Bosnia, the Banja Luka Serbs might provide a more moderate alternative Serb leadership to that of the war criminals in Pale (an expectation that turned out to be true, to some degree), and I think this weighed on his decision.

Was it the right decision? If Banja Luka had fallen, it surely would have spelled the end of the extremist, fascist, Pale clique that had brought war to Bosnia. With the Croatians and Bosnians in control of most of the country, we may have achieved a more rational settlement in Bosnia, one that would have made it easier to maintain the unity of the country. On the other hand, would it have been possible to recreate a multi-ethnic Bosnia after all the Serbs had fled? And did we risk trading greater Serbia for greater Croatia? Like all "what ifs" of history, we'll never know.

Throughout the war and the peace negotiations, the United States had certain goals. These included respect for the borders of the successor states of the former Yugoslavia, insistence on the right of refugees to return to their homes, and justice for the war crimes committed in the war. These principles are embodied in all three American-negotiated agreements ending the wars in the former Yugoslavia (i.e., the Washington Agreement, the Dayton Accords, and the Erdut Agreement reintegrating Eastern Slavonia into Croatia) and were a constant in our diplomacy. The problems now faced, particularly with regard to refugees returning to Bosnia, are a failing not of the peace agreements but of their implementation. Had the agreements compromised on these points, the current situation would be even worse.

The diplomacy of ending a war can be as messy as the war itself. Certainly us diplomacy in the Bosnia conflict involved a number of complicated decisions. I cannot say we made the right choices at each turning point. I can say that the outcome, however imperfect, was better than continued war.

NOTE

1 Edited transcript of a speech presented to the conference at the University of Western Ontario, May 1999.

The Dayton Accord Elections in Bosnia-Herzegovina 1996

JOHN M. REID

INTRODUCTION

I arrived in Sarajevo, Bosnia-Herzegovina, at the end of January 1996, having been recruited by the Government of Canada as a senior deputy for the Organization of Security and Cooperation in Europe (OSCE) mission to Bosnia-Herzegovina. I was to serve as an election expert in the work of the Provisional Election Commission, which had been established under Article III of the Dayton Peace Accords. When I arrived, NATO troops were still flooding into Bosnia-Herzegovina, the country was only beginning to realize that the fighting was not going to break out again in the spring, and a multitude of Western outsiders was beginning to appear.

I found myself the only one in the OSCE who knew anything about election organization and law, that elections were primary in the OSCE agenda, and that they had to be held by the middle of September. Urgent elections were important because, if successful, the NATO alliance would have an exit strategy in place. What we also learned later was that "successful" elections were also vital to the US's continued participation in Bosnia-Herzegovina and, especially, to the forthcoming US presidential elections in November 1996. Elections had little to do, therefore, with the restoration of "normality" in Bosnia-Herzegovina or with the legitimacy of the existing governments, but much to do with the politics of the NATO alliance and its dominant member.

DAYTON PEACE ACCORDS

I am a strong supporter of the Dayton Peace Treaty. It stopped the killing in Bosnia-Herzegovina. The war ended because the contending factions were exhausted and because the international community stepped in to force a truce at the crucial moment. That is what was created by the Dayton Peace Accords: a truce, enforced by the very considerable military might of NATO. Even after a series of elections, that truce endures today, but there is not yet a peace in Bosnia-Herzegovina. Before that comes about, considerable time and effort will have to go into the process of healing and confidence building. The recent sudden rise of Kosovo as a serious problem is an indication of how quickly issues in the Balkans can escalate, growing out of control. It is also an indication of how little understood the Balkans are by the Western world.

One of the long-term objectives of the Dayton Peace Accords is to reassemble and recreate a country that has been torn apart by civil war. Bosnia-Herzegovina has been defined by bitter fighting among its three ethnic groups: Croats, Muslims, and Serbs. The memories of war, and all that they entail in terms of bitterness, a desire for revenge, and a profound lack of trust within and between ethnic groups, are still strong. Civil wars are especially bitter, and this war was one of the worst. Implicit in the Accords is the attempt to create circumstances that will lead to the development of a multiethnic society, one of the failed projects of the Tito Government, which in turn led to the civil war. The efforts to reunite Bosnia-Herzegovina in any form will not be easy, if at all possible, but if this project is to have a chance of success, the international community will need to be aggressive and consistent in pushing the peace process. The subsequent events in Kosovo will, at best, significantly stall an already painfully slow process of recovery and reconciliation.

The OSCE was chosen to lead the western effort in the fields of elections, human rights, and military cooperation. The previous incarnation of the OSCE had been charged with running conferences between eastern and western Europe in order to ensure that all participants in the then divided Europe were aware of each other's position and military resources. The OSCE was chosen for the Bosnia-Herzegovina mission because, after the UN debacle in Bosnia-Herzegovina, the UN would clearly have been unacceptable. However, the OSCE had no experience in large-scale enterprises of this nature: it knew nothing of elections or human rights on a broad scale, although it did have expertise in military cooperation. It was also bruised by the fight between the Americans and the French over who would head the mission; the Americans won, and the French were conspicuously absent from the OSCE mission, but not from the NATO force. Consequently, we had tremendous difficulty getting organized for this election, given the obligations in the Dayton Peace Accords as to how the elections were to be fought, the lack of resources, and especially the OSCE's lack of expertise at both the political and bureaucratic levels, to say nothing of the lack of understanding of the issues at the OSCE mission level.

ELECTIONS

Holding elections was one of the three tasks imposed on the OSCE by the Dayton Peace Agreement. The Agreement established a Provisional Election Commission (PEC) to write an election act, to organize an election team that would administer the elections, and to provide general supervision of the electoral structure. The PEC was made up of one member and a deputy from each of the three ethnic groups; a chairman, the OSCE head of mission, Ambassador Frowick, who had the power to make unilateral decisions when he deemed it necessary; a representative from the Office of the High Representative (OHR); and two outsiders, one who acted as de facto chairman, Sir Kenneth Scott, and myself. While the Western diplomats had no experience or knowledge of elections, fortunately the three locals and their deputies were very knowledgeable about the electoral process used in the elections of 1990 and '91 in the former Yougoslavia. They brought to the table a range of expertise and common sense concerning electoral matters that was badly needed. They were also well plugged into their respective governments, which ensured that for the governments, at least, there would be no surprises.

What the Dayton Peace Accords provided was an apparent political agreement on the general principles under which elections would be held. Bosnia-Herzegovina had no election act, so one had to be written. I designed the architecture of the act and wrote about 60 per cent of the text, which was then amended as necessary and approved by the PEC. However, since the principles that had been agreed to in the Dayton Peace Accords were not fully spelled out, their potential implementation caused great difficulties and led to a number of impasses at many turns. Our problems, moreover, were compounded by the following factors: we did not have the staff expertise we needed, we had to base the election list on the 1991 census, we had to treat the one-third of the population living as refugees abroad the same as those still resident in Bosnia-Herzegovina, we had to account for the fact that another one-third of those living in Bosnia-Herzegovina were refugees within their own country, and we were supposed to ensure that all voted where they had lived during the census of 1991.

The Dayton Peace Accords created a very complex constitutional structure for Bosnia-Herzegovina. Not counting elections in the municipalities, there were 650 nominated candidates for the other levels of government, and not every party provided full lists of candidates. With the municipalities included, there were over 28,000 candidates on party lists, representing forty-one political parties. The number of parties was a great surprise, but the number of candidates was an even greater shock to the OSCE and the election team, especially since the Provisional Election Commission had tried to ensure that only serious parties would be in the field. The large amount of political activity, to say nothing of money, needed to keep such a complex system going is astonishingly for a total population of between 4 and 4.5 million people, many of whom are scattered around the world and at least one-third of whom are displaced within their former country. It will not be an easy system to manage – or to afford.

The elections held on 14 September 1996 in Bosnia-Herzegovina were successful. The circumstances were not ideal, considering that nine months earlier electors had been tying to kill each other. Nobody was killed during these and subsequent elections, although there were serious beatings, including that of one party leader. But these elections were designed to be quick, provisional, temporary, and, given the reality of the situation, imperfect. New elections were required in two years, as the mandate for all elected under the Provisional Election Commission's rules and regulations was limited to 15 September 1998. Those elections took place on schedule and were also successful, although there continued to be the usual difficulties associated with elections under these kinds of circumstances, such as massive population movements both inside and outside the Bosnia-Herzegovina among those with the right to vote.

There was great enthusiasm for the election by the opposition parties. With a significant international presence to ensure fair play, they felt that this would be their best opportunity to develop a political presence. The OSCE was able to find money to provide some funding for all parties, while limiting the amount that went to the three largest parties, the Muslim-run Party for Democratic Action (SDA), the Serbian Democratic Party (SDS), and the Croatian Democration Union (HDZ), which has strong ties to the HDZ of Croatia. Coupled with the activities of outside non-governmental organizations (NGOs), specialized in training political parties, these two initiatives provided more than ample motivation. When party registration was closed, fifty political parties had registered. After coalitions had been formed, forty-one parties and coalitions were prepared to fight the five elections in the Republika Srpska and the Federation of Bosnia-Herzegovina. The political parties produced over 28,000 candidates for the positions to be filled. The PEC had the mammoth job of ensuring that none of these candidates was a war criminal (we found two) and that each met the rest of the criteria. Of course, when municipal elections were postponed because of controversy over where refugees from outside of Bosnia-Herzegovina could vote, the number of parties and candidates participating in the elections dropped off significantly.

Excellent work was done by NGOs from the US and Western Europe to educate and train the opposition political parties. The elections were a success, however, because the big nationalist parties, the SDS, SDA, and HDZ, decided that it was in their own best interests to cooperate in the elections in order to ensure that they were conducted properly. This was vital to the success of the elections since these three parties controlled the Local Election Commissions (LCD); without the LCD's active and effective involvement there could have been no elections. The ruling parties did not cooperate, however, until they had assured themselves that they would be the major beneficiaries of the election process, which was the case: they were elected to office with significant majorities and, in Western eyes, obtained full legitimacy. Most Western politicians also counted the election a success because no one was killed.

These elections were the first in the world to attempt to treat all citizens equally, regardless of where they were located. For electoral purposes, refugees in Canada, Australia, and Germany, for example, were to receive the same treatment as those citizens in Bosnia-Herzegovina who still lived where they had in 1991. The OSCE did not understand this obligation (although the PEC and its election team understood it from the beginning) until late in the game, at which time an organization was thrown together to handle the problem as best it could. Although the odds were against achieving the goal of equality even if a start had been made at the beginning, the various countries hosting refugees from Bosnia-Herzegovina worked very hard to meet this mammoth obligation. Nevertheless, their efforts were not a great success.

The idea behind giving the vote to the refugee population was to encourage refugees to return home. However, the Office of the United Nations High Commissioner for Refugees (UNHCR) reports that three years after the initial elections, few have been able to return because, in most cases, if they came from an area that had been "cleansed," their homes have been taken over (where their homes survived) by members of other ethnic groups or even by members of their own group since housing was in such short supply after the destruction of the war. This part of "normalization" has not worked, as ethnic cleansing, even after the signing of the Dayton Peace Accords, has continued, albeit more slowly than before.

CONSTITUTION

The Dayton Peace Agreement established a new constitutional structure for Bosnia-Herzegovina. It created a very weak central government and somewhat stronger entity governments in the Republika Srpska and the Federation of Bosnia-Herzegovina. On the federation side, it created ten cantons (similar to Canada's provinces) comprising the Bosnia-Herzegovina Federation. In both entities, municipalities exist that are more akin to Canada's regional governments than to municipalities.

The intent of the Dayton constitutions was to devolve power to the local levels of government on the assumption that this was where the moderates would have the greatest clout. Normally, however, the moderates have their greatest influence at the top levels, and the radicals have theirs at the local levels. The jury is still out on this fundamental Dayton assumption. It is also out on the idea that power can be diverted downward from governments that have survived a civil war. The people in charge are tough warlords who have endured a vicious civil war, and it is doubtful that these people will want to give up their power to governmental structures below them, which they do not control and over which they do not have extensive influence. Initially, they were not interested in elections for the same reasons, but they were successful in the elections and thus remain in power. The exception is with the SDS, the major Serb party, which split apart because of fighting between its major sponsors. Constitutions are interesting documents, but they do not always provide an accurate road map as to how the power in a community flows.

The presidency of Bosnia-Herzegovina is a three person rotating institution. Each of the main ethnic groups will elect a representative to the presidency, a Muslim and a Croat from the federation and a Serb from the Republika Srpska.

There are very elaborate controls to ensure that each ethnic group has a veto over anything that anyone else wants to do, whether that person is in the presidency or in one of the joint legislatures. Under the central government there are two entities, the Republika Srpska and the Federation of Bosnia-Herzegovina.

The Federation of Bosnia-Herzegovina is a very complex structure, as it houses both Croats and Muslims in the same territory, who, in some regions, fought bitterly against each other; that battle continues to this day within the federation. The federation has a base of municipalities with significant constitutional power, which are grouped into ten cantons. In addition to their normal duties, the cantons elect representatives to the second chamber of the federation. The proportionally elected Federation House of Representatives has 140 members. It elects the president of the Federation of Bosnia-Herzegovina, who then appoints the prime minister, who then selects his government. In contrast to the federation, the Republika Srpska is lean and mean: a presidency and a legislature of eighty-three members. It is modelled on the US state system. The legislature is elected by proportional representation. It too shares the same municipal base as the federation, but there are no cantons; it is a unitary system.

MILITARY REALITIES

As the instrument to stop the fighting and to separate the three warring factions, the Dayton Peace Accords have been an unqualified success to date. The annexes dealing with military responsibilities are precise and detailed. The lessons learned from the days of the United Nations Protection Force (UNPROFOR) were understood by the Western negotiators of the Peace Accords. The NATO command has the power to implement its part of the agreement without reference to the other organizations in the Peace Accords that have different responsibilities. NATO has carried out its responsibilities with distinction. It can be argued, however, that NATO has had the easiest mission of all the international agencies since it came with sufficient force to overwhelm any faction or combination of factions that wanted to take it on. This has not prevented the former warring factions from testing NATO at all times and in all places. Almost every day, there have been reports from NATO of new challenges thrown out by the former warring factions that it has had to deal with. But its mandate was unambiguous, and NATO has filled it well. Its success was a precondition for any other action by members of the international community.

Remember, there is no peace yet among the various parties to the Dayton Peace Accords in Bosnia-Herzegovina. So it will be necessary to continue deploying NATO forces for a considerable time. If there were not sufficient international military forces in Bosnia-Herzegovina, I believe it would not take long for fighting to resume. Having entered the fray, the international community now has an obligation to keep strong military forces in Bosnia-Herzegovina until the memories of the bitter civil war recede and some sense of "normalization" returns. It will be some time before there is a peace to keep.

CONFLICT RESOLUTION

A good part of the Dayton Peace Accords is based on conflict resolution. For example, the concept of elections being held within nine months of the formal signing of the Accords is one of a number of items. The Regional Stabilization Programme, designed to create mutual confidence between the armies of the former warring factions, is an initiative with which the OSCE has had considerable experience in Europe. The OSCE and the Office of the High Representative have human rights programs in place to support the ombudsman projects of the UN. In contrast to the deliberate powers given to NATO to ensure a military truce, the Peace Accords gave little, if any, power to the international-community organizations responsible for bringing about political change in Bosnia-Herzegovina.The OSCE has the power to convince, but it has no stick and few carrots; the high representative has more sticks but few carrots.

The purpose of military conflict resolution is to provide another way of settling disputes. It is designed to ensure that there are no military or intelligence surprises, that all parties have the relevant information, and that the rules of engagement and discussion are clear and understood by all parties. It works best if the parties become caught up in pursuing objectives that are important to them and from which all parties can "win." This is more easily said than done. For example, in the case of the OSCE Regional Stabilization Programme, it means keeping the military commanders talking while obtaining the information needed from each party to ensure that there are no surprises. In a truce situation, this is not an easy task.

An example of the ongoing political activities of the former warring factions is the continuing phenomena of ethnic cleansing. Annex 7 of the Dayton Peace Accords gives refugees and displaced persons the right to return home – i.e., to where they lived before the war broke out in 1991. It is a key part of the Accords. After the truce, however, ethnic cleansing continued unabated. The UNHCR reported in late August 1996 that the number of people who had been removed from their homes and had become either displaced persons in Bosnia-Herzegovina or refugees abroad since 14 December 1995 (the date of the signing of the Dayton Peace Accords) was over 90,000 more than the number that had been resettled to where they had lived in 1991. As A. Izetbegovic, the president of the Republic of Bosnia-Herzegovina, stated, "the war continues, but by other means." As a result, the UNHCR has been unable to meet any of its goals in resettling refugees and displaced persons. Annex 7 is presently a dead letter. This is only one example of the lack of power and authority of the international community.

In my judgment, the defining moment in the Dayton peace process came in late February 1996 when the Republika Srpska government put enormous pressure on Serbs living in Sarajevo to relocate to the Serb-held territory. They used terrorist tactics on their own people to force them to move away from Sarajevo, aided and abetted by the Federation of Bosnia-Herzegovina. The international community was unable to prevent this forced movement of Serbs out of Sarajevo. Many Serbs departed out of fear because law and order had broken down in their municipalities; people who did not want to leave were beaten up. Some left out of conviction as well. The Bosnia-Herzegovina Federation police stood by and watched. NATO took no action. When the Serbs left, they went with everything they owned or could grab. Fires were lit, and residences were destroyed.

This incident demonstrated the powerlessness of the Dayton Peace Accords' political agencies, the OSCE, OHR, and UN, to name but three. It demonstrated the limits of the activities that NATO was prepared to undertake. It clearly indicated to the former warring factions how far the international community was prepared to go to defend the Dayton Peace Accords. The entities understood from this exercise exactly what power the international-community agencies had and, more important, what international will there was to interfere in their domestic activities. They became much more aggressive in following their policies of ethnic cleansing and in creating little "statelets" out of the entity border. This was the apogee of the international community's influence in Bosnia-Herzegovina.

RECOVERY AND ECONOMICS

What the international community is trying to deal with in Bosnia-Herzegovina is a collapsed communist structure. One of the reasons for the war was the deteriorating economic circumstances in the former Yougoslavia in the 1980s. If you ask the citizens of Bosnia-Herzegovina what they want, they answer that they would like to go back to the good old days of the 1970s under Tito. They had work, there was peace and prosperity, they had leisure. They could travel. The political leadership in Bosnia-Herzegovina appears to accept this goal; in fact, they themselves would like to return to the 1970s since this would mean more power for them. The current political leadership does not want to give power away, lest it lose control of the country's economic life; on the contrary, it wishes to amass as much power as possible. To decentralize, to sell off state assets, to privatize state industries (what is left of them), to devolve power to lower levels of government, to admit that elections are a legitimate way of changing governments: these are all foreign concepts, and, if understood at all, they are rejected out of hand by many of the main actors, even if they dare not say so publicly.

Economics and politics are the Siamese twins of communist countries, and Bosnia-Herzegovina, as part of the former Yougoslavia, was immersed in the marriage of those concepts as well. With the collapse of the old communist country and the impact of the civil war, to say nothing of the attempt by the West to impose some of its values on the country's political and legal systems, it is as if the old system imploded into a black hole. These conflicting tendencies are evident in the three ruling political parties (the SDA, SDS, and HDZ) that emerged from Tito's communist party organization, but they are also part of the ethos of the various other political parties that emerged after the war. For the international community to convince Bosnians of all stripes to undertake those Western changes will be a difficult political challenge, especially since we ourselves are still debating these ideas. Still, progress must be made on the economic front, or there will be no peace. Most of the industrial installations were destroyed in the war, but because they were built on a massive scale, many of them were already obsolete in any case; however, the physical asset has been destroyed.

There have been some small but useful international initiatives to establish some economic activity. The British, for example, have offered loans on easy terms to all those who ran small enterprises before the war. The World Bank has launched a similar project in other regions of the international community. Restoration of buildings and various infrastructure projects comprise the current economic engine, supported entirely by the international community. In the aftermath of the war, there is little funding within Bosnia-Herzegovina itself to support reconstruction of the economy.

CONCLUSION

What did the elections accomplish?

First, they satisfied the strictures of the Dayton Peace Accords, which called for elections by 14 September. This was probably of more importance to the international community than to the citizens of Bosnia-Herzegovina.

Second, the new Dayton Peace Accords constitutions were established.

Third, while elections legitimized the existing governments in the eyes of the international community, these governments were already legitimized in the eyes of the Bosnia-Herzegovina citizens.

Fourth, to some degree, they legitimized the various opposition parties in the consciousness of the electors and in the political structures of Bosnia-Herzegovina. This was accomplished in the face of vicious attacks against the opposition by the three dominant nationalist parties, who openly campaigned on the slogan that a vote cast for any other party was a vote for another ethnic group. It remains to be proven that the opposition parties can survive without assistance from the international community.

Fifth, and the most optimistic projection hoped for by the international community, the elections opened the possibility for some "normalization" of the situation in order to allow the citizens to put the war behind them and to plan for the future – though the Kosovo situation has greatly hindered this possibility.

The truce in Bosnia-Herzegovina established by the Dayton Peace Accords continues. The great failure has been the inability of refugees to return home. The further development of a peace will depend on time and a strong military presence. The Kosovo affair is clearly a distinct hindrance because Kosovo is where the disintegration of the former Yougoslavia started and because the issue in the Kosovo conflict, ethnic cleansing and ethnic supremacy, is exactly the same issue that prompted the civil war. There are a number of other areas where fighting could easily break out again within Bosnia-Herzegovina. The elections and the passage of time have diminished the authority that the international-community organizations had, even though the high representative has seen fit to dismiss the elected president of the Republika Srpska. Yet the international presence is important because there are pressures that the international community can bring to bear from time to time, notably the movement of assistance funds that act as a carrot.

Having intervened to end the war, the international community has no other choice but to stick it out for the longer term. The events in Kosovo reinforce this situation, for if the international community does not stay, it will lose its investment in peace and good will, and will inevitably be dragged back to Bosnia-Herzegovina to try to deal with the next outbreak of civil war – as we have seen with Kosovo. And if this should be the case, then the situation in Bosnia-Herzegovina will be immeasurably worse the second time around.

No Fire in a Vacuum: Distraction, Disinterest, Distortion, and Disunity in Formulating Western Policy towards the Former Yugoslavia

GRAHAM N. GREEN*

Since the beginning of the wars in the former Yugoslavia in 1991, it has become fashionable to try to attach blame for the outbreak of fighting to the actions – or lack of actions – of the international community. There are some who believe that timely intervention by Western countries could have prevented the wars, while there are others who believe that no outside intervention, however timely, could have forestalled the violence.

One thing is clear: the Yugoslav wars were not imported. There was plenty of home-grown tinder in Yugoslavia in the latter years of the 1980s with which to prepare the fires and still more fuel available to keep the fires burning once they had started. Nor did the sparks that ignited the blaze come from beyond Yugoslavia's borders. Equally clear, however, is that the Yugoslav wars were not inevitable. Although the domestic protagonists seemed incapable of averting the inferno, there were opportunities for outsiders to step in to help prevent it from starting.

The key question, therefore, is when did Yugoslavia pass the point of no return so that its destruction became unstoppable. Like fire, which needs three elements to burn – air, fuel, and heat – so too was Yugoslavia's collapse precipitated by three essential ingredients. Each element was destabilizing, but on its own none was enough to plunge Yugoslavia into war, nor would any two have been enough. Together, however, they formed a lethal poison that killed Yugoslavia.

The first key ingredient was the rise of Serbian nationalism, stoked and encouraged by Slobodan Milosevic, who built a strong power base that delighted Serbs throughout Yugoslavia but created considerable unease amongst the country's many other ethnic communities, notably the Slovenes and the Croats.[1] Ironically, leaders around Yugoslavia initially welcomed Milosevic's political triumphs in 1987,[2] as did many in the West who saw him as an economic reformer and a hope for the future.[3]

The second key ingredient was Slovenia's steady movement towards independence, which began in the mid-1980s and accelerated following the events of the "Slovene Spring" in 1988,[4] leading to Slovenia's declaration in 1989 that is was a sovereign republic but still within Yugoslavia.[5]

The third and final key ingredient was the rise of Croatian nationalism, which had been spurred on by the developments in Serbia and Slovenia. Franjo Tudjman became the leader who best exploited this new wave of nationalism, which had been kept in check since its last incarnation had been crushed by Tito in 1971.[6]

It was in this explosive environment that the Yugoslav Communist Party held its Fourteenth Extraordinary Conference in January 1990, during which both the Slovenes and the Croatians walked out in protest at Milosevic's efforts to block proposed amendments to the conference's final resolution. This marked the end of the Yugoslav Communist Party,[7] which, ominously, left the Yugoslav National Army (JNA) as the only effective pan-republican institution in Yugoslavia.

Thus, by the end of January 1990, all of the ingredients were in place for the violent break-up of Yugoslavia, yet nobody outside the country seemed to have noticed. The US deputy secretary of state, Lawrence Eagleburger, visited Yugoslavia the following month and expressed America's preference for a united Yugoslavia, but he also said that if Yugoslavia did break up, the US would have to accept it.[8]

Following this visit, the US began urging its European allies to publicly support unity and democracy in Yugoslavia and to avoid any actions that could encourage secession by the republics, but these exhortations were greeted in Europe "with a yawn."[9] The Europeans, for the most part, dismissed the warnings, not because they were unconvinced but because there did not appear to be any threat to the interests of the major powers. Only the Austrians had urged throughout 1990 that attention be paid to developments in

Yugoslavia, but Austria was not yet a member of the European Community (EC), whose members, in any event, saw these pleadings as part of Austria's policy to support Slovenian independence.[10]

By the time an analysis by the Central Intelligence Agency was leaked to the *New York Times* in the autumn of 1990 predicting that Yugoslavia would likely break up within two years,[11] the war in Croatia was already unofficially underway, following the so-called "log revolution" of August 1990.[12] Unfortunately, by this point world attention was focused on the growing tensions in the Middle East resulting from Iraq's invasion of Kuwait and the build up to the subsequent Gulf War.

Events then moved rapidly during the first few months of 1991. In January, Milosevic and Slovenian president Milan Kucan reached an agreement that Slovenia had the right to secede from Yugoslavia. In March, after failing to get the federal presidency to declare a state of emergency in response to mass demonstrations in Belgrade, Milosevic declared that "Yugoslavia is finished." On the same day, the Croatian Serbs in the *krajina* region (who had mounted the "log revolution") declared their independence from Croatia.[13]

On 31 March, after the first casualties of the Croatian war, the JNA separated the two sides in the area around Titova Korica, as it had done for the first time the previous month in Pakrac, in effect removing parts of Croatian territory from Zagreb's control.[14] The Slovenians saw the JNA deployments as an attempt to redraw Yugoslavia's internal boundaries, and their assembly quickly adopted a declaration of sovereignty, fearing a military coup. Croatia followed suit, pronouncing its preference for a reconstituted Yugoslavia of sovereign states but vowing that it would not stay "one day longer" if Slovenia decided to leave.[15]

The confederation idea was abandoned in early May after twelve Croat police were killed in a Serbian ambush in Borovo Selo. Tudjman warned Croats that they faced the beginning of open warfare against Croatia, a warning that was reinforced the next day when the federal presidency authorized the JNA to intervene to separate Serbs and Croats.[16] Two weeks later, on 19 May, Croatia held its referendum on independence. Not surprisingly, given such an atmosphere, 93 per cent of those voting declared themselves in favour of independence. The *krajina* Serbs boycotted the vote, having held their own referendum the previous August, with 99 per cent of their voters opting to remain in Yugoslavia.[17]

The next day, the EC made the first of many misguided interventions in Yugoslavia by linking a proposed association agreement with Yugoslavia to the country's continued unity. This was reiterated during a subsequent visit to Yugoslavia by EC president Jacques Delors, who promised to try to get $4.5 billion in EC aid to support Yugoslavia's political reforms, but only if the country remained united as a single state. These appeals for unity were unlikely to have much effect on the Slovenes or the Croats,[18] however, and shortly after the Delors visit, both countries continued their preparations for independence, which was now set for 25 June.[19]

American secretary of state James Baker then visited Yugoslavia and urged Slovenia and Croatia not to implement their independence declarations so that further negotiations could be held, stressing once again the US policy of unity and democracy. He then warned Milosevic that Washington rejected any Serbian territorial claims beyond its republican borders and did not agree that Milosevic could use force to keep Yugoslavia together. Baker's position was somewhat unclear, however, as he gave no indication that the US was prepared to use military force to stop a Serbian/JNA attack on either Croatia or Slovenia. The US ambassador to Belgrade at the time, Warren Zimmerman, has written that he believes Baker's messages, coming as they did just four days before the independence declarations, were too late and should have been made six months earlier, although he recognizes that this would have been impossible given the US preoccupation at that time with preparations for the Gulf War.[20]

As expected, Croatia and Slovenia went ahead anyway, with Slovenia immediately seizing control of border and customs posts, which the JNA tried to retake on 27 June, resulting in the first battles of the Slovenian war. The EC then issued a declaration calling for the restoration of constitutional order and respect for the territorial integrity of Yugoslavia,[21] although some EC leaders began to realize that this had inadvertently given the JNA a "green light" to use force.[22] The EC troika of foreign ministers[23] then arrived in Yugoslavia confident in their ability to broker a peaceful outcome, but their approach was condescending to say the least, as they proceeded to lecture the Yugoslavs "as if they were all unruly schoolchildren."[24]

The Europeans were now trying to reduce a complex conflict to a simple border dispute while ignoring its underlying causes, but they did not have the military means to deter further use of force[25] and could only rely on moral suasion and economic incentives and penalties to try to resolve the situation.[26] (The prospect of international recognition of the newly independent countries was another instrument available to the EC, but that was squandered before the year was out.)

On 8 July, the EC reversed its position on preserving Yugoslavia's territorial integrity by brokering the Brioni Agreement between Yugoslavia and Slovenia,[27] thereby tacitly recognizing Slovenia's independence. This was another mistake by the Europeans because, by separating the Slovenian situation from the rest of the Yugoslav crisis, they were trying to deal with the different elements of the Yugoslav problem in a piecemeal fashion, ignoring the effects this would have on the other republics.

Unarmed European monitors were sent to Yugoslavia as part of the Brioni Agreement, but there was still no support for a peacekeeping force. The EC had begun discussing some kind of interposition force by the beginning of August, but there was no support from the United Nations Security Council, with the Soviet Union opposed and Yugoslavia citing non-interference in its internal affairs.[28] This changed, however, in late September after Croatian forces surrounded JNA barracks and installations and fighting broke out across Croatia. Yugoslavia now welcomed a resolution,[29] which imposed a mandatory arms embargo as a way to prevent Croatia from obtaining further weapons while preserving the JNA's vast superiority in firepower. Belgrade was also thinking ahead to depriving its next target – Bosnia-Herzegovina – of weapons, although the international community had not foreseen this consequence when it adopted Resolution 713.[30]

On 7 September, the EC gave its newly appointed mediator, Lord Carrington, just two months to negotiate a comprehensive settlement throughout Yugoslavia. As Carrington later admitted, this was "absolutely ridiculous" and showed how ignorant the EC was about how difficult a task it would be.[31] Nevertheless, Carrington forged ahead, working from the premise that Yugoslavia could not be put back together again but holding out the "carrot" of EC recognition of Slovenian and Croatian independence as an inducement to get their agreement on a comprehensive package. His efforts were undermined less than two weeks later, however, when the EC expressly ruled out military intervention,[32] thereby removing one of the potential "sticks" that might have been used to persuade the Serbs.

Carrington's efforts were further undermined on 8 October when former US secretary of state Cyrus Vance was appointed the special representative of the UN secretary general.[33] Unlike Carrington, Vance had an open-ended timeframe, a mandate to deal only with Croatia, no prejudgment by the UN of the final political outcome,[34] and the option of recommending a peacekeeping force if a ceasefire could be arranged. Although Vance promised to work in close coordination with Carrington, both Belgrade and Zagreb preferred the Vance process as it offered more immediate benefits: for the Croats, the "internationalization" of the conflict through the deployment of international peacekeepers; for the Serbs, the consolidation by the UN of Serbian territorial gains in Croatia, thereby allowing the JNA to withdraw and prepare for the next round of fighting in Bosnia.[35] Once again, the international community had not thought this far ahead.

World public opinion, meanwhile, was turning strongly in favour of Slovenia and Croatia in light of the ongoing JNA shelling of Vukovar and Dubrovnik, and pressure was growing for some kind of international intervention.[36] Vance brokered his first ceasefire in Croatia on 23 November (although it remained unsigned until 2 January 1992). The Security Council then expressed its willingness to send a UN peacekeeping force to Croatia, although it noted that appropriate conditions for its deployment had not yet been established.[37]

The Carrington process was finally killed off by Germany in mid-December when it insisted that the EC recognize Slovenia and Croatia in what it described as "preventive recognition."[38] Britain and the Netherlands were opposed but were not prepared to put Yugoslavian unity ahead of European unity, particularly so soon after the Maastricht Treaty had been signed.[39] The UN also opposed early recognition on the grounds that it would prejudge the outcome of future political negotiations,[40] but on 15 January 1992 the EC and many other countries – but not the United States – formally recognized the independence of Slovenia and Croatia.[41] Once again, the Europeans were treating the Yugoslav problem in a piecemeal fashion, ignoring the consequences of their actions on Bosnia-Herzegovina. At the same time, they had allowed political expediency to destroy the first experiment in developing a common European foreign policy.

The EC focus now shifted to Bosnia. An agreement was eventually reached in Lisbon that would preserve Bosnia's external borders while recognizing three national territorial units, each with the right to self-determination. Both the Bosnian Serbs and Bosnian Croats accepted the "Cutileiro Plan"[42] and, to many people's surprise, so did Bosnian president Alija Izetbegovic, who until that point had steadfastly rejected any division of Bosnia along ethnic lines. He rescinded that acceptance, however, after further reflection once he had returned to Sarajevo.

At this point, American and European policies came into collision, further pushing Bosnia towards war. The United States was under pressure from its Croatian lobby to join the Europeans and Canada in recognizing Croatia, but its policy remained to extend recognition simultaneously only to the four republics that had requested it.[43] It began pressing the EC to recognize Bosnia and Macedonia, even though the Europeans now felt that Bosnia was no longer capable of constituting a sovereign state. The US continued to push, however, resulting in Bosnia's recognition on 6 April 1992[44] (although Macedonia was not recognized, in deference to Greek intransigence[45]). This international recognition prompted the Bosnian Serbs to proclaim their own independent republic in Bosnia, thus marking the formal beginning of the Bosnian war.

The United Nations then began implementing a series of piecemeal measures that were often contradictory and sometimes unenforceable in response to various Security Council resolutions. Meanwhile, any pretense of a coordinated international policy to end the war in Bosnia now disappeared and would not reappear for more than three years. The UN started with the deployment of the United Nations Protection Force (UNPROFOR),[46] designed to keep the peace in Croatia but headquartered in Sarajevo, in the misguided hope that its mere presence in the city could forestall fighting.[47] Before the year was over, the Security Council had: decided to have UNPROFOR take control of Sarajevo airport "for humanitarian purposes";[48] threatened to use "other measures" to deliver humanitarian aid to Sarajevo;[49] approved the use of force if necessary to get humanitarian aid into Bosnia[50] (although the British defence minister quickly said this did not mean that the UN would "fight their way through"[51]); assigned UNPROFOR to escort humanitarian convoys;[52] imposed a "no-fly zone" over Bosnia[53] (but with no enforcement mechanism for the first six months[54]); and authorized a "preventive" deployment of UN troops to Macedonia.[55]

Enforcement of the "no-fly zone" was approved in March 1993[56] after a series of Bosnian-Serb attacks on the town of Srebrenica. When the attacks continued, Srebrenica was declared a UN "safe area,"[57] followed by five more locations (including Sarajevo)[58] against which UNPROFOR was mandated to deter attacks – through, if necessary, the use of air power.[59] The UN secretary general complained that the inherent contradictions between traditional peace-keeping and the newer concept of peace enforcement could undermine the viability of peace-keeping operations and endanger its personnel,[60] but the Security Council continued to support the safe areas concept, even though there was never any intention of providing the means to render them safe.[61]

While all of this was going on, the diplomatic rivalries and muddle continued. An attempt was made to bring them into some sort of coordination in August 1992 with the creation of the International Conference on the Former Yugoslavia (ICFY), with Cyrus Vance representing the UN and Lord Owen (who had replaced Lord Carrington) representing the EC. Owen had been an early advocate of using air power against the Bosnian Serbs[62] but quickly abandoned that position once he became an ICFY co-chair. In fact, Western countries were doing everything possible to avoid becoming combatants in Bosnia, often citing "ancient ethnic hatreds" or Balkan savagery as reasons to stay out of the conflict. Another common response was to point to ceasefire violations committed by all sides as evidence of the guilt of all the "warring parties"[63] or even to accuse each side of killing their own people to try to garner international support.[64]

The focus, therefore, remained exclusively on the diplomatic front. Although the ICFY had brought together the UN and EC efforts, the United States continued its own diplomatic initiatives, often contradicting those of the co-chairmen. This was highlighted by the Clinton administration's opposition to the Vance-Owen Peace Plan[65] in favour of its preferred option of "lift and strike."[66] Owen had publicly accused the US of lacking the moral authority to criticize the plan because the US refused to send ground troops to Bosnia.[67] This, and the Europeans' refusal to support "lift and strike" in May 1993, created deep rifts between the ICFY and the US and prompted Secretary of State Warren Christopher to say that he found nothing but "indifference, timidity, self-delusion and hypocrisy" amongst the Europeans.[68] He declared Bosnia "a European problem"[69] and launched a new American policy of "containment,"[70] whose overriding purpose was to avoid sending any US ground troops to Bosnia.[71]

[Another reason for the abrupt shift in American policy at this juncture has been attributed to the reading of *Balkan Ghosts*[72] by President Clinton, which convinced him that nothing could be done by outsiders to deal with long established ethnic hatred in the Balkans.[73] In a later speech, President Clinton expressed his regret at this "gross oversimplification and misreading of history."[74]]

Not surprisingly, all of this acrimony and division among Western countries made it impossible to put sufficient pressure on the Bosnian parties to reach a negotiated settlement. Meanwhile, the fighting on the ground continued and the atrocities mounted, including repeated attacks on the UN "safe areas." In November 1994, after the Serbs attacked the Bihac safe area, the United States once again pressed for NATO air strikes against Serbian strategic installations, but Britain and France said that this would put NATO and the United Nations in direct conflict and that, in such a situation, they would side with the UN. The United States then decided to back down, choosing the unity of NATO over the safety of the Bihac pocket.[75]

It was not until May 1995 that the international community finally took decisive action that eventually resulted in the Dayton Peace Agreement. Once again, however, it was enlightened self-interest that motivated Western action, not an over-arching concern for Bosnia's fate.

On 25 May 1995, NATO bombed Bosnian-Serb positions after the Serbs had again shelled Sarajevo and other "safe areas." The Serbs responded by taking 350 UN personnel hostage, forcing NATO to call off the air strikes. In June, while some of the hostages were still being held, NATO troop contributing countries began actively discussing their possible withdrawal from UNPROFOR. This would have triggered activation of a highly-classified NATO plan (Op-Plan 40–104), which, in part, envisaged 20,000 American troops helping to evacuate the UN forces. In theory, the US could still have refused to commit its forces to the operation, but had it done so, Washington believed that the extreme resentment caused amongst other NATO partners would most probably have destroyed NATO as an effective military alliance. President Clinton therefore decided that the US had to find a way to avoid a UN failure in Bosnia.[76]

By July, the Bosnian Serbs had overrun Srebrenica and massacred more than 7,000 people who had been sheltering there.[77] After Zepa also fell to the Serbs, NATO drew "a line in the sand" at the remaining eastern enclave of Gorazde and, significantly, decided that it alone would determine whether to use force, thereby removing the "dual key" that had been held by the UN and which the UN had been highly reluctant to use.[78]

Events moved rapidly after that. On 4 August, Zagreb launched "Operation Storm" to recover the remaining Serb-held territory in Croatia. The Croatian army joined forces with the Bosnian army to start recovering Serb-held land in Bosnia. NATO carried out a two-week campaign of air strikes against Bosnian-Serb positions, and US mediator Richard Holbrooke embarked on a "last-ditch, all-out"[79] negotiating effort that culminated on 14 December with the signing in Paris of the "Treaty of the Élysée,"[80] which, after more than three and a half years of fighting, finally ended the Bosnian war.

Even before the signing ceremony was over, however, the questions began. Why hadn't the world acted sooner to stop the war in Bosnia? More importantly, why hadn't the world done something to prevent the Yugoslav wars from beginning in the first place? The answers can be summed up in four words: distraction, disinterest, distortion, and disunity.

From 1987 to 1989, when the three principal ingredients of the Yugoslav inferno were being assembled, international attention was focused elsewhere, particularly on the impending collapse of communism throughout Eastern Europe. Yugoslavia was losing its geo-strategic importance to the West, and a higher priority was being placed on nurturing countries like Poland, Hungary, and Czechoslovakia towards democracy and a market economy.

In 1990, as events gathered momentum in Yugoslavia, the West continued its preoccupation with events elsewhere in Eastern Europe and the Soviet Union. In August 1990, the number-one priority became how to deal with the Iraqi invasion of Kuwait and preparations for the Gulf War.

In 1991, before fighting broke out in Yugoslavia, the international community continued to devote its attention to the Gulf War and its aftermath. By the time it finally realized how serious things had become in Yugoslavia, events had progressed so far that they could not possibly be reversed in time. This was particularly true of Slovenia's determination to declare its independence, the single most important event in triggering what followed. After the fighting started, the international community showed itself to be ill-informed about the root causes of the war, disunited in the remedies it was prescribing, unwilling to commit the necessary resources to applying those remedies it could agree on, and more interested in preserving its traditional alliance relationships than in taking strong military action to impose a solution on the parties.

The concerted international response in the second half of 1995 that finally did end the Bosnian war did not arise out of some belated sense of responsibility to its victims, but rather because the continuation and escalation of the war at that point posed too great a threat to the future of the North Atlantic alliance. In other words, a vital Western interest was now at risk, and that – not humanitarian concerns – is what compelled the West to put aside its differences and to match its military actions to its political objectives.

NOTES

* GRAHAM N. GREEN was Canadian ambassador to the Republic of Croatia from 1995 to 1997. He also dealt with issues relating to the former Yugoslavia in the Department of Foreign Affairs and International Trade from 1993 to 1994. He served at the Canadian Mission to the United Nations in New York from 1988 to 1992 and was one of Canada's representatives to the Security Council in 1989 and 1990.

1 Silber and Little 1995, 77.
2 Ibid., 47.
3 Woodward 1995, 152. See also Zimmerman 1996, 59.
4 Silber and Little 1995, 55.
5 Ibid., 77–82.
6 Ibid., 87.
7 Ibid., 84–6.
8 Zimmerman 1996, 62.
9 Ibid., 65; see also Glenny 1992, 177.
10 Woodward 1995, 148.
11 Zimmerman 1996, 84.
12 Silber and Little 1995, 107–11.

13 Ibid., 139.

14 Ibid., 146–50.

15 Ibid., 151.

16 Ibid., 154–6.

17 Ibid., 167–8.

18 Woodward 1995, 160.

19 Silber and Little 1995, 164.

20 Zimmerman 1996, 133–6.

21 The EC had decided on 23 June 1991 not to recognize any unilateral declarations of independence by either Slovenia or Croatia.

22 Silber and Little 1995, 175.

23 Jacques Poos (Luxembourg), Hans van den Broek (Netherlands), Gianni de Michelis (Italy).

24 Zimmerman 1996, 147.

25 Woodward 1995, 164–5.

26 Ibid., 175.

27 Silber and Little 1995, 180–2.

28 Woodward 1995, 174–5.

29 United Nations Security Council Resolution 713 (1991), 25 September 1991.

30 Zimmerman 1996, 155.

31 Silber and Little 1995, 209.

32 Woodward 1995, 180.

33 Yugoslavia hoped that the appointment of an American indicated that the UN was acting as a proxy of the United States (see ibid., 180), although there is no indication that this was the case. Nevertheless, by November 1991 it was clear that there were few if any takers for the Yugoslavia file within the State Department in Washington, as the whole issue had become a "tar baby" that nobody wanted to touch with a presidential-election year approaching. "It was seen as a loser" (Zimmerman 1996, 170–1).

34 On the day that Vance was appointed, the EC's Badinter Commission decided that Yugoslavia was "a state in the process of dissolution," which was both a step towards recognizing Slovenia and Croatia and an indication that the EC would not consider the remnants of Yugoslavia to be the successor state (Woodward 1995, 180).

35 Belgrade also anticipated the imminent international recognition of Slovenia and Croatia and wanted to avoid having the Security Council brand the JNA an "occupying force" in Croatia (Silber and Little 1995, 217).

36 NATO did, apparently, draw up contingency plans to stop the
    shelling of Dubrovnik, but there was no support for military inter-
    vention in 1991. Zimmerman believes that, had such action been
    taken, it might have sent a message to Belgrade about Western
    resolve, but instead it sent the completely opposite message
    (1996, 158).
37 United Nations Security Council Resolution 721 (1991), 27 Novem-
    ber 1991.
38 Woodward 1995, 183.
39 Silber and Little 1995, 219.
40 Woodward 1995, 188.
41 Both Bosnia-Herzegovina and Macedonia had also applied to the EC
    for recognition. The Badinter Commission decided that only
    Slovenia and Macedonia fully met the EC criteria, but Greece
    blocked Macedonia's recognition, and Germany insisted that Croatia
    be recognized (Ibid., 195).
42 Named after the Portuguese diplomat, José Cutileiro, who had
    presided over the negotiations.
43 Slovenia, Croatia, Bosnia-Herzegovina, Macedonia.
44 The United States delayed its recognition of Bosnia-Herzegovina
    until 7 April in order not to offend Serb sensitivities: 6 April was
    the anniversary of Hitler's bombing of Belgrade in 1941
    (Zimmerman 1996, 194).
45 Woodward 1995, 196–7.
46 United Nations Security Council Resolution 749 (1992), 7 April
    1992.
47 MacKenzie 1993, xvii.
48 United Nations Security Council Resolution 758 (1992), 8 June
    1992.
49 United Nations Security Council Resolution 761 (1992), 29 June
    1992.
50 United Nations Security Council Resolution 770 (1992), 13 August
    1992.
51 Malcolm Rifkind, quoted in Vulliamy 1994, 159.
52 United Nations Security Council Resolution 776 (1992), 14 Septem-
    ber 1992.
53 United Nations Security Council Resolution 781 (1992), 9 October
    1992.
54 United Nations Security Council Resolution 816 (1993), 31 March
    1993.

55 United Nations Security Council Resolution 795 (1992), 11 December 1992.
56 United Nations Security Council Resolution 816 (1993), March 1993.
57 United Nations Security Council Resolution 819 (1993), 16 April 1993.
58 United Nations Security Council Resolution 824 (1993), 6 May 1993.
59 United Nations Security Council Resolution 836 (1993), 4 June 1993.
60 See, for example, Report of the Secretary-General on the Work of the Organization, UN Document A/50/60; S/1995/1, 3 January 1995, para. 35.
61 "The term 'safe area' (like 'protection force') quickly became a cruel misnomer. The safe areas were among the most profoundly unsafe places in the world" (Silber and Little 1995, 303).
62 Owen 1995, 13–16.
63 Silber and Little 1995, 280.
64 One of the earliest and most widely reported quotes along these lines was attributed to Canadian major general Lewis MacKenzie, the first commander of UN forces in Sarajevo, who is reported to have said on 21 July 1992: "If I could convince both sides to stop killing their own people to impress CNN, perhaps we could have a ceasefire" (MacKenzie 1993, 308).
65 Owen 1995, chap. 3.
66 "Lift and strike" refers to lifting the UN-imposed arms embargo against Bosnia-Herzegovina and launching NATO air strikes as required against Bosnian-Serb forces attacking the Bosnian armed forces.
67 Owen 1995, 109.
68 Quoted in Vulliamy 1994, 284.
69 Quoted in Owen 1995, 168.
70 Silber and Little 1995, 319–20.
71 Owen 1995, 162.
72 Kaplan 1993.
73 Holbrooke 1998, 22.
74 "There are those who say Europe and its North American allies have no business intervening in the ethnic conflicts of the Balkans. They are the inevitable result, these conflicts, according to some, of centuries-old animosity which were unleashed by the end of the

Cold War restraints in Yugoslavia and elsewhere. I, myself, have
been guilty of saying that on an occasion or two, and I regret it now
more than I can say. For I have spent a great deal of time in these
last six years reading the real history of the Balkans. And the truth
is that a lot of what passes for common wisdom in this area is a
gross oversimplification and misreading of history." Speech by
President William Jefferson Clinton to the Veterans of Foreign Wars,
Eisenhower Hall, Ft. McNair, 13 May 1999 (as released by the
Office of the Press Secretary, the White House, Washington, DC).

75 Silber and Little 1995, 387.
76 Holbrooke 1998, 65–8.
77 Figures provided by the International Committee of the Red Cross,
quoted in ibid., 70.
78 Ibid., 71–2.
79 Ibid., 73–4.
80 The name given to the Dayton Peace Agreement by the French
Foreign Ministry "in a strange, almost touching footnote to its sense
of injured pride" (Ibid., 322).

Bosnia: Some Policy Dilemmas

DONALD W. SMITH

As I am a relative newcomer to the Balkans, the conference held at the University of Western Ontario was very much a learning experience for me. Much has been said about the complexity of the problems in the Balkans, and in fact there is a great deal to be learned before one can begin to appreciate some of the forces behind what is currently happening there. I am reminded of what an Irish friend used to say about the Irish "question": "If you think you are confused you are beginning to understand."

Nevertheless, my time with the Canadian Embassy in Zagreb – a small embassy of fairly recent establishment created, in large part, to serve Canada's interest in regional security – has afforded me some insight into the situation in the Balkans. Indeed, much of the embassy's political reporting is related in one way or another to security issues, including those affecting Bosnia.

In particular, I would like to address what I see as a policy dilemma for Western countries in using the military to enforce human rights norms. This dilemma has affected the recent involvement of Western countries in the Balkans, including Bosnia, but has been especially relevant to the development of events in Kosovo. The dilemma is that Western governments are compelled to take action to prevent or curb human-rights abuses, but situations sometimes arise in which the use of force is the only viable tool available to them. When this is the case, many of the same reasons that lead Western countries to support human rights severly constrain their ability to use military force promptly and effectively.

In the twentieth century some of the most important developments in international relations and international law have been in the area of human rights and humanitarian law, and it has been fairly common among Western countries to adopt the promotion of human rights as a foreign-policy objective. This has been paralleled by the development of human-rights rules in domestic legal systems. As a result, in Western democracies, there is a political imperative to take action against human-rights abuses, both at home and abroad. In the context of dealing with human-rights abuses this imperative to act is not necessarily a dilemma if the situation can be resolved through some form of negotiated settlement. It does, however, become a dilemma when a situation arises in which a solution can only be achieved through the use of military force.

The dilemma arises partly from a general ambivalence in Western countries over the use of the military (although I would exclude Germany from the core of this analysis because it is a very special case). In fifty years of hard work, traditional enemies in western Europe have overcome differences and operated together peacefully, both directly and within a number of international organizations. It is almost inconceivable, for instance, that there might now be armed conflict between Germany and France, whereas until the middle of the century, some form of armed conflict between them was a regular occurrence. The same could be said about almost any combination of western European countries. In North America we have not experienced modern warfare on our own territory. The trauma of the Vietnam War still haunts the body politic in the United States and affects American views on military engagement. We are also very reluctant to ask our own citizens in the military to kill or be killed. Western countries maintain strong military establishments but also an extreme reluctance to use military force it if is likely to cause civilian casualties.

Modern media coverage, particularly television, intensifies both sides of this dilemma. On the one hand, coverage of human-rights abuses increases the pressure on governments to act. On the other hand, the inevitable coverage of the consequences of military action increases their reluctance to consider its use. Also, Western governments, in dealing with military situations, are obliged to maintain transparency almost to the extent that they must maintain transparency in their purely civilian actions. This creates a challenge for military commanders in carrying out effective military operations.

I am not suggesting in any respect that we have lost the capacity to mount effective military actions or that we should be questioning the usefulness of militaries. But how far do political and other constraints permit us to go in using military action to achieve our human rights and humanitarian goals? I think the answer is "not very far, and it is a difficult process." This a serious handicap when we are dealing with somebody like President Milosevic in situations in which it is essential that we have military action or the credible threat of military action as one of our negotiating tools.

Here I should say something about the nature of negotiation because we often hear criticism of the NATO bombing of Yugoslavia on the grounds that diplomacy should have been given more of a chance to reach a solution. Diplomacy in many circumstances is simply another word for a process of negotiation. In most negotiations one side has something to offer, the other side has something to offer, and they make an exchange. In Bosnia there were a number of parties, and each had something that the others wanted. Although external duress provided a catalyst, they were able to reach a negotiated settlement on the basis of an exchange of tangible benefits. With Kosovo, the situation is somewhat different. NATO did not have much on the table in the way of tangible benefits that Yugoslavia wanted. Virtually the only thing that was on the table on our side during the negotiations was the threat of force. Milosevic knew from past experience that Western countries are reluctant to use force. He was also well aware of how cumbersome the international machinery is in organizing military action. He knew, because we told him, that ground forces were unlikely to be used. Demands, often heard in the debates in Western countries, that NATO have an "exit strategy" gave the impression that even if NATO moved in, it would pull out quickly. At some point before the bombing, Milosevic must have realized he had miscalculated, but I am sure that he believed for a long time he could call NATO's bluff and win without any form of military action being taken against him.

I would like to comment briefly on a second possible dilemma arising out of a potential conflict between our own values and objectives that has been brought to light by the recent indictments issued by the International Criminal Tribunal for the Former Yugoslavia against President Milosevic and four other senior Yugoslav officials. The dilemma will arise only if the necessity of dealing with Milosevic to reach some kind of settlement in Kosovo forces decision makers to consider diminishing their support for the Tribunal. There has been some comment that the Tribunal should have postponed the indictments because they will complicate or delay the resolution of the Kosovo situation. The Tribunal was set up as an independent body based on a model that resembles common law courts, in which prosecutors have considerable independence in deciding which cases will proceed. It was given a mandate intended to keep it free from the necessity of making political judgments in conducting its operations. For all proponents of the Tribunal there has been a danger from the beginning that, although they support it in principle, they might find themselves backing away from it for strategic reasons or when its activities are in conflict with their own vital national interests. In the Kosovo situation, the issuing of the indictments may indeed complicate the reaching of a resolution as Milosevic is obviously a key player. However, I think Chief Prosecutor Arbour was right when she said that is not a problem for the Tribunal itself to resolve or be concerned about. It is a political problem for governments to resolve without compromising the independence of the Tribunal. I do not think the issuance of the indictments at this delicate time will necessarily be harmful to the Tribunal, nor do I think it will seriously compromise the process of dealing with Milosevic. We will have to wait and see.

I would like to review briefly some context and constraints on governments that have been relevant in the Balkans. Neither the military engagement in Bosnia nor the NATO action in Yugoslavia is a discrete event, but part of a progression. You can choose your point in time to mark the beginning of the progression, but in modern times I would go back only to the death of Tito and the start of the disintegration of Yugoslavia, which then lead to the rise of Milosevic, the beginnings of the war in Slovenia, and the spread of war to Croatia, to Bosnia, and now to Kosovo. This, of course, is obvious, and it has been said before, but we often hear commentators speak as if the events in Kosovo and Bosnia were taking place in a vacuum. These events are treated as if they suddenly appeared on the international scene and as if they can be approached as though all conceivable options were open to decision makers in dealing with them. Unfortunately, decision makers have no such luxury. They are constrained not only by past developments, including the experiences of previous mistakes, but also by existing commitments in other areas. They approach these problems with a whole set of baggage from what has gone on before and from what is going on elsewhere, while at the same time trying to look to the future.

The disintegration of the former Yugoslavia and the resulting hostilities developed at the same time as other major international events were unfolding, including the breakup of the Soviet Union, the reunification of Germany, and the Gulf War. More generally, debates were taking place on who should be responsible for European security and on the role of NATO after the collapse of the Soviet Union. Bilateral alignments within Europe were shifting. The expansion of NATO was being debated and implemented. The more strategic effects of NATO military action in Yugoslavia on our relations with Russia and China had to be considered. The broader context made the decision-making process more complex and the decisions more difficult. It also explains to some extent why decisions were made that now, when the memory of the context has faded, may look like mistakes.

Moving more specifically to Bosnia, I do not agree, as we often hear, that the sole cause of the recent conflict was ancient hatreds and that it is impossible for Muslims, Serbs, and Croats to live together in some form of peace. My own impression is that there is no single cause for what happened, but a coincidence of conditions and events. There is no denying that hatreds, tensions, and grievances are part of the problem and that they have been deliberately perpetuated. Somewhat different, although related, is the existence of strong elements of nationalism that had been suppressed for significant periods of time and that still require some avenue for legitimate expression. With the breakup of the former Yugoslavia, an existing legal and social order disintegrated. Such a development, wherever it occurs, creates an unstable, unpredictable, and therefore dangerous situation. The final element that secured the progression toward tragedy was the emergence of leaders willing to exploit the breakdown of the existing order and to pursue conflict in order to further their own personal interests and the national aspirations of their own ethnic groups.

I do not believe it is impossible for the various groups in Bosnia-Herzegovina to live together peacefully. To what might be called historic animosities has been added the more serious problem of atrocities committed within living memory during and subsequent to World War II. Croatia and Bosnia are very personal places. People know one another and they know who did what. It will be very difficult for many people to forgive. It will be impossible for them to forget. However, given a period of stability, some outlet for legitimate expression of nationalism, and the absence of leaders inciting them to violence and destruction, it is possible that the various groups will be able to live together. Perhaps they will not like each other very much, but they can still guide their conduct in a way that will produce political stability again and be economically and socially productive.

To succeed in any conflict, we must know the psychology and values of opponents. But we must also be clear as to our own values and how they affect the options open to us. One of the objectives of Canadian foreign policy is to promote Canadian values abroad. The activities pursued by the Milosevic government through Croatia, Bosnia, and Kosovo are simply incompatible with Canadian values. The Canadian values that dictate that we take action in response to human-rights abuses are going to remain. The Canadian values that limit our ability to use military force effectively to enforce human rights norms will remain as well, and, to the extent that we encounter situations when military action is essential to achieving our goals, this will be a dilemma. I do not share the pessimism of many about the NATO air campaign. I think it will succeed, but like many others, I cannot say how or when.

Finally, I would like to say a brief word about the argument sometimes heard that the international community has failed to act against human-rights violations in other areas and therefore should not be acting in Kosovo. I believe our view of human rights and our human-rights objectives must be the same everywhere throughout the world. Unfortunately, there are constraints on governments. We cannot be everywhere and do everything. Decisions have to be made as to where our resources can best be deployed to achieve results.

There are sound reasons for Canada's engagement in the Balkans, but we must look to the future and plan what will happen after the war is over. The military action in Kosovo is simply a stepping stone to get us to a "diplomatic" settlement, and there will be one. If there is to be lasting peace and stability, there must be no attempt to ascribe collective guilt. We cannot condemn one particular group of people for the crimes of their leaders. We must also be prepared to accept that significant resources will have to be allocated to the Balkans for a considerable period of time if our policy decisions are to be implemented.

Peacekeeping with No Peace to Keep: The Failure of Canadian Foreign Policy in Bosnia

NADER HASHEMI

It's ... important to know that we are doing good things [in Bosnia].

Barbara McDougall

On 11 November 1993, a Serbian artillery shell landed outside of a school in the Alipasino polje district of Sarajevo. It was a typically indiscriminate attack against the civilian population with typically devastating results: nine children and one teacher were killed instantly by flying shrapnel. "We were writing when we heard something fired somewhere. Suddenly I heard screaming and noise," recalled Mirza Huskic, one of the wounded children. The Bosnian government reacted by calling on the United Nations Security Council to either help end the siege of Sarajevo – now into its second year – or lift the arms embargo so that the Bosnians could attempt to do it themselves.[1] Both requests were denied, and the daily siege and bombardment of Sarajevo continued. It dominated the news in November 1993 as the international community grappled with one of the most pressing and difficult crises in the post-Cold War era. Coincidentally, at this time, Jean Chrétien was meeting with US president Bill Clinton in Seattle. Both were in town attending the Asia-Pacific Economic Council Summit. While the subject that brought them together was global economic relations, during the course of their conversation Clinton asked his Canadian counterpart for advice on how to deal with the slaughter in Bosnia. "That's a very tough one. I don't know," replied Chrétien. After a few moments of embarrassed silence the president moved onto the topic of Haiti. This vignette, while a mere passing moment in the 1990s, perfectly captures the failure of Canadian foreign policy in Bosnia.[2]

The thesis of this essay is that Canadian foreign policy toward the break up of Yugoslavia was structurally flawed. This most clearly manifested itself in Canada's reaction to the war in Bosnia-Herzegovina. Rather than pursuing a just resolution of the conflict based on professed Canadian support for human rights and international law, the policies that Ottawa adopted contributed to the dismemberment of a multi-ethnic society, rewarded aggression, and prolonged the war in the Balkans. The variable that best explains Canada's behaviour is its over dependence on United Nations peacekeeping as the main vehicle for expressing its foreign policy. Notwithstanding Canada's stellar record in this domain, UN peacekeeping – in particular the mantra of impartiality that is its central component – was an inadequate response to events in Bosnia. Though Canada was not a main player in influencing either events on the ground or the international community's response to these events, Canada did play a significant role in Bosnia that in retrospect can be characterized as counterproductive at best, pernicious at worst.

The period under examination extends from 8 April 1992 to 15 December 1995. This approximately coincides with the time between Canada formally recognizing the Republic of Bosnia-Herzegovina and diplomatic relations being established between the two states. The intention of this essay is to scrutinize the policies of the Mulroney and Chrétien governments on the war in Bosnia against the backdrop of the doctrine of UN peacekeeping.

The main point of departure for this study is that "what [has taken] place in Bosnia-Herzegovina was attempted genocide – the extermination of people in whole or in part because of their race, religion or ethnicity." This quote from Human Rights Watch accurately characterizes what took place.[3] Virtually every human rights organization that investigated – Physicians for Human Rights, Médicins sans Frontières, the UN Commission on Human Rights, the American Jewish Congress, the Anti-Defamation League, the International League for Human Rights, etc. – reached the same conclusion about the nature of the war in Bosnia.[4]

Genocide, it should be emphasized, is the worst crime known to humankind. Internationally, among the bodies authorized to make a legal determination that the crime of genocide has occurred are the UN Security Council's Commission of Experts, the International Court of Justice, and the International Criminal Tribunal for the former Yugoslavia (ICTY). After examining mountains of evidence, all three international bodies reached the same conclusion: Serbian political and military leaders perpetrated a systematic campaign of genocide against one of Europe's last remaining minority populations, the Bosnian Muslims.

Despite this critical determination, Canada refused to treat the Bosnia war as a case of genocide. It is impossible to locate any Canadian government document that contains the word "genocide" and "Bosnia" in the same sentence. This applies not only to government discussion, but also to mainstream scholarship in Canadian academia. A lead article in *Canadian Foreign Policy* by two professors of political science at Simon Fraser University is a case in point.[5]

Instead, in formulating Canadian policy, political leaders preferred to characterize the conflict in Bosnia exclusively as a "civil war" of "ancient ethnic hatreds" in which moral parity existed between the protagonists. The view of Canada's most famous soldier, Major General Lewis MacKenzie, epitomized this perspective. "Dealing with Bosnia," he affirmed, "is a little bit like dealing with three serial killers. One has killed 15, one has killed 10, one has killed 5. Do we help the one that has only killed 5?"[6]

CANADA'S RESPONSE TO THE BREAK-UP OF YUGOSLAVIA

It should be re-emphasized that Canada was not a major player in determining the international community's response to the collapse of Yugoslavia and the subsequent genocide in Bosnia-Herzegovina. From the outset, when the Serbian-dominated Yugoslav National Army (JNA) attacked Slovenia in the summer of 1991, it was the United Nations Security Council, led by Britain and France, that played the leading role, followed by a disinterested United States and, far behind it, the Russian Federation. As a middle power, Canada, as with most international crises, was reactive to events in the region. On the rhetorical level, however, Ottawa was a leading voice for intervention.[7]

Prime Minister Brian Mulroney, in a speech given in September 1991 at Stanford University, was one of the first world leaders to call for international action in response to the break-up of Yugoslavia. During his convocation address he lamented that

Some Security Council members have opposed intervention in Yugoslavia, where many innocent people have been dying, on the grounds of national sovereignty. Quite frankly such invocations of the principle of national sovereignty are as out of date and offensive to me as the police declining to stop family violence simply because a man's home is supposed to be his castle.[8]

Around the same time, the secretary of state for External Affairs, Barbara McDougall, speaking before the United Nations General Assembly, affirmed that the "concept of sovereignty must respect higher principles including the need to preserve human life from wanton destruction." Urging international action in Yugoslavia, she added that "[s]hould it be decided that a United Nations peace-keeping operation would contribute to such a solution, I want to assure you that Canada will do its part."[9]

As a result of the Serb-Croat cease-fire brokered by United Nations representative Cyrus Vance on 3 January 1992, Canada eagerly contributed 1,200 of the 13,000 personnel that constituted the United Nations Protection Force (UNPROFOR) in what was now the independent Republic of Croatia. Following the lead of the European Community and Australia, Canada recognized Slovenia and Croatia as independent states on 15 January 1992, arguing that the "Yugoslav Federation as we have known it no longer exists and cannot be reconstituted by force." Ottawa disbursed $1 million in humanitarian aid to Croatia, Slovenia, and Yugoslavia, and six Canadian officers joined the UN Liaison Mission to the region in preparation for the dispatch of UNPROFOR.[10] This is how things stood on the eve of the Bosnian genocide.

In Belgrade, Slobodan Milosevic and his aide Borislav Jovic, anticipating international recognition of Bosnia, devised a scheme to withdraw all JNA soldiers who were not Bosnian Serbs and replace them with Bosnian Serbs who had been stationed in Serbia. This gave the radical Serbian nationalists a 90,000-strong fighting force, backed by some of the best weaponry in the JNA arsenal, which they unleashed with full fury on the nascent Republic of Bosnia-Herzegovina in early April 1992.[11] Before the fighting in Bosnia began, the roots of the turmoil in the Balkans, as Ottawa understood it, had already been enunciated. It is important to highlight the fact that the mass killings in Bosnia in no way informed Ottawa's position. The Government of Canada's official explanation for the break-up of Yugoslavia and the subsequent genocide in Bosnia was to go unchallenged by nearly everyone in Canada who commented on the Balkans. Given its centrality in determining Canadian attitudes in general and Canadian policy toward Bosnia in particular, it merits careful scrutiny.

"ANCIENT ETHNIC HATREDS" AND THE "DOCTRINE OF MORAL EQUIVALENCE"

Like the rest of the world, the war in the Balkans came as a surprise to most Canadians. Sarajevo, site of the 1984 Winter Olympic Games, was perhaps the only identification people had with the region, and those who remembered their high-school history would recall that Bosnia was where Archduke Franz Ferdinand, heir to the Hapsburg throne, was assassinated by Gravilo Princip, thus triggering the First World War. Unfamiliarity with the history and politics of the region was best exemplified by former American president Jimmy Carter, who travelled to Bosnia to broker a cease-fire in December 1994. Confusing names and places, he allowed himself to be used by the Bosnian Serbs in a much-needed propaganda exercise following their assault on the safe area of Bihac the month before. With Ratko Mladic and Radovan Karadzic standing by his side, Carter announced before the international media that this was "one of the rare chances to let the world know the truth … I cannot dispute your statement that the American public has had primarily one side of the story."[12]

The Canadian government lauded the Carter peace mission to Bosnia. Ottawa also internalized Jimmy Carter's model for understanding the politics and history of the region. In short, like Carter, Canada held that this was a war of "ancient ethnic hatreds." An unstated proposition of this paradigm is that it was exclusively a "civil war" with "deep historical roots" that defy human comprehension. In the subtext of all the commentary that took place in Canada about the Balkans, there were unambiguous overtones that this was in essence a dispute between peoples with equally unpronounceable names, in an obscure corner of Europe, who had "been fighting for centuries," in the words of then opposition leader Lucien Bouchard.[13]

Major General Lewis MacKenzie's extensive commentary in the media helped solidify this view in the minds of Canadians. Responding to a reporter's question, "Who fired the first shot [in Bosnia]?" MacKenzie replied, "some son of a bitch 400 years ago."[14] In short, Bosnia was viewed by Canadian politicians as another Somalia, where Alija Izetbegovic was an Ali Mahdi, Radovan Karadzic another Farah Aideed, and Canadian troops were caught in the middle. No issue of principle was considered at stake. The Genocide Convention, the UN Charter, the Security Council resolutions, and international humanitarian law were all deemed irrelevant. Ottawa's unstated policy was that the Bosnian war, like a forest fire burning out of control, simply had to burn itself out. In light of these deep-seated animosities, "there is nothing you or I can do in the Balkans to make it what it isn't," lamented Canadian defense minister Kim Campbell.[15]

In one of the first public statements on the war in Yugoslavia, the Government of Canada revealed that it had internalized this essentialist view of the region as the primary cause of conflict. Speaking in an emergency debate in the House of Commons on the situation in Yugoslavia, External Affairs Minister Barbara McDougall enunciated Canadian policy: "I would like to have a formula that would convince the parties to drop their weapons and negotiate a fair and lasting settlement," she stated. "*But the politics and emotions of this region defy any such straightforward solution.*" Elaborating further, she asked the members of parliament to

[C]onsider, for a moment, the *complex ethnic interrelationships in this region*: Serbs make up 66 per cent of the people in Serbia, but in one part of its territory – the province of Kosovo – 90 per cent are Albanian. In Croatia, 75 per cent of the people are Croatian, but fully 12 per cent are Serbian. The *ethnic mix is even more complex* in Bosnia-Herzegovina, where 44 per cent of the people are Slavic Muslims, 31 per cent are Serbs and 17 per cent are Croats. Establishing peace and stability in a region of such *entrenched ethnic tension* is not easy. But I want to assure the House and the people of Canada that we have not backed away (emphasis added).[16]

The Canadian government's position, therefore, was that the fundamental cause of war in Yugoslavia lay in the ethnic composition of the region, not in the policies of Slobodan Milosevic. The political leaders of the Yugoslav republics and their respective ideologies were *not* causal factors in the war. In other words, from a Canadian perspective, the pursuit of political power was irrelevant; culture, ethnicity, and biology mattered more.

In attempting to understand human conflict, one cannot avoid looking at the human agents of decision making. The crucial questions that must be asked are these: why does the conflict assume the shape and proportion it does at a particular point in time? Is the conflict due to "ancient ethnic hatreds" and thus irrational, or can the conditions that have produced a series of events be identified? The obvious place to look for these conditions is in the decisions made by the political actors involved in the conflict. In other words, who ordered the attacks? Who formulated the policy of ethnic cleansing? Who orchestrated the siege of Sarajevo? Is there a clear chain of command and control? Is a pattern detectable, etc.? None of these important questions were asked by Canadian political leaders.

The theory of "ancient ethnic hatreds" is linked to what the historian Noel Malcolm has termed the "doctrine of moral equivalence."[17] All sides in Bosnia shared the same moral guilt, and as Canadian officials repeatedly stated, there were no white hats in the war. If the Serbs had killed more, the doctrine states, it was only because the Bosnians had not had the opportunity to do the same. In Ottawa's conception of the conflict, "the Serbs were expressing ancient Serb hatred, the Muslims ancient Muslim hatred, etc., and one bundle of hatred can be no better and no worse than another."[18] All were warring factions, or to quote one of Canada's leading historians, "Serbs, Croats and Bosnian Muslims vie[d] to see who [could] commit the most appalling atrocities."[19] An unfortunate detail that had to be ignored was the fact that one of the "warring factions" was the democratically elected and internationally recognized government of Bosnia, made up of Serbs, Croats, Muslims, and Jews, and that this government was struggling to preserve a multi-ethnic and secular state. As Malcolm perceptively observes:

[T]he reduction of the Bosnian war to an upswelling of "ancient ethnic hatreds" did not only lower the status of the elected government of that country, [but also had the negative affect of raising] the status of the rebel Serb leadership, who now tended to be regarded not as a gang of ambitious local politicians egged on from Belgrade, but as representative figures, through whom the deep, historic forces of ancient Serb hatred found their natural outlet.[20]

Canadian policy was premised on the belief that rational intervention to halt the war in Bosnia was impossible. The rules of
civilization counted for little and could not be applied in this
instance. The hatred allegedly ran too deep.

There is no evidence of any inquiry undertaken by the Government of Canada into the war aims of the parties. They were *pre-
sumed* to be identical despite the evidence to the contrary. In the
transcripts of the House of Commons Foreign Affairs Committee
hearings from 1991–95, not one question or comment is related
to the political objectives of Radovan Karadzic or Slobodan
Milosevic and how they compared or contrasted with those of the
Bosnian government. Canadian government officials and foreign-
affairs analysts completely overlooked the pattern of political
intrigue that led to the rise of Slobodan Milosevic, from his calcu-
lated takeover of Vojvodina and Montenegro, his removal of
Kosovar autonomy in 1989, and his mobilization of Serbian nationalist sentiment, to the constitutional coup against the federal presidency, the Serbian economic blockade against Slovenia and
Croatia in 1990, and the incitement and arming of Serbian paramilitary units in Croatia and Bosnia.[21]

When forced to comment on Bosnia, government officials and
members of the opposition would simplistically state that "all sides"
were guilty. There was unanimity across the Canadian political
spectrum on this point. From the beginning, it was axiomatic to
posit moral parity between victim and victimizer. The documentation compiled by governments, the United Nations' own special
rappoteur for human rights for the former Yugoslavia, and many
non-governmental organizations was ignored. All of this documentation was in agreement that the atrocities committed by the Bosnian
Serbs and their Belgrade benefactors were quantitatively and qual-
itatively different from those of the other parties. Nonetheless,
Canada's position remained unshakeable.

THE MULRONEY GOVERNMENT: ESTABLISHING THE BASIC CONTOURS OF CANADIAN POLICY

There was noticeable concern about events in Bosnia as evidenced
by public statements made by senior ministers in the Mulroney
cabinet. In contrast to the succeeding Liberal government, Brian

Mulroney used forceful language and demonstrated a distinct interest in speaking to the issue whenever the opportunity arose. In July 1992, in a speech before the Conference on Security and Cooperation in Europe (CSCE), his External Affairs minister, Barbara McDougall, compared international inaction in Bosnia with that of the world's reaction to the Nazi Holocaust. She was to use the aggressive behaviour of Nazi Germany as an analogy to events in the region on other occasions as well.[22]

Following Brian Mulroney's widely cited policy speech at Stanford University, he was quoted on several occasions making robust statements as the war spread to the Republic of Bosnia-Herzegovina. "What is going on in Yugoslavia is unspeakable and unacceptable," reported the *Globe and Mail*. The Mulroney government was also known to be pressing the Security Council "to get off the dime," as the prime minister put it, and intervene with force to stop the bloodshed.[23] In a December 1992 speech at the John F. Kennedy School of Government at Harvard University, Mulroney went as far as calling for a Gulf War type of operation to end the conflict in Bosnia. During the question and answer session he stated: "[w]e must take the action we have taken elsewhere because it's the only thing that works."[24] He went on to say that "Canada would strongly support an initiative designed by the United Nations and only under the aegis of the Security Council that would be designed to not keep the peace in Bosnia, because we know that can't be done, but to make the peace."[25]

Brian Mulroney's relatively strong opinions on the war in Bosnia had a personal dimension and arguably for this reason were not reflected in government policy. Jeff Sallot, parliamentary bureau chief for the *Globe and Mail*, in a feature article on Canada's Balkan policy, observed that "Mr. Mulroney is on familiar ground" in commenting on Bosnia. "His wife, Mila, was born in Sarajevo," and he "has spent many long hours discussing the country with his in-laws." The Mulroneys honeymooned in Yugoslavia and "[f]riends say Mr. Mulroney was shocked by the TV footage of the shelling of Dubrovnik, the romantic Adriatic port city where he and Mrs. Mulroney went on their honeymoon."[26] Notwithstanding these facts there is no evidence to support the claim that Mila Mulroney influenced Canada's Bosnia Policy.

Arguably, the Reagan and Bush world-view ideologically influenced Mulroney, who cultivated close relationships with both men.

He was a strong supporter of Operation Desert Storm and was one of the few Western leaders who endorsed the American bombing of Libya in 1986. Margaret Thatcher's strong opinions on Bosnia arguably influenced Mulroney as well. When it came to the implementation of policy, however, Canada took a back seat to the Europeans and the Americans. This was clearly evident a week after Mulroney's forceful words at Harvard University, when he was visited by two European leaders.

In December 1992, British prime minister John Major and European Community president Jacques Delors travelled to Ottawa. The rapidly deteriorating situation in Bosnia, augmented by the onset of winter, naturally placed it high on the agenda. The following day, headlines in the Canadian press read, "PM softens stance."[27] It was clear there was a conflict of views with John Major, one of the architects of UN Security Council policy towards Bosnia. The press reported that after their meeting, Mulroney "[had] toned down his tough talk on military action in Bosnia." This about face was "in sharp contrast to Mulroney's sabre-rattling last week [at Harvard] when he said the time [had] come for peacekeepers in Bosnia to become peacemakers."[28]

Canada's posture on Bosnia, both under the Conservative government of Brian Mulroney and Jean Chrétien's Liberals, was to mirror that of Britain and France. On all of the key issues – air strikes, lifting of the arms embargo, and UN versus NATO control over military policy – Canada aligned itself with the Europeans instead of the Americans. In May 1993, the Canadian government made several important statements pertaining to its Bosnia policy. This established the core framework for Canadian policy until the signing of the Dayton Accords in December 1995.

In a major interview on 13 May 1993 on CBC television, External Affairs Minister Barbara McDougall spoke specifically about Canada's concerns and its policies in Bosnia-Herzegovina. "It's a choice," she said, "between doing what we're doing, which the Europeans and ourselves think has some real value, and perhaps the military action that the United States is proposing." What concerned her most was "a split in the transatlantic alliance," as she stressed in her interview. In regards to specific policy positions, McDougall stated that "nothing was ruled out, except ... lifting the arms embargo for the Muslims."[29] In fact, Canada's position on the arms embargo was second only to the positions taken by Britain and France in terms of its rigidity. The internationally recognized Bosnian state was not recognized as having the right to defend itself against what McDougall herself at one point called "savage aggression."[30] On this point, Canada would not budge. In fact, whenever the subject was raised, Canadian officials would dismiss the suggestion with emotive words rarely used in denouncing Serbian war crimes. "The level-playing field argument is insane," exclaimed McDougall several months earlier. "It is madness," she added,[31] convinced that lifting the arms embargo would prolong the war and increase atrocities.

In short, Canada adopted a minimalist approach to the war in Bosnia. It refused to make human rights the centrepiece of its foreign policy – let alone genocide – and had no known position on the inviolability of the borders of a UN member state. Nor did it have a position on state-sponsored aggression. By insisting that the UN Security Council take the lead in determining policy, Canada was in effect siding with the Europeans against the Americans. The tough talk on Bosnia was not heard again from Mr Mulroney as he prepared to step down as party leader in anticipation of a federal election. Instead, he adopted the perspective of his British and French counterparts, who, as the situation in Bosnia deteriorated, attempted to deflect public criticism away from their failed policy and onto the victims. In one of his last public statements on the region, Mulroney directed angry words at the "architects of this tragedy, all of whom are in Bosnia-Herzegovina itself" and are "100 per cent to blame" for the bloodshed.[32] The absence of any reference to Slobodan Milosevic in influencing the conflict in Bosnia is significant to point out here. In October 1993, the Liberal government of Jean Chrétien came to office, and Canadian policy shifted from bad to worse.

JEAN CHRÉTIEN AND THE LIBERALS:
NAPPING IN THE MIDST OF GENOCIDE

In their introduction to the annual publication put out by Carleton University's Norman Paterson School of International Affairs, *Canada Among Nations,* Fen Hampson and Maureen Molot observe that Canadian "foreign policy is one area where there has been a surprising degree of national consensus over the last fifty years." This is particularly true in the area of peacekeeping, which is not only fundamental to Canada's external relations, but also an integral part of Canada's national identity. In this domain, Hampson and Molot add, "there are no national divisions."[33]

Jean Chrétien's Liberals uncritically accepted all of the positions on Bosnia adopted by the previous Conservative government. In actuality, there were no significant policy differences between the two governments. What separated the Liberal and Conservative approaches to events in the region was that the Liberals were noticeably more uncomfortable with the issue as a whole. Like their posture toward Quebec nationalism, they secretly wished it would simply go away. Speaking to reporters near the end of the Bosnian war, Chrétien publicly admitted that he had always been apprehensive about Canada's role in the former Yugoslavia. "Since I became Prime Minister I've never been completely comfortable with our position in Bosnia," he said.[34] "We're there to maintain peace. We're not there to make peace, and sometimes there is no peace to keep. It's an extremely difficult role to play."[35]

The lack of interest in Bosnia on the part of the new Canadian government was evident in cutbacks in the amount of aid it sent to the region. Following the February 1994 partial cease-fire around Sarajevo, the United Nations spearheaded an effort to restore basic utilities to the city. Canada was "the only G7 country to give us nothing," remarked a senior UN official involved in the project. In commenting on this development, the *Globe and Mail* reported that this "underscores a significant, albeit unannounced, policy shift by the Liberal government of Jean Chrétien. While the former Conservative government was front and centre every time the UN sought assistance in the former Yugoslavia, the Chrétien government has been content to slip into the background."[36]

Two embarrassing episodes demonstrated the new Canadian government's disinterest in dealing with Bosnia and in a larger sense epitomized Ottawa's indifference towards the region. In his international debut as Canada's new prime minister, Jean Chrétien travelled to Brussels for a NATO meeting in January 1994. The following day, the subtitle on the front page of the *Ottawa Citizen* read: "Caught Napping." Juliet O'Neill reported that, "While British officials were briefing the press on proposals to bomb the Serbs, the small Chrétien party had gone to bed for the night ... Canadian policymakers had literally been caught napping while France and Britain were cooking up their wee-hour plan that would have American planes drop a few bombs near Srebrenica."[37] She added that Chrétien's insistence on travelling light, without experts and a large team of foreign-affairs advisors, "had led to near diplomatic disaster."[38]

A similar incident occurred later in the same year. The first Canadian diplomat to visit Sarajevo since the war began was sent to attend a UN meeting on reconstruction efforts for the besieged Bosnian capital. As reported in the *Globe and Mail*, "during the meeting, according to officials from the [UN's] special co-ordinator's office, the [Canadian] diplomat nodded off."[39] The symbolism behind these incidents of napping in the midst of an international crisis is hard to miss.

As the Serbian nationalist siege of Bosnia intensified, the issue of air strikes was placed on the international agenda. Canada was to distinguish itself in this area as well.

CANADA AND NATO AIR STRIKES IN BOSNIA

At approximately 12:37 P.M. on Saturday, 5 February 1994, a Serbian mortar fell on the main market square in Sarajevo instantly killing sixty-nine people and wounding over 200 more. This was to be one of the worst war-time atrocities in the Bosnian capital. President Izetbegovic called an immediate news conference and said it was a "black and terrible day. We Bosnians feel condemned to death. Every government which supports the arms embargo against this country is an accomplice to acts of atrocity such as this."[40] The international community was forced to react. At a NATO meeting a rare consensus began to emerge calling for the bombing of Serbian artillery positions around Sarajevo if they did not withdraw their heavy weapons from the surrounding hills. The US, France, and Britain were all in favour of the proposal to use air strikes to halt the bombardment of Sarajevo. *Canada* was the lone dissenter.

"In Ottawa, Defense Minister David Collenette emphasized that NATO air raids on Serb ground forces in Bosnia remain unacceptable," the *Ottawa Citizen* reported. "Our first priority is the safety of our troops," explained Collenette.[41] As for the civilian population trapped inside Sarajevo, subjected to daily bombardment and starvation in what was to become the longest siege of a city in modern European history, Canada had no position. In fact, the only known statement by a Canadian official on the subject was made by the Canadian UN spokesperson in Sarajevo, Barry Frewer. The previous summer to everyone's amazement, echoing Radovan Karadzic, he declared before the world media that Sarajevo was no longer under siege. Serb forces were in a "tactically advantageous position ... but I [wouldn't] call it a siege," he affirmed.[42] Within hours the Bosnian government declared him persona non grata.

This was the second time in a month that "Canada's new Liberal government ... [had] blocked a British-French-US plan to deliver a similar ultimatum backed by the threat of air strikes."[43] The first was in August of 1993, when "Canada, apparently alone, objected strongly to the United States proposal" to bomb Serbian forces in Bosnia, the *New York Times* reported.[44] After two phone calls from President Clinton to Mr Chrétien, "Canada, under intense pressure from its closest allies, agreed reluctantly" to join the NATO consensus.[45] After bowing to international coercion and doing everything it could to soften the language of the NATO communiqué, Chrétien was anxious to proclaim that "the Serbs have agreed to accept the UN ultimatum in Sarajevo ... There will be no need to have air strikes."[46] It should be pointed out that Canada's vociferous and steadfast opposition to air strikes was not backed by alternative proposals on how to deal with Serbian ethnic cleansing in Bosnia. There were only vague references from Ottawa that negotiations, not war, were the only road to peace.

UN PEACEKEEPING AND THE NEUTRALITY DILEMMA IN BOSNIA

There are two types of United Nations mandates that involve the deployment of military forces. They are distinguished from each other by adjacent chapters in the United Nations Charter: Chapter VI, "peacekeeping" missions, and Chapter VII, "peacemaking" missions. Chapter VI of the UN Charter allows the Security Council to assist parties in reaching a peaceful settlement of a dispute based on their mutual consent. Most of the previous UN missions have fallen under this category and are known as "classical" peacekeeping operations. Typically, following the establishment of a cease-fire, UN forces will interpose themselves between the parties, monitoring and maintaining the separation of forces until political negotiations can foster a settlement. Chapter VII of the UN Charter, on the other hand, relates to acts of aggression and threats to international peace and security and allows the Security Council to authorize member states to take appropriate military action by air, land, and sea. Chapter VII initiatives do not require the consent of the parties and permit the affirmative use of force to realize the objectives of the mandate.[47]

There has been some debate as to whether the UN mandate in the former Yugoslavia was legally a Chapter VI or Chapter VII mandate. In considering nearly 100 resolutions passed by the Security Council since 1991, Paul Williams and Michael Scharf write that it was "clearly a Chapter VII [peacemaking] mandate" that permitted "the affirmative use of force to promote the delivery of humanitarian aid and the prevention of ethnic cleansing." They note that "the fact that the Security Council has specifically invoked the use of force provisions of Chapter VII is particularly important, as in all other 'peacekeeping' mandates prior to 1990, the UN had not chosen to base the UN mandate on any particular Charter provisions, let alone Chapter VII."[48] The problem with the UN mission in Bosnia was that for *raisons d'etat*, mainly British and French, it was interpreted by the UN Secretariat and the Department of Peacekeeping Operations as exclusively a Chapter VI classical peacekeeping mandate. As noted above, such a mandate requires the consent of the parties to the dispute, which in the context of the Bosnian war meant Serbian consent.

For the entire course of its precarious 3½-year existence, those who ran the UNPROFOR mission in Bosnia would not budge from their insistence that their mandate was consent-based and absolutely prohibited the use of force. A central axiom of a Chapter VI peacekeeping mandate is that UN forces must not take sides in the dispute and must remain neutral at all costs. Canadian military historian Sean Maloney notes that "impartiality ... must be demonstrated by PK [peacekeeping] forces at all times and in all situations – operational, administrative and social. No belligerent point of view can be favoured. To do so puts the mission in jeopardy."[49] In Bosnia, the UNPROFOR mission was dedicated solely to treating the symptoms of the war, not its causes. This translated into protecting humanitarian activities based on the approval of the parties. In order to comprehend where the mission went wrong and how it became part of the problem instead of a solution, it is necessary to draw upon David Rieff's important study of the United Nations operation in Bosnia, particularly with reference to his widely acclaimed book, *Slaughterhouse: Bosnia and the Failure of the West.*

David Rieff spent two and a half years riding humanitarian convoys in Bosnia and observing firsthand the activities of the Office of the United Nations High Commissioner for Refugees (UNHCR) and UNPROFOR. He also spent considerable time at the United Nations head office in New York speaking extensively with members of its bureaucracy, particularly those in charge of the mission in the former Yugoslavia. His biggest contribution to our understanding of events in the region is his systematic and exhaustive analysis of the ethos of UN peacekeeping in the post-Cold War era, particularly in the context of genocide.

As the atrocities and ethnic cleansing escalated in Bosnia, the UN's position remained the same. We are here "to protect humanitarian activities during wartime," Marrack Goulding, former head of the Department of Peacekeeping Operations stated,[50] or in the words of Michael Rose, the head of UN forces in Bosnia, "we are not here to protect anything other than ourselves and our convoys."[51] All the United Nations could do was alleviate the consequences of the war, not deal with its root causes, because, as UN officials constantly repeated, this was the mandate that the Security Council had given them. "If all the United Nations intended to do was to bring in food and medicine, didn't this just amount to keeping people alive longer so the Serbs would have more chances to kill them?" Rieff wondered as he attempted to understand the UN's behaviour in Bosnia. "Wasn't it incongruous that UN soldiers ... lost their lives to bring in food to isolated areas, but steadfastly refused to silence the guns that were causing the emergency? It seemed unimaginable that the United Nations would be content to go on this way indefinitely."[52] Yet it did, for three and a half years.

One of the biggest criticisms levelled at UNPROFOR was its insistence on remaining neutral in the war. This mantra of impartiality, which underpinned everything the UN did in the region, while suitable for peacekeeping operations in which there was a durable cease-fire, was meaningless in the context of an ongoing war, particularly when one side was committing genocide. Rieff observes that holding fast to the belief that one had to be impartial between war criminals and their victims "[a]t times ... could be positively grotesque, as when Yasushi Akashi, the Secretary General's Special

Envoy, left a meeting in Pale and declared to the press that he believed Radovan Karadzic to be 'a man of peace,' boasting of the 'friendship' that had developed between them."[53]

One peacekeeping official, in an attempt to justify the UN's posture, told Rieff that "You can't denounce people you need to do business with." UN officials in Bosnia, in order to carry out their mission, needed to be trusted by the parties, and that effectively meant the jettisoning of human rights. The "mandate" didn't allow it. The UN's main priority was getting convoys past Serbian checkpoints and assuring that when Yasushi Akashi went to Pale he got a hearing. The men and women associated with UNPROFOR "were bound to always choose discretion, to stand up for the [UN] mission rather than for the principles on which the United Nations' authority, both moral and practical, [were] actually based."[54]

In explaining the reaction of the UN's Department of Peacekeeping Operations to the establishment of safe areas in Bosnia, Rieff amply demonstrates the contradictions and flaws of the UN mission. The reaction on the part of UNPROFOR to Security Council resolution 836 (4 June 1993) dealing with the protection of the six safe areas in Bosnia was that the resolution "was not impartial enough." In order to ensure that they remain even-handed, the safe areas should be disarmed, argued UNPROFOR officials; otherwise they will become staging grounds for the Bosnia army. "In peacekeeping terms this made sense." However, if carried to its logical conclusion, disarmament would have resulted in the dismembering of the Bosnian state and the dispossession of its people. Elaborating further, Rieff adds:

The problem was that if UNPROFOR had really been able to disarm Bosnian troops in … Sarajevo, in the second largest city under its control, Tuzla, and in the enclaves that were the last areas of Bosnian resistance in a part of the country that had otherwise been all but completely ethnically cleansed, they would have effectively abolished the Bosnian state in the name of protecting Bosnian citizens from Serb attack.[55]

As the mandate evolved in Bosnia, UNPROFOR took the concept of impartiality to new heights by looking for any excuse to both downplay the atrocities committed by Serbs and, on the other hand, expose the actions of the Bosnian government. Often this involved regurgitating Serbian propaganda verbatim. For the

United Nations, this is what it meant to be even-handed in Bosnia. For example, Canadian UN spokesman Barry Frewer stated that Karadzic's Serbs did not have Sarajevo under siege but rather were "enjoying a tactically advantageous position," "encircling the city," and "preventing a military breakout."[56] This echoed what the Bosnian Serbs were saying when asked by the media why their forces were besieging and terrorizing the Bosnian capital.

United Nations apologetics for Serbian behaviour were rooted not only in attempting to remain neutral in Bosnia, as peacekeeping dogma required, but in a real "convergence of interest ... [that] actually played itself out on almost a daily basis."[57] "As time went on, many, particularly within UNPROFOR ... grew increasingly frustrated by what they saw as the Bosnian government's refusal to accept its own defeat." Their rationale, Rieff notes, however immoral, did make sense. UNPROFOR's job was to assist the UNHCR's delivery of humanitarian aid. "What was getting in the way? The fighting. And who was keeping the fighting going? The Bosnian government side, which was not prepared to accept the dismemberment of the country."[58] When viewed in these terms, "wasn't a surrender on the part of the [Bosnian] government the surest road to peace?"[59] For UN officials, the rights and wrongs of the conflict did not matter. They wanted peace at any price – genocide or not – and from their viewpoint it was the Bosnian government that was the most intransigent party.

Testifying before United States Congress, Lewis MacKenzie, reflecting UN thinking, made this abundantly clear: "The Serbs, at present, will talk any time, any place, any where, at any level, because they basically have what they want ... They are prepared to negotiate ... The political solution is to pull the rug of intervention out [from under the Bosnian government] and force people to sit down and discuss. One side [the Serbs] has already said it is prepared to do that today. The other side [the Muslims] has not got the message yet."[60]

As the war dragged on, the UNPROFOR mission continued to deteriorate. Relief convoys were repeatedly turned back, sometimes by a lone gunman manning a checkpoint, and the Sarajevo airport was frequently shut down at the whim of the Serbs. The Bosnian capital now had the distinction of being a European city under the longest siege in modern history and the first city whose siege was actually monitored and administered by the United Nations. Michael Ignatieff has perceptively observed that by waiting so long before trying to reverse Serbian aggression, the West became complicit in the destruction of Bosnia and its capital city. The UN allowed itself to become the administrator of the Serbian siege of Sarajevo. The UN both prevented the city from starving to death, and yet, by doing nothing to break the siege, it helped to prolong the city's suffering. Moral results could hardly be more ambiguous than this.[61]

By 1995, while UN officials were still proclaiming that their humanitarian aid effort had saved thousands of lives, the first deaths by starvation were being reported in Bosnia.[62] Not only was the UN unable to protect relief convoys, but it proved unable to protect its own troops, who were routinely taken hostage as a shield against NATO air strikes. It is revealing to note that United Nations commanders grew increasingly frustrated, not with the Serbs but with the Bosnian government. "Why, countless United Nations officials would demand, did the Bosnians insist on fighting on when it was clear that they had lost?" The perversion of the UN mandate had reached such a low point that in "the minds of many UN officials, Bosnian resistance," over time, "itself became a sort of crime against humanity. If the victims would only accept their victimhood, there was so much the international community could do for them."[63] To these sentiments, the beleaguered and out-gunned Bosnian government could only respond: "We make no apology to those who would find it more convenient if we would just disappear rather than serve as a constant reminder to them of their betrayal of principles."[64]

How could the United Nations and its supporters rationalize such behaviour? How could a noble organization whose moral authority embodied the hopes of so many for just world order explain and justify its open sympathy and collusion with Serbian ethno-nationalism? What David Rieff found interesting was that individual UN officials were aware of "how debased the institution was becoming" due to its Bosnia endeavour; however, "corporately the UN simply refused to accept that this was what had happened." The fault lay elsewhere, "with the mandate, or the spinelessness of the great powers, or simply the savagery and ruthlessness of the belligerents themselves."[65]

In his carefully constructed attempt to comprehend the philosophical rationale of UN behaviour in Bosnia, Rieff places his finger on the problem by comparing the United Nations to the Roman Catholic Church. He uses this analogy to explain why the "UN rejected the insights it could have drawn at any time about the real nature of its mission in Bosnia"; it was due to "an ingrained sense of its own special virtue." Developing this idea further, Rieff picks up on a curious phrase he would often hear UN officials uttering: "I believe in the United Nations." *Belief* is usually reserved for a religion or an ideology, yet Rieff points out that for many UN officials their uncritical belief in the organization they served, especially the holy concept of peacekeeping, was akin to a religious conviction. He continues:

[Such a conviction] helps explain why from the beginning it was so difficult for the United Nations officials to accept the idea that the Bosnian disaster could be even in part their fault, and why when foreign journalists or officials of the Bosnian government accused them bitterly of complicity, by the failure to act or to speak up, in the genocide of the Bosnian Muslims, they found that accusation to be not only baseless but terribly unjust. For them, such a charge was not only wrong in fact – "Don't blame us, blame your governments," Secretariat officials liked to say – but was what in philosophy is known as a category mistake. A government can be in the wrong, as a country can be in the wrong. But a Church cannot be in the wrong.[66]

This is an accurate assessment of what motivated many in UNPRO-FOR and blinded them to the genocide that was unfolding around them. Tom Gjelten touches upon Rieff's theory in his attempt to understand Lewis MacKenzie's actions in Bosnia, in particular MacKenzie's unsubstantiated charge that the Bosnian government was shooting its own people in order to attract international sympathy. Gjelten quotes a UN political officer who worked with MacKenzie in Sarajevo. Speaking on condition of anonymity, the officer stated that at the time MacKenzie was looking for some reason to blame the Bosnian government because "[p]sychologically, he needed it," explained the official. "We had been blaming the Serbs for everything and it was uncomfortable for MacKenzie, meeting with them all the time. *He felt this need to balance it.*"[67] Gjelten points out that when MacKenzie arrived in Bosnia he was a veteran peacekeeper of thirty years who "brought to his work the instincts of a professional UN soldier. He was predisposed to find a place in the middle without considering the rights or wrongs of any side's position." Recall from Rieff's discussion of the United Nations that the first axiom of UN peacekeeping is impartiality at all costs. The facts do not matter, neutrality does. MacKenzie's "disdain for thoughtful analysis," Gjelten continues, "merely reflects what UN service instils in its peacekeepers ... Many of the organization's officials are uncomfortable with moral clarity, especially if it impedes their work. Theirs is a world in which the assignment of responsibility is often governed not by judgements of fact and principle but by considerations of convenience."[68]

There was never any parity in Bosnia between the actions of the democratically elected and internationally recognized government in Sarajevo and the Belgrade-backed rebel Serbs, whose leaders have been indicted by the International Criminal Tribunal for the former Yugoslavia. A simple inquiry into the war aims of the protagonists is telling in this regard. Warren Zimmerman, American ambassador to Yugoslavia at the time of its break-up, recognized this. In his memoir, he writes that "Karadzic, whom I had first met during the Bosnian election campaign, was the polar opposite to Izetbegovic. Where the Muslim preached reconciliation, the Serb habitually used the language of confrontation. 'Boycott,' 'war,' 'violence,' 'demand,' 'unacceptable,' 'genocide,' 'hell,' and 'annihilation,' peppered his vocabulary."[69] Yet, as Rieff perceptively observes, "for the UN to have acknowledged any of this would have meant that the entire rationale for its behaviour in Bosnia would have had to be re-examined."[70] For UN ideologists, "impartiality" necessitated that all sides be considered "serial killers." How else could one carry on in the midst of a genocide? Reality had to be inverted in order to remain true to the cause of United Nations peacekeeping. The facts were an inconvenience that needed to be manipulated in order for UN officials to reach a predetermined conclusion.

The preceding analysis of the United Nations is not meant to absolve the great powers from their responsibility for events in Bosnia-Herzegovina. From the very beginning, "they have tried to use their military presence in Bosnia as part of their diplomacy," which meant pressuring the Bosnian government to accept the de facto if not de jure partition of its state.[71] What is more pertinent for this paper is understanding both the philosophical underpinnings of United Nations peacekeeping policy and the motives of those who served it loyally and uncritically for three and a half years in Bosnia.

What does this have to do with Canadian foreign policy on Bosnia? In short, everything. The *Montreal Gazette* has accurately noted that "Peacekeeping has become the foundation on which much of Canada's foreign and defense policy is built."[72] If ever there were a country that internalized the ideology of UN peacekeeping, it was Canada. Canada's most prominent diplomat, Lester Pearson, is credited with inventing the concept, and since then Canadian nationalism has been inextricably linked to it. Every argument, justification, and position put forth by UNPROFOR to explain its posture in Bosnia was echoed by Canadian officials. "Ottawa urges neutrality in Bosnia" was how the *Globe and Mail* described Canada's reaction as the Serbs overran the UN safe area of Bihac in November 1994.[73] High ranking government officials, when asked to denounce Serbian crimes against humanity, would repeatedly make statements such as: "I'm not going to get into who's right and who's wrong" (Defense Minister David Collenette) because it "doesn't enhance the cause to say these are the good guys and those are the bad guys" (Foreign Affairs Minister André Ouellete).[74]

When confronted with the charge that it was immoral to disarm the citizens of Srebrenica – as Canadian soldiers attempted to do in April 1993 – Foreign Affairs officials were unable to comprehend the point. Any argument that Canada's refusal to support a lifting of the arms embargo put it in a de facto alliance with Serbian war aims and that alternatively Canada *should* take sides in the war was met with anger and derision. In a Canadian context, these suggestions were blasphemous.

Canada's foreign policy in Bosnia, more than the foreign policy of any other member of the United Nations, embodied the abnegation that paralyzed the UNPROFOR mission. So deeply entrenched in the political culture was the ethos of UN peacekeeping that Ottawa could not see, as David Rieff again points out, "[how] all its actions in the former Yugoslavia led it not to impartiality or good works, but to collusion with aggression."[75] Even after the Serbian assault on Srebrenica, when Ratko Mladic rounded up and murdered every male he could get his hands on from the ages of twelve to sixty in an orgy of violence not seen in Europe since Hitler, the Canadian government still could not fathom the idea of Bosnian self-defense. This was amply demonstrated by the emotional reaction of Canada's defense minister to the US Senate resolution on 26 July 1995 to lift the arms embargo against the beleaguered Bosnian state. With a befuddled look on his face, David Collenette said: "I can't believe that rational people today, in 1995, in our various electorates, whether the United States, Canada or other places in the world, are going to take that attitude. That takes us back 1,000 years to almost prehistoric, tribal-type conflicts."[76]

CANADIAN FOREIGN POLICY AND THE PROBLEM OF UN PEACEKEEPING

Jack Granatstein has drawn attention to the connection between the ideology of UN peacekeeping and political paralysis in Canadian foreign policy. He observes that "for too many Canadians peacekeeping has become a substitute for policy and thought ... [S]ome countries ... try to deal with problems by throwing money at them; our people and, to some substantial extent, our governments try to deal with the world's problems by sending peacekeepers."[77] The genocide in Bosnia is a perfect illustration of this point.

World attention was focused on the Balkans in April 1992 as Milosevic's greater Serbia project spread from Croatia to Bosnia. Canada, instead of taking a stand against territorial aggression and virulent nationalism and in defense of human rights and multiculturalism – positions it routinely invokes as being the foundations upon which Canadian foreign policy is based – instinctively offered to send in peacekeepers as a panacea for the region's problems.

Ottawa's obsession with peacekeeping has put Canadian foreign policy in a straitjacket. It is structurally oriented to be indifferent to ethnic cleansing and mass slaughter and has become such a dominating characteristic of Canada's internationalism that it inhibits Canadians from seeing the world's problems clearly or critically.[78] The claim that Ottawa pursued or even considered alternative approaches toward the conflagration in Bosnia that did not involve the dispatch of UN blue helmets is bereft of any evidentiary support. Instead, Ottawa went to great lengths to sanitize the UN's Bosnia mission, whose mandate was not only impossible to implement, but more importantly an inappropriate response to genocidal Serbian nationalism.

Tadeusz Mazowiecki, the only senior United Nations official to resign over Bosnia, remarked that the UNPROFOR mandate was essentially sick. What then can we conclude about those who repeatedly stated – in the face of Europe's worst slaughter since the Third Reich – that "we are doing good things" in Bosnia?[79]

The confusion and contradictions that enveloped Canadian policy were evident in the public comments made by Canadian leaders. Prime Minister Chrétien explained that Canadians were in Bosnia "to maintain peace. We're not there to make peace." Yet in the same breath he would acknowledge that "sometimes there is no peace to keep."[80] This begs the question: why were Canadian troops deployed in the first place if the primary condition of their deployment had not been met or could not be met? Like the proverbial surgeon who proclaims the operation a success even though the patient has died, Canadian leaders similarly engaged in the manufacture of illusions to justify their failed policy. In the same issue of the *Globe and Mail*, for example, one could read comments by Jean Chrétien praising the humanitarian work of Canadian soldiers and, only a few pages down, a United Nations account of "the first deaths by starvation" in Bosnia.[81]

Looking back over the previous fifty years, Canada's middle power status and its role as an intermediary on the world stage has been a legacy that Canadians can be proud of. In past conflicts, where the threshold of violence was relatively low and the fighting had abated, Canada has been able to play a constructive role in creating the conditions for a durable political settlement. Canadian involvement in United Nations missions in the Middle East, Central America, and Southeast Asia come to mind. In the face of an ongoing genocide, however, when one side is engaging in "the extermination of a people in whole or in part because of their race, religion or ethnicity," to cite Human Rights Watch's description of Serbian nationalist behaviour, neutrality is meaningless.

In the context of genocide there are two important lessons that should be learned as this century comes to a close. Genocide and the regimes that perpetrate them are only defeated by the use of overwhelming military force. The genocide of European Jewry, the killings fields of Cambodia, and the genocides in Rwanda and Bosnia all came to an end as the result of serious and sustained military action, in particular the use of ground troops.

Secondly, political leaders who engage in war crimes – genocide in particular – need to be pursued and punished by the international community. The governments of Brian Mulroney and Jean Chrétien (prior to the Kosovo war) refused to acknowledge the xenophobic and neo-fascistic underpinnings of Serbian (and to a lesser extent Croatian) nationalism. A consent-based UN "classical" peacekeeping operation was never an appropriate response to Serbian ethnic cleansing and the territorial ambitions of the Zagreb and Belgrade regimes. Neutrality was complicity in this context. Canada's unshakeable support for UN policy in Bosnia and its ironclad commitment to peacekeeping reminds one of the wise words of Fred Cuny, a humanitarian relief worker in Sarajevo. In expressing his frustrations with the United Nations in Bosnia, he observed that had the UN been around in 1939, we all would be speaking German.[82]

NOTES

I would like to thank András Riedlmayer, Ausma Khan, Roy Gutman, Emran Qureshi, Norman Cigar, and Daniel Kofman for their feedback on this essay.

1 Final Report of the United Nations Commission of Experts established pursuant to United Nations Security Council Resolution 780 (1992), Annex VI – part 9/10, Chronology of the Battle and Siege of Sarajevo, 11 November 1993.

2 Greenspon and Wilson-Smith 1996, 92.

3 *War Crimes in Bosnia-Hercegovina*, vol. 2, New York: Human Rights Watch, 1993, 2.

4 See the "Joint Policy Statement on Bosnia," 31 July 1995, where the signatories decry "the slaughter in Bosnia as genocide, one of the most heinous crimes known to humanity." Also, *Life, Death and Aid: The Médicins Sans Frontières Report on World Crisis Intervention*, London: Routledge, 1993, 89–96. Furthermore, the reports filed by Tadeusz Mazowiecki, special rapporteur of the UN Commission on Human Rights, are essential reading. They can be obtained online at http://www.haverford.edu/relg/sells/reports/mazowiecki.html.

5 Cohen and Moens 1999.

6 "Bosnian Muslim state practical, ex-general says," *Globe and Mail*, 27 May 1993.

7 In an emergency debate in the House of Commons on the situation in Yugoslavia, the secretary of state for External Affairs stated that "Canada was the first country to request a meeting of the United Nations Security Council on the Yugoslav situation" ("Statement by The Honourable Barbara McDougall, Secretary of State for External Affairs, On the Situation in Yugoslavia in the Emergency Debate in the House of Commons," 18 November 1991, no. 91/59).

8 Prime minister of Canada, "Address by Prime Minister Brian Mulroney on the Occasion of the Centennial Anniversary

Convocation, Stanford University," Palo Alto, California, 29 September 1991.

9 Secretary of State for External Affairs, "Statement by the Secretary of State for External Affairs, the Honourable Barbara McDougall, to the Forty-Sixth Session of the United Nations General Assembly," New York, 25 September 1991.

10 *Canadian International Relations Chronicle* (January-March 1992), 16.

11 Silber and Little 1995, 240. See also comments by Borislav Jovic that appear in his book, *The Last Days of the Socialist Federation of the Republic of Yugoslavia*, which implicate Milosevic in the destruction of Yugoslavia (cited in Jane Perlez, "Serb chief painted as warmonger by ex-aide," *New York Times*, 16 December 1995).

12 Editorial, "Merry Christmas, Mr. Karadzic," *New Republic*, 9 January 1995.

13 *Hansard*, House of Commons, 29 March 1995, 11228.

14 Cited by Christopher Young, "Yugoslavia's death throes must be contained," *Ottawa Citizen*, 16 October 1992.

15 Jeff Sallot, "Canadian troops may have to leave," *Globe and Mail*, 24 February 1993.

16 Earlier in her speech McDougall stated that the "roots of the conflict reach deep into history, and the base human desire for revenge and retribution has increased rather than diminished over time." *Hansard*, House of Commons, 18 November 1991, 4962.

17 Malcolm 1995a, 5.

18 Malcolm 1995b, 121.

19 Jack L. Granatstein, a professor of history at York University, made these remarks before the House of Commons Standing Committee on National Defense and Veteran Affairs, "Peacekeeping," no. 30, 9 February 1993, 10.

20 Malcolm 1995b, 122. For further references on the theory of "ancient ethnic hatreds" and the "doctrine of moral equivalence" see the introduction to Malcolm 1996.

21 Malcolm 1995b, 120. Silber and Little 1995, along with their accompanying BBC documentary, provides the most authoritative reference to Milosevic's role in the break-up of Yugoslavia.

22 Linda Hossie, "France, U.S. at odds over Bosnia," *Globe and Mail*, 8 August 1992. At the International Conference on the Former Yugoslavia held in London in late August 1992, in reaction to the suggestion that it was too late to save Bosnia because it had ceased to exist as a country, McDougall fired back that during World War II

the Netherlands had also ceased to exist but was eventually liberated and restored (cited by Paul Koring, "Leaders shy away from using force in Bosnia conflict," *Globe and Mail*, 27 August 1992).

23 "UN backs force, if needed, to aid battered Bosnians," *Globe and Mail*, 14 August 1992.

24 Tim Harper, "End horror in Bosnia, PM urges," *Toronto Star*, 11 December 1992.

25 Robert Fife, "PM urges force in Bosnia," *Ottawa Sun*, 11 December 1992.

26 Jeff Sallot, "How a Balkan policy eludes Canada," *Globe and Mail*, 17 May 1993.

27 Peter Stockland, "PM softens stance," *Ottawa Sun*, 18 December 1992.

28 Ibid.

29 CBC *Newsworld* Interview, 13 May 1993, 7:40 A.M.

30 Secretary of state for External Affairs, "Canada Supports International Pressure to End the Violence in Bosnia-Hercegovina," *News Release*, no. 94, 12 May 1992.

31 Paul Koring, "West still stymied on Bosnian action," *Globe and Mail*, 17 December 1992. McDougall was clearly relieved that when the new Clinton administration announced its Bosnia policy, lifting the arms embargo was not an option. "Relieved isn't the right world," she said in reference to US Foreign policy and the arms embargo, "I'm very pleased, obviously" (Murray Campbell, "Canada gives blessing to U.S. peace efforts in Bosnia," *Globe and Mail*, 12 February 1993).

32 Norman Greenaway, "Celebrate unpopularity, PM tells Clinton," *Ottawa Citizen*, 3 June 1993.

33 Hampson and Molot 1996, 5.

34 *Calgary Herald*, 6 July 1996.

35 Hugh Windsor, "Bosnia shows up UN's weakness, PM says," *Globe and Mail*, 6 July 1996.

36 Paul Koring, "Canada refuses to join Sarajevo aid plan," *Globe and Mail*, 3 September 1994.

37 Juliet O'Neill, "PM's frugality nearly led to diplomatic disaster," *Ottawa Citizen*, 13 January 1994.

38 Ibid.

39 Paul Koring, "Canada refuses to join Sarajevo aid plan," *Globe and Mail*, 3 September 1994.

40 Silber and Little 1995, 343.

41 Juliet O'Neill and Julian Beltrame, "Europe, U.S. back use of air strikes to end siege," *Ottawa Citizen*, 8 February 1994.

42 John Pomfret, "U.N. shifting Bosnian focus from protection to partition," *Washington Post*, 17 August 1993. Cited in Maass 1996, 262.

43 Paul Koring, "Canada agrees to ultimatum," *Globe and Mail*, 10 February 1994. See also Juliet O'Neill, "Dutch can replace Canadians in Srebrenica, Serbs promise," *Ottawa Citizen*, 13 January 1994.

44 Craig R. Whitney, "NATO declines to support a U.S. plan to bomb Serbs: Canada balks at Washington's plan to help Sarajevo," *New York Times*, 3 August 1993. Brian Mulroney, after meeting with British prime minister John Major, publicly attacked US senator Joe Biden's suggestion that the Western alliance adopt a policy of "lift and strike" in response to Serbian atrocities in Bosnia (see Paul Koring, "PM opposes Bosnia airstrike," *Globe and Mail*, 12 May 1993).

45 Paul Koring, "Canada agrees to ultimatum," *Globe and Mail*, 10 February 1994. For reference on the Clinton phone calls to Chrétien, see Jeff Sallot, "Push from Clinton swayed Ottawa," *Globe and Mail*, 10 February 1994.

46 Paul Koring, "Canada agrees to ultimatum," *Globe and Mail*, 10 February 1994.

47 For references, see Rikhye 1984 and Diehl 1994.

48 Williams and Scharf 1995, 35.

49 Maloney 1996, 19.

50 Rieff 1995, 138.

51 Cited in Anzulovic 1999, 172.

52 Rieff 1995, 140.

53 Ibid., 166

54 Ibid., 239.

55 Ibid., 175.

56 John Burns, "A siege by any other name would be as painful," *New York Times*, 17 August 1993.

57 Rieff 1995, 175.

58 Rieff 1995, 139.

59 Ibid., 194.

60 Cited in Cigar 1995, 152–3.

61 Ignatieff 1995, 31.

62 "UN convoy reaches Bosnian enclave," *Globe and Mail*, 6 July 1995.

63 Rieff 1995, 221.

64 Bosnia foreign minster, Muhammad Sachirbey, quoted in Maass 1996, 263.

65 Rieff 1995, 220.

66 Ibid., 243.

67 Emphasis added. Tom Gjelten, "Blaming the Victim," *The New Republic*, 20 December 1993, 20.

68 Ibid.

69 Zimmerman 1996, 174–5.

70 Rieff 1995, 249.

71 Noel Malcolm, "How the UN helps the Serbs to win the war," *Sunday Telegraph*, 4 June 1994. For evidence of Western pressure to force Bosnian capitulation see the details of Lord Carrington's visit to Sarajevo on 23 April 1992 in Silber and Little 1995, 279–80. In July 1993 the spokesperson for Lord Owen and Thorvald Stoltenberg told the world press, "The message to the Muslims is *negotiate or perish* ... If they want to be practical they can secure a solid future" (emphasis added, cited in Almond 1994, 317).

72 Cited in Granatstein 1993, 280.

73 Jeff Sallot, "Ottawa urges neutrality in Bosnia," *Globe and Mail*, 25 November 1994.

74 The first quotation appears in "A Canadian Perspective," *Maclean's*, 12 June 1995, 24, and the second is cited in Paul Koring, "Bias blurs UN's role in Bosnian conflict," *Globe and Mail*, 3 June 1995.

75 Rieff 1995, 248.

76 Julian Beltrame and Joe Lauria, "End arms ban, US Senate says," *Ottawa Citizen*, 27 July 1995.

77 Granatstein 1992, 234.

78 English and Hillmer 1992, viii.

79 Interview with Barbara McDougall, 13 May 1993, CBC *Newsworld*, 7:40 A.M.

80 Hugh Windsor, "Bosnia shows up UN's weakness, PM says," *Globe and Mail*, 6 July 1995.

81 Compare ibid. with Reuters, "UN convoy reaches Bosnian enclave," *Globe and Mail*, 6 July 1995.

82 Cited in Rieff 1995, 140.

References

Agee, C., ed. 1998. *Scar on the Stone: Contemporary Poetry from Bosnia.* Newcastle upon Tyne: Bloodaxe Books.

Allen, B. 1996. *Rape Warfare: The Hidden Genocide in Bosnia-Herzegovina and Croatia.* Minneapolis, MN: University of Minnesota Press.

Almond, M. 1994. *Europe's Backyard War.* London: Heinemann.

Anderson, B. 1991. *Imagined Communities.* London & New York: Verso.

Andrić, I. 1977. *The Bridge on the Drina.* Trans. L. Edwards. Chicago: University of Chicago Press.

– 1990. *The Development of Spiritual Life in Bosnia under the Influence of Turkish Rule.* Chapel Hill: Duke University Press.

Anzulović, B. 1999. *Heavenly Serbia: From Myth to Genocide.* New York: New York University Press; London: Hurst & Company.

Babić, P., and M. Zovkić, eds. 1986. *Katolička crkva u Bosni i Hercegovini u XIX i XX stoljeću.* Sarajevo: Vrhbosanska visoka teološka škola.

Ballard, R. 1996. "Islam and the Construction of Europe." In W.A.R. Shadid and P.S. Koningsveld, eds, *Muslims in the Margin: Political Responses to the Presence of Islam in Western Europe.* The Hague: Kok Pharos publishing.

Banac, I. 1984. *The National Question in Yugoslavia: Origins, History, Politics.* Ithaca: Cornell University Press.

Benac, A., and O. Bihalji-Merin. [1963]. *Bogomil Sculpture.* New York: Harcourt, Brace & World.

Bhabha, H. 1994a. "Of Mimicry and Men: The Ambivalence of Colonial Discourse." In H. Bhabha, *The Location of Culture.* London: Routledge.

– 1994b. "The Postcolonial and the Postmodern: The Question of Agency." In H. Bhabha, *The Location of Culture*. London: Routledge.

Blažina, V. 1996. "Mémoricide ou la purification culturelle: la guerre et les bibliothèques de Croatie et de Bosnie-Herzégovine." *Documentation et bibliothèques* 42: 149–64.

Boutros-Ghali, B. 1999. *Unvanquished: A US-U.N. Saga.* New York: Random House.

Bringa, T. 1995. *Being Muslim the Bosnian Way: Identity and Community in a Central Bosnian Village*. Princeton: Princeton University Press.

– 2002. "Averted Gaze: Genocide in Bosnia-Herzegovina 1992–1995." In A. Hinton, *Annihilating Difference: The Anthropology of Genocide*. Berkeley: University of California Press.

Butler, T. 1993. "Yugoslavia mon amour." *Mind and Human Interaction* 4: 120–8.

Buturović, A. 1995. "Producing and Annihilating the Ethos of Bosnian Islam." *Cultural Survival Quarterly* 19, no. 2: 29–33.

– 1996. "National Quest of the Anguish of Salvation: Bosnian Muslim Identity in Meša Selimović's *The Dervish and Death*." *Edebiyat* 7: 41–57.

– 2001. "Re-Asserting Authenticity: Bosnian Identity, Religion and Landscape in the Poetry of Mak Dizdar." In J. Scott and P. Simpson-Housley, eds, *Mapping the Sacred: Religion, Geography, and Postcolonial Literatures*. Amsterdam & Atlanta: Editions Rodopi BV.

Campbell, D. 1998. *National Deconstruction: Violence, Identity, and Justice in Bosnia*. Minneapolis: University of Minnesota Press.

Čengić, A., and F. Duraković, eds. 1994. *Cultural Institutions and Monuments in Sarajevo*. Budapest: Open Society Institute, [1995].

Cigar, N. 1995. *Genocide in Bosnia: The Policy of "Ethnic Cleansing" in Eastern Europe*. College Station: Texas A&M University Press.

Cohen, L., and A. Moens. 1999. "Learning the Lessons of UNPROFOR: Canadian Peacekeeping in the Former Yugoslavia." *Canadian Foreign Policy* 6 (Winter): 85–101.

Connor, W. 1994. "A Nation is a Nation, is a State, is an Ethnic Group, is a …" In J. Hutchinson and A. Smith, eds, *Nationalism*. Oxford & New York: Oxford University Press.

Corwin, P. 1999. *Dubious Mandate: A Memoir of the UN in Bosnia, Summer 1995*. Durham, NC: Duke University Press.

Cvijić, J. 1986. *Balkansko poluostrvo i južnoslovenske zemle*. Belgrade. (Reported in Emmert 1990.)

Daniel, N. [1960]. *Islam and the West: The Making of an Image*. Edinburgh: Edinburgh University Press, 1980; Oxford: Oxford University Press, 1993.

Denison, O. 2001. "The New Idolatry." *Q-News*, no. 30 (April): 33.

Diehl, P. 1994. *International Peacekeeping.* Baltimore: Johns Hopkins Press.

Dizdar, M. 1973. *Kameni Spavač [Stone Sleeper].* Mostar: Prva književna komuna.

– 1995. *Antologija starih bosanskih tekstova [Old Bosnian Texts].* Sarajevo: Alef.

– 1996. *Kameni spavač [Stone Sleeper].* Sarajevo: Veselin Masleša.

– 1999. *Kameni spavač: Stone Sleeper.* Trans. F.R. Jones. Sarajevo: DiD.

Donia, R., and J. Fine. 1994. *Bosnia and Hercegovina: A Tradition Betrayed.* London: C. Hurst & Company; New York: Columbia University Press.

Društvo arhitekata Sarajevo. 1994. *Warchitecture.* Sarajevo: OKO.

Duraković, E. 1979. *Govor i šutnja tajanstva: poetsko djelo Marka Dizdara.* Translation by F. Jones *[The Saying and Unsaying of Secrecy: The Poetic Work of Mak Dizdar].* Sarajevo: Svjetlost.

– ed. 1995. *Antologija bošnjačke poezije XX vijeka [An Anthology of Twentieth-Century Bosniak Poetry].* Sarajevo: Alef.

Eickelman, D., and J. Piscatori. 1990. "Social Theory in the Study of Muslim Societies." In D. Eickelman and J. Piscatori, eds, *Muslim Travelers: Pilgimage, Migration, and the Religious Imagination.* London: Routledge.

Emmert, T.A. 1990. *Serbian Golgotha: Kosovo, 1389.* New York: Columbia University Press.

English, J., and N. Hillmer, eds. 1992. *Making a Difference?: Canada's Foreign Policy in a Changing World Order.* Toronto: Lester Publishing.

Evans, Sir A. 1971. *Through Bosnia and Herzegovina on Foot.* New York: Arno Press & The New York Times.

Filipović, M., ed. 1987. *The Art Treasures of Bosnia and Herzegovina.* Sarajevo: Svjetlost.

Fine, J. 1975. *The Bosnian Church: A New Interpretation – A Study of the Bosnian Church and its Place in State and Society from the 13th to the 15th Centuries.* Boulder: East European Quarterly; New York: distributed by Columbia University Press.

– 1987. *The Late Medieval Balkans: A Critical Survey from the Late Twelfth Century to the Ottoman Conquest.* Ann Arbor: University of Michigan Press.

– 1994. "The Medieval and Ottoman Roots of Modern Bosnia." In M. Pinson, ed., *The Muslims of Bosnia-Herzegovina.* Cambridge: Harvard University Press.

Fischer, M. 1986. "Ethnicity and the Post-Modern Art of Memory." In J. Clifford and G. Marcus, eds, *Writing Culture: The Poetics and Politics of Ethnography.* Berkeley & Los Angeles: University of California Press.

Gellner, E. 1983. *Nations and Nationalism.* Oxford: Basil Blackwell.

216 References

Gjelten, T. 1995. *Sarajevo Daily: A City and its Newspaper under Siege*. New York: Harper Collins Publishers.

Glenny, M. 1992. *The Fall of Yugoslavia: The Third Balkan War*. New York: Penguin.

Gow, J. 1997. "After the Flood: Literature on the Context, Causes and Course of the Yugoslav War – Reflections and Refractions." *Slavonic and East European Review* 75, no. 3 (July): 446–84.

Granatstein, J.L. 1992. "Peacekeeping: Did Canada Make a Difference? And What Difference Did Peacekeeping Make to Canada?" In J. English and N. Hillmer, eds, *Making a Difference?: Canada's Foreign Policy in a Changing World Order*. Toronto: Lester Publishing.

– 1993. "Canada and Peacekeeping: Image and Reality." In J.L. Granatstein, ed., *Canadian Foreign Policy: Historical Readings*. Rev. ed. Mississauga, ON: Copp Clark-Pitman Ltd.

Greenspon, E., and A. Wilson-Smith. 1996. *Double Vision: The Inside Story of the Liberals in Power*. Toronto: Doubleday.

Gutman, R. 1993. *A Witness to Genocide*. New York: Macmillan.

Hampson, F.O., and M.A. Molot, eds. 1996. *Canada among Nations 1996: Big Enough to Be Heard*. Ottawa: Carleton University Press.

Handžić, A. 1994. *Population of Bosnia in the Ottoman Period*. Istanbul: IRCICA.

Helsinger, E. 1997. *Rural Scenes and National Representation*. Princeton: Princeton University Press.

Hickok, M. 1997. *Ottoman Military Administration in Eighteenth-Century Bosnia*. Leiden: Brill.

Hobsbawm, E. 1990. *Nations and Nationalism since 1780*. Cambridge: Cambridge University Press.

Holbrooke, R. 1998. *To End a War*. New York: Random House.

Hourani, A.H. 1991. *Islam in European Thought*. Cambridge: Cambridge University Press.

Huntington, S. 1996. *The Clash of Civilizations and the Remaking of the World Order*. New York: Touchstone.

Idrizbegović, A. 1996. "Introduction." In M. Dizdar, *Kameni spavač [Stone Sleeper]*. Sarajevo: Veselin Masleša.

Ignatieff, M. 1995. "The Seductiveness of Moral Disgust." *Index on Censorship* 24, no. 5 (September–October): 22–38.

Imamović, M. 1997. *Historija Bošnjaka*. Sarajevo: Bošnjačka zajednica kulture.

Janowitz, A. 1990. *England's Ruins*. Cambridge: Basil Blackwell.

Judah, T. 1997. *The Serbs: History, Myth, and the Destruction of Yugoslavia.* New Haven: Yale University Press.

Kaplan, R.D. 1993. *Balkan Ghosts: A Journey through History.* New York: Vintage.

Kinross, L. 1977. *The Ottoman Centuries: The Rise and Fall of the Turkish Empire.* New York: William Morrow.

Kofman, D. 2001. "Self-determination in a Multi-ethnic State: Bosnians, Bosniaks, Croats, and Serbs." In Dž. Sokolović and F. Bieber, eds, *Reconstructing Multi-ethnic Societies: The Case of Bosnia-Herzegovina.* Aldershot: Ashgate Publishing.

Kostović, N. 1995. *Sarajevo izmedju dobrotvorstva i zla [Sarajevo between Philanthropy and Evil Times].* Sarajevo: El-Kalem.

Krzović, I. 1987. *Arhitektura Bosne i Hercegovine 1878–1918 [Architecture of Bosnia and Herzegovina 1878–1918].* Sarajevo: Umjetnička galerija Bosne i Hercegovine.

Kurspahić, K. 1997. *As Long as Sarajevo Exists.* Trans. C. London. Stony Creek, Conn.: Pamphleteer's Press.

Lefèvre, A.-C. 1996. "Bosnie et Croatie: un désastre cuturel sans précédent." *Archéologia*, no. 328 (November): 26–35.

Loos, M. 1974. *Dualist Heresy in the Middle Ages.* Prague: Academia Publishing.

Lovrenović, I. 1998. *Unutarnja zemlja: kratki pregled kulturne povijesti Bosne i Hercegovine [The Inner Land: A Brief Survey of the Cultural History of Bosnia and Herzegovina].* Zagreb: Durieux.

Maass, P. 1996. *Love Thy Neighbour: A Story of War.* New York: Knopf.

MacKenzie, L. 1993. *Peacekeeper: The Road to Sarajevo.* Vancouver: Douglas & McIntyre.

Mahmutćehajić, R. 2000a. *Bosnia the Good: Tolerance and Tradition.* Budapest: Central European Press.

– 2000b. *The Denial of Bosnia.* State College, PA: Pennsylvania State University Press.

Malcolm, N. 1994. *Bosnia: A Short History.* London & New York: New York University Press.

– 1995a. "Bosnia and the West: A Study in Failure." *The National Interest,* no. 39 (Spring): 3–14.

– 1995b. "Impartiality and Ignorance." In B. Cohen and G. Stamkoski, eds, *With No Peace to Keep: United Nations Peacekeeping and the War in the Former Yugoslavia.* London: Grainpress Limited.

– 1996. *Bosnia: A Short History.* Rev. ed. New York: Macmillan.

Maloney, S. 1996. "Insights into Canadian Peacekeeping Doctrine." *Military Review* 126 (March–April): 12–23.

Marković, M.S. 1983. "The Secret of Kosovo." In V.D. Mihailovich, ed., *Landmarks in Serbian Culture and History.* Pittsburgh, PA: Serb National Federation.

Mehmedinović, S. 1998. *Sarajevo Blues.* San Francisco: City Lights.

Mernissi, F. 1996. "Palace Fundamentalism and Liberal Democracy: Oil, Arms and Irrationality." *Development and Change* 27: 251–65.

Mitchell, W.J.T. 1980. "Spatial Form in Literature: Toward a General Theory." In W.J.T. Mitchell, ed., *The Language of Images.* Chicago: University of Chicago Press.

– 1986. *Iconology, Image, Text, Ideology.* Chicago: University of Chicago Press.

Nonneman, G., T. Niblock, and B. Szajkowski, eds. 1996. *Muslim Communities in the New Europe.* Lebanon: Ithaca Press.

Nora, P. 1996. *Realms of Memory.* Vol. 1. Trans. A. Goldhammer. Ed. L.D. Kritzman. New York: Columbia University Press.

Norris, H.T. 1993. *Islam in the Balkans.* Columbia, SC: University of South Carolina Press.

Obradović, S. 1994. "Tuzla: The Last Oasis." *Uncaptive Minds* 7, no. 3 (Fall–Winter).

Off, C. 2000. *The Lion, the Fox, and the Eagle: A Story of Generals and Justice in Rwanda and Yugoslavia.* Toronto: Random House Canada.

Owen, D. 1995. *Balkan Odyssey.* London: Victor Gollancz.

Pašić, A. 1994. *Islamic Architecture in Bosnia and Hercegovina.* Trans. M. Ridjanović. Istanbul: Research Centre for Islamic History, Art, and Culture.

– 1995. *The Old Bridge (Stari Most) in Mostar.* Istanbul: Research Centre for Islamic History, Art, and Culture.

Peić, S. 1994. *Medieval Serbian Culture.* London: Alpine Fine Arts Collection.

Pinson, M., ed. 1993. *The Muslims of Bosnia-Herzegovina.* Cambridge: Harvard University Center for Middle East Studies.

Popović, S., D. Janca, and T. Petovar. 1990. *Kosovski čvor: dresiti ili seći?* [*Kosovo Knot: To Untie or to Cut?*]. Belgrade: Udruženje za jugoslovensku demokratsku inicijativu.

Price, D. 1999. *History Made, History Imagined: Contemporary Literature, Poiesis, and the Past.* Urbana & Chicago: University of Illinois Press.

Prpa, B. 2000. "Vojislav Koštunica: Milošević's Opponent or Successor?" *Nacional* (Zagreb) (24 August).

Rakić, S. 2000. *Serbian Icons from Bosnia-Herzegovina: Sixteenth to Eighteenth Century.* New York: A. Pankovitch Publishers.

Riedlmayer, A. 1994. *Killing Memory: Bosnia's Cultural Heritage and Its Destruction.* Videocassette. Haverford: Community of Bosnia.

– 1995. "Erasing the Past: The Destruction of Libraries and Archives in Bosnia-Herzegovina." *Middle East Studies Association Bulletin* 29 (July): 7–11.

– 2001. "Convivencia under Fire: Genocide and Book Burning in Bosnia." In J. Rose, ed., *The Holocaust and the Book: Destruction and Preservation.* Amherst: University of Massachusetts.

Rieff, D. 1995. *Slaughterhouse: Bosnia and the Failure of the West.* New York: Simon & Schuster.

Rikhye, I.J. 1984. *The Theory and Practice of Peacekeeping.* London: C. Hurst & Company.

Runciman, Sir. S. 1960. *The Medieval Manichee: A Study of the Christian Dualist Heresy.* Cambridge: Cambridge University Press.

Said, E.W. 1978. *Orientalism.* London: Penguin Books.

– 1999. "The Treason of the Intellectuals." *Al-Ahram Weekly,* no. 435 (24–30 June).

Šanjek, F. 1976. *Les Chrétiens bosniaques et le mouvement cathare: XIIe–XVe siècles.* Louvain: Nauwelaerts.

Schick, I. 1999. *The Erotic Margin: Sexuality and Spatiality in Alteritist Discourse.* New York & London: Verso.

Sells, M. 1996. *The Bridge Betrayed: Religion and Genocide in Bosnia.* Berkeley: University of California Press.

– 1998. *The Bridge Betrayed: Religion and Genocide in Bosnia.* Rev. ed. Berkeley: University of California Press.

Shadid, W.A.R., and P.S. Koningsveld, eds. 1996. *Muslims in the Margin: Political Responses to the Presence of Islam in Western Europe.* The Hague: Kok Pharos publishing.

Sharenkoff, V. 1927. *A Study of Manichaeism in Bulgaria with Special Reference to the Bogomils.* New York: Carranza & Co.

Sijarić, Ć. 1996. "Neither a Church nor a Mosque." Translation by A. Buturović. *Edebiyat* 7, no. 1: 63–88.

Silber, L., and A. Little. 1995. *The Death of Yugoslavia.* New York: Penguin.

Soja, E. 1989. *Postmodern Geographies.* London & New York: Verso.

Sorić, A., J.D. Avdagić, et al., eds. 1988. *Franjevci u raskršću kultura i civilizacija: blago franjevačkih samostana Bosne i Hercegovine [Franciscans on the Crossroad of Cultures and Civilizations: The Treasures of the Franciscan Monasteries of Bosnia and Herzegovina].* Zagreb: Muzejsko Galerijski Centar.

Spasojević, B. 1999. *Arhitektura stambenih palata austrougarskog perioda u Sarajevu [Architecture of Residences and Mansions of the Austro-Hungarian period in Sarajevo].* 2nd ed. Sarajevo: Rabić.

Subotić, G. 1998. *Art of Kosovo: The Sacred Land.* New York: Monacelli Press.

Vertovec, S., and C. Peach, eds. 1997. *Islam in Europe: The Politics of Religion and Community.* London: Macmillan; New York: St Martin's Press.

Volkan, V.D. 1997. *Bloodlines: From Ethnic Pride to Ethnic Terrorism.* New York: Farrar, Straus, and Giroux.

– 1999a. *Das Versagen der Diplomatie: Zur Psychoanalyse nationaler, ethnischer und religiöser Konflikte [The Failure of Diplomacy: The Psychoanalysis of National, Ethnic and Religious Conflicts].* Giessen: Psychosozial-Verlag.

– 1999b. "Psychoanalysis and Diplomacy Part I: Individual and Large Group Identity." *Journal of Applied Psychoanalytic Studies* 1: 29–55.

– and E. Zintl. 1993. *Life after Loss: The Lessons of Grief.* New York: Charles Scribner's Sons.

– and N. Itzkowitz. 1994. *Turks and Greeks: Neighbours in Conflict.* Cambridgeshire, England: Eothen Press.

Vulliamy, E. 1994. *Seasons in Hell: Understanding Bosnia's War.* New York: St Martin's Press; London & New York: Simon & Schuster.

Wenzel, M. 1965. *Ukrasni motivi na stećcima [Ornamental Motifs on Tombstones from Medieval Bosnia and Surrounding Regions].* Sarajevo: Veselin Masleša.

– 1993. "Bosnian History and Austro-Hungarian Policy: The Zemaljski Muzej, Sarajevo, and the Bogomil Romance." *Museum Management and Curatorship* 12: 127–42.

West, R. 1994. *Tito and the Rise and Fall of Yugoslavia.* New York: Carroll & Graf.

Williams, P., and M. Scharf. 1995. "The Letter of the Law." In B. Cohen and G. Stamkoski, eds, *With No Peace to Keep: United Nations Peacekeeping and the War in the Former Yugoslavia.* London: Grainpress Limited.

Woodward, S.L. 1995. *Balkan Tragedy: Chaos and Dissolution after the Cold War.* Washington: The Brookings Institute.

Young-Bruehl, E. 1996. *The Anatomy of Prejudice.* Cambridge, MA: Harvard University Press.

Zimmerman, W. 1996. *Origins of a Catastrophe.* New York: Times Books.